Blender 2.49 Scripting

Extend the power and flexibility of Blender with
the help of Python: a high-level, easy-to-learn
scripting language

Michel Anders

BIRMINGHAM - MUMBAI

Blender 2.49 Scripting

First published: April 2010

Production Reference: 1230410

Published by Packt Publishing Ltd.
32 Lincoln Road
Olton
Birmingham, B27 6PA, UK.

ISBN 9781849510400

www.packtpub.com

Cover Image by Vinayak Chittar (vinayak.chittar@gmail.com)

Credits

Author
Michel Anders

Reviewer
Pang Lih-Hern

Acquisition Editor
Sarah Cullington

Development Editor
Mehul Shetty

Technical Editor
Namita Sahni

Indexers
Hemangini Bari

Rekha Nair

Editorial Team Leader
Akshara Aware

Project Team Leader
Lata Basantani

Project Coordinator
Shubhanjan Chatterjee

Proofreader
Jeff Orloff

Graphics
Geetanjali Sawant

Production Coordinator
Melwyn D'sa

Cover Work
Melwyn D'sa

About the Author

Michel Anders, after completing his chemistry and physics studies, where he spent more time on computer simulations than on real world experiments, he realized that his real interests lay with IT and Internet technology. He has worked as an IT manager for several different companies, including an Internet provider and a hospital.

Currently he manages the R&D department of Aia Software—a leading developer of document composition software. He lives happily on a small, converted farm with his partner, 3 cats, and 12 goats.

He has been using Blender since version 2.32, although he will be the first one to acknowledge his artwork is naive at best. He loves to help people with Blender and Python-related questions and may be contacted as "varkenvarken" on `blenderartists.org`.

First, I would like to thank all the wonderful people at Packt Publishing. Without their help this book would not have been written. Also, I would like to thank my partner and my colleagues at work for putting up with my endless talks about Blender. Finally, I'd like to thank all those people in the Blender community who have together made Blender such a wonderful application.

About the Reviewer

Pang Lih-Hern is a computer game engine programmer with five years of industry experience. He started programming when he was 12, learning the quick Basic language. After graduating with a degree in Software Engineering and Games Design from Multimedia University Malaysia he started his freelancing endeavor that eventually lead him to be part of the core technical team of John Galt Games (Malaysia). He was part of the decision making group in designing and implementing the company's proprietary game engine. Lih-Hern is also actively involved in the open source front, often submitting fixes and features for the popular open source Ogre3D engine. One notable contribution is the Parallel Split Shadow Map feature that enhances the shadow rendering of a 3D scene. He is also a strong advocate of Blender and is currently holding the position of maintaining the Blender exporter to Ogre3D's mesh format.

After leaving John Galt Games (Malaysia), Lih-Hern co-founded Liquid Rock Games with his fellow artist partner Yap Chun Fei. The goal was to create innovative AAA quality games without the need for huge budget cost by the means of using open source technology and tools such as Blender, Gimp, and Ogre3D. As of now, Liquid Rock Games is in the process of developing its first racing title named Aftershock— an online multiplayer post-apocalyptic racing game. The game's artwork is modeled and textured using Blender and Gimp, showing the capability of such tools in the commercial market.

First of all, I would like to thank the publisher, Packt publishing, for giving me the opportunity to review this book. I would also like to thank my family and the co-partner of my company for allowing me the spare time and support to review this book. I hope that the readers will benefit from this book and be inspired to produce more amazing useful tools for Blender.

For Clementine

Table of Contents

Preface

Blender is no doubt the most powerful, and versatile, open source 3D package available. Its power comes close to, or even surpasses, many professional packages. Blender's built-in Python interpreter plays an important role in tapping this power and allows artists to extend the functionality even further. Yet, mastering a scripting language and getting familiar with the many possibilities that Blender offers through its Python API can be a daunting venture.

This book will show how to get the most out of Blender by showing practical solutions to many realistic problems. Each example is a complete working script, which is explained step-by-step in a very detailed manner.

What this book covers

Chapter 1, Extending Blender with Python, gives you an overview of what can and cannot be accomplished with Python in Blender. It teaches you how to install a full Python distribution and how to use the built-in editor. You also learn how to write and run a simple Python script and how to integrate it in Blender's menu system.

Chapter 2, Creating and Editing Objects, introduces objects and meshes and you will see how to manipulate them programmatically. Specifically, you learn how to create configurable mesh objects, design a graphical user interface, and how to make your script store user choices for later reuse. You also learn how to select vertices and faces in a mesh, parent an object to another, and how to create groups. Finally, this chapter shows how to run Blender from the command line, render in the background, and how to process command-line parameters.

Chapter 3, Vertex Groups and Materials, tells you about the many uses of vertex groups and how versatile they can be. You get to know how to define vertex groups and how to assign vertices to a vertex group. You will also learn how you can use those vertex groups for modifiers and armatures. You also look into the application of different materials to different faces and how to assign vertex colors to vertices.

Chapter 4, Pydrivers and Constraints, shows how you can associate built-in constraints with Blender objects and how to define complex relationships between animated properties by using the so-called **pydrivers**. You also define new complex constraints that may be used just like the built-in constraints. Specifically, you see how to drive one **IPO** from another by a Python expression, how to work around some limitations inherent in **pydrivers**, and how to restrict the motion of objects and bones by adding constraints. This chapter teaches you how to write a constraint in Python that will snap an object to the closest vertex on another object.

Chapter 5, Acting on Frame Changes, focuses on writing scripts that may be used to act on certain events. You can learn what script links and space handlers are and how they can be used to perform activities on each frame change in an animation. You also see how to associate additional information with an object, how to use script links to make an object appear or disappear by changing its layout or changing its transparency, and how to implement a scheme to associate a different mesh with an object on each frame. Finally, you can look into ways to augment the functionality of the 3D view.

Chapter 6, Shape Keys, IPOs, and Poses, discovers that there is more to IPOs that can prove useful in animated scenes. Although IPOs were introduced in *Chapter 4,* here you learn how to define IPOs on all kinds of objects, associate shape keys with a mesh, and how to define IPOs for those shape keys. You also look into posing armatures and combining poses into actions.

Chapter 7, Creating Custom Shaders and Textures with Pynodes, introduces Pynodes and you get to know how they enable you to define completely new textures and materials. You learn how to write Pynodes that create simple color patterns, Pynodes that produce patterns with normals, and you also learn how to animate Pynodes. This chapter also explains about Pynodes that produce height and slope-dependent materials and even create shaders that react to the angle of incident light.

Chapter 8, Rendering and Image Manipulation, turns to the rendering process as a whole. You can automate this rendering process, combine the resulting images in various ways, and even turn Blender into a specialized web server. Specifically, you learn how to automate the rendering process, create multiple views for product presentations, and create billboards from complex objects. You get to know about ways to enhance Blender with some external libraries to manipulate images, including render results.

Chapter 9, Expanding your Toolset, is less about rendering and more about making life easier for the day-to-day use of Blender by extending its functionality. In this chapter, you learn how to list and archive assets such as image maps, publish a rendered image automatically with FTP, extend the functionality of the built-in editor with regular expression searches, speed up computations by using Psyco—a just-in-time compiler, and add version control to your scripts with Subversion.

Appendix A, Links and Resources, gives you a list of most resources used in this book along with some generally useful information.

Appendix B, Common Pitfalls, highlights some of the common questions that pop up more often than others as do some mistakes.

Appendix C, Future Developments, is the final appendix that tries to show what the future holds in store and how this may affect you as both Blender and Python are constantly developed further.

What you need for this book

All examples in the book use Blender 2.49 (available at `www.blender.org`) and its built-in Python 2.6.x language. Many examples assume that you have a full Python (`www.python.org`) distribution. In *Chapter 1, Extending Blender with Python,* you are shown how to install a full distribution—if you don't have one already. Blender and Python are platform independent and all examples should run equally well on Windows, Linux, and Mac. Some additional modules are used as well and suitable download instructions are provided where appropriate. All examples can be downloaded from the publisher's website (`http://www.packtpub.com`).

Who is this book for

This book is for users comfortable with Blender as a modeling and rendering tool and who want to expand their skills to include Blender scripting to automate laborious tasks and achieve results otherwise impossible. Blender experience is essential as is some experience in Python programming.

Conventions

In this book, you will find a number of styles of text that distinguish between different kinds of information. Here are some examples of these styles, and an explanation of their meaning.

Code words in text are shown as follows: "The Python file with the mesh building blocks is called `mymesh.py` so the first part of our code contains the following `import` statement."

A block of code is set as follows:

```
def event(evt, val):
    if evt == Draw.ESCKEY:
        Draw.Exit() # exit when user presses ESC
    return
```

When we wish to draw your attention to a particular part of a code block, the relevant lines or items are set in bold:

```
def error(text):
    Draw.Register(lambda:msg(text), event, button_event)
```

Any command-line input or output is written as follows:

blender -P /full/path/to/barchart.py

New terms and **important words** are shown in bold. Words that you see on the screen in menus or dialog boxes, for example, appear in the text like this: "Then we can apply this vertex group to the density parameter in the **extra** panel of the particles context to control the emission."

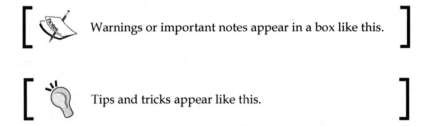

Warnings or important notes appear in a box like this.

Tips and tricks appear like this.

Reader feedback

Feedback from our readers is always welcome. Let us know what you think about this book—what you liked or may have disliked. Reader feedback is important for us to develop titles that you really get the most out of.

To send us general feedback, simply send an e-mail to `feedback@packtpub.com`, and mention the book title via the subject of your message.

If there is a book that you need and would like to see us publish, please send us a note in the **SUGGEST A TITLE** form on `www.packtpub.com` or e-mail `suggest@packtpub.com`.

If there is a topic that you have expertise in and you are interested in either writing or contributing to a book on, see our author guide on www.packtpub.com/authors.

Customer support

Now that you are the proud owner of a Packt book, we have a number of things to help you to get the most from your purchase.

 Downloading the example code for the book
Visit https://www.packtpub.com//sites/default/files/downloads/0400_Code.zip to directly download the example code.
The downloadable files contain instructions on how to use them.

Errata

Although we have taken every care to ensure the accuracy of our content, mistakes do happen. If you find a mistake in one of our books — maybe a mistake in the text or the code — we would be grateful if you would report this to us. By doing so, you can save other readers from frustration and help us improve subsequent versions of this book. If you find any errata, please report them by visiting http://www.packtpub.com/support, selecting your book, clicking on the **let us know** link, and entering the details of your errata. Once your errata are verified, your submission will be accepted and the errata will be uploaded on our website, or added to any list of existing errata, under the Errata section of that title. Any existing errata can be viewed by selecting your title from http://www.packtpub.com/support.

Piracy

Piracy of copyright material on the Internet is an ongoing problem across all media. At Packt, we take the protection of our copyright and licenses very seriously. If you come across any illegal copies of our works, in any form, on the Internet, please provide us with the location address or website name immediately so that we can pursue a remedy.

Please contact us at copyright@packtpub.com with a link to the suspected pirated material.

We appreciate your help in protecting our authors, and our ability to bring you valuable content.

Questions

You can contact us at questions@packtpub.com if you are having a problem with any aspect of the book, and we will do our best to address it.

1
Extending Blender with Python

Before we start crafting scripts in Blender we must check whether or not we have all the necessary tools available. After that we will have to familiarize ourselves with these tools so that we can use them with confidence. In this chapter, we will look at:

- What can and cannot be accomplished with Python in Blender
- How to install a full Python distribution
- How to use the built-in editor
- How to run a Python script
- How to explore built-in modules
- How to write a simple script that adds an object to a Blender scene
- How to register a script in the Blender scripts menu
- How to document your script in a user-friendly way
- How to distribute a script

With so many things possible there is an awful lot to learn, but fortunately the learning curve is not as steep as it might seem. Let's just type in a quick few lines of Python to put a simple object into our Blender scene, just to prove we can, before we head into deeper waters.

1. Start Blender with an empty scene.

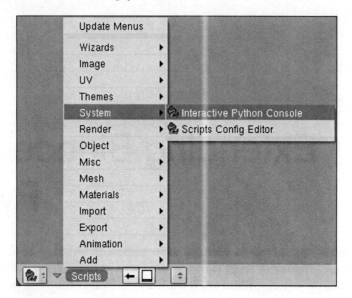

2. Open the interactive Python console (refer to the preceding screenshot to see where to find it).

3. Type in the following lines (end each one with a *Enter/Return*).

```
mesh = Mesh.Primitives.Monkey()
Scene.GetCurrent().objects.new(mesh, 'Suzanne')
Window.RedrawAll()
```

Voila! That's all that is needed to add Suzanne, Blender's famous mascot, to the scene.

The Blender API

Almost anything in Blender is accessible from Python scripts but there are some exceptions and limitations. In this section, we illustrate what this means exactly and which notable features are not accessible to Python (for example, fluid dynamics).

The Blender API consists of three major areas of interest:

- Access to Blender objects and their properties, for example a `Camera` object and its `angle` property or a `Scene` object and its `objects` property
- Access to operations to perform, for example adding a new `Camera` or rendering an image
- Access to the graphical user interface, either by using simple building blocks or by interacting with the Blender event system

There are also some utilities that do not fit well in any of these categories as they concern themselves with abstractions that have no direct relation to Blender objects as seen by the end user, for example functions to manipulate vectors and matrices.

A lot of power

Taken together this means we can achieve a lot of things from Python scripts. We can:

- Create a new Blender object of any type, including cameras, lamps, meshes, and even scenes
- Interact with the user with a graphical user interface
- Automate common tasks within Blender such as rendering
- Automate maintenance tasks outside of Blender such as cleaning up directories
- Manipulate any property of a Blender object that is exposed by the API

That last statement shows one of the current weaknesses of the Blender API: any object property that the developers add in the Blender C source must be provided separately in the Python API. There is no automatic conversion from internal structures to the interface available in Python and this means that efforts must be duplicated and may lead to omitted functionality. For instance, in Blender 2.49 it is not possible at all to set up a fluid simulation from a script. Although it is possible to set up a particle system, there is no way to set the behavioral characteristics of a boids particle system.

Another problem of the 2.49 Python API is that many of the actions a user may choose to perform on an object have no equivalent in the API. Setting simple parameters such as the camera angle or performing a rotation of any object is easy and even associating for example, a subsurface modifier to a mesh is just a few lines of code but common actions, especially on mesh objects, such as subdividing selected edges or extruding faces are missing from the API and must be implemented by the script developer.

These problems led the Blender developers to completely redesign the Blender Python API for the 2.5 version, focusing on feature parity (that is, everything possible in Blender should be possible using the Python API). This means that in many situations it will be far easier to get the same results in Blender 2.5.

Finally, Python is used in more places than just standalone scripts: **PyDrivers** and **PyConstraints** enable us to control the way Blender objects behave and we will encounter them in later chapters. Python also allows us to write custom textures and shaders as part of the nodes system as we will see in *Chapter 7, Creating Custom Shaders and Textures*.

Also, it is important to keep in mind that Python offers us far more than just the (already impressive) tools to automate all sorts of tasks in Blender. Python is a general programming language with an extensive library of tools included, so we do not have to resort to external tools for common system tasks such as copying files or archiving (zipping) directories. Even networking tasks can be implemented quite easily as a number of render farm solutions prove.

Some batteries included

When we install Blender, a Python interpreter is already part of the application. This means that it is not necessary to install Python as a separate application. But there is more to Python than just the interpreter. Python comes with a huge collection of modules that provide a wealth of functionality. Anything from file manipulation to XML processing and more is available, and the best bit is that these modules are a standard part of the language. They are just as well maintained as the Python interpreter itself and (with very few exceptions) available on any platform that Python runs on.

The downside is, of course, that this collection of modules is fairly large (40MB or so), so the Blender developers chose to distribute only the bare minimum, primarily the math module. This makes sense if you want to keep the size of the Blender downloads manageable. Many Python developers have come to depend on the standard distribution because not having to reinvent the wheel saves huge amounts of time, not to mention it's not an easy task to develop and test a full-fledged XML library say, just because you want to be able to read a simple XML file. That is why it is now more or less a consensus that it is a good thing to install the full Python distribution. Fortunately, the installation is just as easy as the installation of Blender itself, even for end users, as binary installers are provided for many platforms, such as Windows and Mac, also in 64-bit versions. (Distributions for Linux are provided as source code with instructions on how to compile them, but many Linux distributions either already provide Python automatically or make it very easy to install it afterwards from a package repository).

Check for a full Python distribution

Chances are that you already have a full Python distribution on your system. You can verify this by starting Blender and checking the console window (the term **console window** refers to either the DOSBox that starts in parallel on Windows or the X terminal window where you start Blender from on other systems) to see if it displays the following text:

```
Compiled with Python version 2.6.2.

Checking for installed Python... got it!
```

If it does, then there is nothing you have to do and you can skip to *The interactive Python console* section. If it shows the following message then you do have to take some action:

```
Compiled with Python version 2.6.2.

Checking for installed Python... No installed Python found.

    Only built-in modules are available.  Some scripts may not run.

    Continuing happily.
```

Installing a full Python distribution

The steps toward a full Python installation for Windows or Mac are as follows:

1. Download a suitable installer from http://www.python.org/download/. At the moment of writing, the latest stable 2.6 version is 2.6.2 (used in Blender 2.49). It is generally a good thing to install the latest stable version as it will contain the latest bug fixes. Make sure, however, to use the same major version as Blender is compiled with. It is fine to use version 2.6.3 when it is released even as Blender is compiled with version 2.6.2. But if you use an older version of Blender that is compiled with Python 2.5.4 you have to install the latest Python 2.5.x release (or upgrade to Blender 2.49, if that is an option).

2. Run the installer: On Windows the installer offers you to choose where to install Python. You can choose anything you like here, but if you choose the default, Blender will almost certainly find the modules installed here without the need to set the PYTHONPATH variable. (see below)

3. (Re) start Blender. The Blender console should show the text:

```
Compiled with Python version 2.6.2.
Checking for installed Python... got it!
```

If it doesn't, it might be necessary to set the PYTHONPATH variable. Refer to the Blender wiki for detailed information:

`http://wiki.blender.org/index.php/Doc:Manual/Extensions/Python`

On Ubuntu Linux, the first step is not needed and installing can be done by using the built-in package manager:

```
sudo apt-get update
sudo apt-get install python2.6
```

Other distributions might use a different package management system so you might have to check the documentation for that. Under Windows it might be necessary to set the PYTHONPATH environment variable, although this is unlikely when using the provided packages.

The interactive Python console

To see where Blender actually looks for modules you may look at Python's sys.path variable. To do this you have to start up Blender's interactive Python console. Note that you use a different and possibly confusing notion of console here — the DOSBox or the terminal window that is started alongside Blender's main application window and where various informational messages are displayed is referred to as **console** as well! The Python interactive console that we want to use now is started from the **script window**:

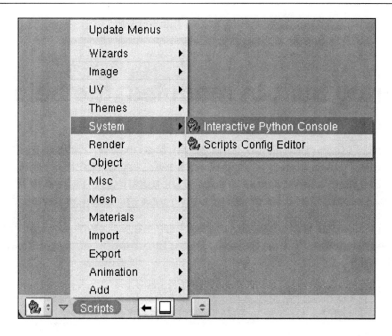

Once the interactive Python console is started, type the following commands:

```
import sys
print sys.path
```

Note that the interactive Python console does not show any prompt (unless when expecting indentation, for example within a for loop) but anything you type will be in a different color (white on black by default) from what is returned (that will be blue or black). The two preceding commands will give us access to Python's sys module that contains various variables with system information. The sys.path variable that we print here will hold all of the directories that will be searched when we try to import a module. (Note that importing sys will always work because sys is a built-in module.) The output will be something similar to:

```
['C:\\Program Files\\Blender Foundation\\Blender', 'C:\\Program
Files\\Blender
Foundation\\Blender\\python26.zip', 'C:\\Python26\\Lib',
'C:\\Python26\\DLLs',
'C:\\Python26\\Lib\\lib-tk', 'C:\\Program Files\\Blender
Foundation\\Blender',
'C:\\Python26', 'C:\\Python26\\lib\\site-packages',
'C:\\Python26\\lib\\site-packages\\PIL',
'C:\\PROGRA~1\\BLENDE~1\\Blender',
'C:\\Documents and Settings\\Michel\\Application Data\\Blender
Foundation\\Blender\\.blender\\scripts', 'C:\\Documents and
Settings\\Michel\\Application Data\\Blender
Foundation\\Blender\\.blender\\scripts\\bpymodules']
```

If your Python installation directory is not in this list then you should set the
PYTHONPATH variable before starting Blender.

Exploring built-in modules, the help() function

The interactive Python console is a good platform to explore built-in modules
as well. Because Python comes equipped with two very useful functions, help()
and dir(), you have instant access to a lot of information contained in Blender's
(and Python's) modules as a lot of documentation is provided as part of the code.

For people not familiar with these functions, here are two short examples, both
run from the interactive Python console. To get information on a specific object
or function, type:

```
help(Blender.Lamp.Get)
```

The information will be printed in the same console:

```
Help on built-in function Get in module Blender.Lamp:

Lamp.Get (name = None):
        Return the Lamp Data with the given name, None if not found, or
        Return a list with all Lamp Data objects in the current scene,
        if no argument was given.
```

The help() function will show the associated docstring of functions, classes,
or modules. In the previous example, that is the information provided with the
Get() method (function) of the Lamp class. A **docstring** is the first string defined
in a function, class, or module. When defining your own functions, it is a good
thing to do this as well. This might look like this:

```
def square(x):
    """
    calculate the square of x.
    """
    return x*x
```

We can now apply the help function to our newly-defined function like we did before:

```
help(square)
```

The output then shows:

```
Help on function square in module __main__:
square(x)
    calculate the square of x.
```

In the programs that we will be developing, we will use this method of documenting where appropriate.

Exploring built-in functions, the dir() function

The `dir()` function lists all members of an object. That object can be an instance, but also a class or module. For example, we might apply it to the `Blender.Lamp` module:

```
dir(Blender.Lamp)
```

The output will be a list of all members of the `Blender.Lamp` module. You can spot the `Get()` function that we encountered earlier:

```
['ENERGY', 'Falloffs', 'Get', 'Modes', 'New', 'OFFSET', 'RGB',
 'SIZE', 'SPOTSIZE', 'Types', '__doc__', '__name__', '__package__',
 'get']
```

Once you know which members a class or module has, you can then check for any additional help information for these members by applying the `help()` function.

Of course both `dir()` and `help()` are most useful when you already have some clue where to look for information. But if so, they can be very convenient tools indeed.

Getting familiar with the built-in editor

It is possible to use any editor (that you like) to write Python scripts and then import the scripts as text files but Blender's built-in text editor will probably be adequate for all programming needs. It features conveniences such as syntax highlighting, line numbering, and automatic indentation, and gives you the possibility to run a script directly from the editor. The ability to run a script directly from the editor is a definite boon when debugging because of the direct feedback that you get when encountering an error. You will not only get an informative message but the offending line will also be highlighted in the editor.

What is more, the editor comes with many plug-ins of which the automatic suggestion of members and the documentation viewer are very convenient for programmers. And of course, it is possible to write additional plug-ins yourself.

You can select the built-in editor by choosing **Text Editor** from the Windows menu:

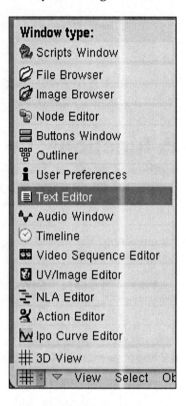

When you start up you are presented with an almost empty area except for a strip of buttons at the bottom:

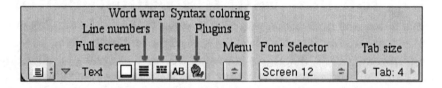

We can select the default empty text buffer TX:Text or create a new empty text by selecting **ADD NEW** from the drop-down menu available when we click on the **Menu** button.

The default name for this new text will be TX:Text.001, but you may change it to something more meaningful by clicking on the name and changing it. Note that if you would like to save this text to an external file (with **Text | Save As...**) the name of the text is distinct from the filename (although in general it is a good idea to keep these the same to avoid confusion). It is not mandatory to save texts as external files; texts are Blender objects that are saved together with all other information when you save your .blend file.

External files may be opened as texts by selecting **OPEN NEW** from the **Menu** button drop-down instead of **ADD NEW**. If for some reason an external file and an associated text are out of sync when Blender is started, an out of sync button is displayed. When clicked, it displays a number of options to resolve the issue.

Once a new or existing text is selected, the menu bar at the bottom of the screen is updated with some additional menu options:

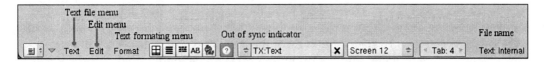

The **Text file menu** gives access to options to open or save a file or to run the script in the editor. It also presents a number of template scripts that may be used as a basis for your own scripts. If you select one of these templates a new text buffer is created with a copy of the selected template.

The **Edit menu** contains **cut-and-paste** functionality as well as options to search and replace text or jump to a chosen line number.

The **Format** menu has options to indent and unindent selected text as well as options to convert whitespace. The latter option can be very helpful when the Python interpreter complains about unexpected indentation levels although there seems nothing amiss with your file. If that happens you possibly have mixed tabs and spaces in way that confuse Python (as they are different as far as the interpreter is concerned) and a possible way out is to convert selected text to spaces first and then back to tabs. This way mixed spaces and tabs will be used in a uniform way again.

An editor example

To get used to the editor, create a new text buffer by choosing **Text | New** and type in the following example lines:

```
import sys
print sys.path
```

Most keys on the keyboard will behave in a familiar way, including *Delete*, *Backspace*, and *Enter*. The shortcut keys for cutting, pasting, and copying are listed in the **Edit** menu as *Alt + X*, *Alt + V*, and *Alt + C* respectively but the *Ctrl* key equivalents *Ctrl + X*, *Ctrl + V*, and *Ctrl + C* (familiar to Windows users) work just as well. A full keyboard map can be consulted on the Blender wiki, `http://wiki.blender.org/index.php/Doc:Manual/Extensions/Python/Text_editor`

Selecting portions of the text can be achieved by clicking and dragging the mouse, but you can also select text by moving the text cursor around while pressing the *Shift* key.

Text will be uncolored by default, but reading scripts can be made a lot easier on the eye by enabling syntax highlighting. Clicking on the little **AB** button will toggle this (it will be black and white when syntax highlighting is off and colored when on.) Like many aspects of Blender, text colors can be customized in the **themes** section of the **User Preferences** window.

Another feature that is very convenient to enable, especially when debugging scripts, is line numbering. (You might write a faultless code in one go, but unfortunately yours truly is less of a genius.) Every Python error message that will be shown will have a filename and a line number, and the offending line will be highlighted. But the lines of the calling function(s), if any, will not be highlighted although their line numbers will be shown in the error message, so having line numbers enabled will enable you to quickly locate the calling context of the trouble spot. Line numbering is enabled by clicking on the **lines** button.

Running a script is done by pressing *Alt + P*. Nothing is displayed in the editor when there are no errors encountered, but the output will be shown on the console (that is, the DOSBox or X terminal Blender started from, *not* the Python interactive console that we encountered earlier).

First steps: Hello world

Tradition demands every book about programming to have a "hello world" example and why would we offend people? We will implement, and run, a simple object instantiating script and show how to integrate this in Blender's script menu. We will also show how to document it and make an entry in the help system. Finally, we will spend some words on the pros and cons of distributing scripts as `.blend` files or as scripts to install in the `scriptdir` by the user.

Let's write some code! You can type in the following lines directly into the interactive Python console, or you can open a new text in Blender's text editor and then press *Alt + P* to run the script. It is a short script but we'll go through it in some detail as it features many of the key aspects of the Blender Python API.

```
#!BPY

import Blender
from Blender import Scene, Text3d, Window

hello = Text3d.New("HelloWorld")
hello.setText("Hello World!")

scn = Scene.GetCurrent()
ob = scn.objects.new(hello)

Window.RedrawAll()
```

The first line identifies this script as a Blender script. This is not necessary to run the script, but if we want to be able to make this script a part of Blender's menu structure we need it, so we better get used to it right away.

You will find the second line (which is highlighted) in virtually any Blender script because it gives us access to the classes and functions of the Blender Python API. Likewise, the third line gives us access to the specific submodules of the Blender module that we will need in this script. We could access them as members of the Blender module of course (for example, Blender.Scene), but importing them explicitly saves some typing and enhances readability.

The next two lines first create a Text3d object and assign that to the variable hello. The Text3d object will have the name HelloWorld in Blender so users can refer to this object by this name. Also this is the name that will be visible in the Outliner window and in the lower-left corner if the object is selected. If there already exists an object of the same type with this name, Blender adds a numerical suffix to the name to make it unique. For example, HelloWorld might become HelloWord.001 if we run the scripts twice.

By default, a newly created Text3d object will contain the text **Text** so we change that to **Hello World!** with setText() method.

A newly created Blender object is not visible by default, we have to associate that with a Scene so the next few lines retrieve a reference to the current scene and add the Text3d object to it. The Text3d object is not added directly to the scene but the scene.objects.new() method embeds the Text3d object in a generic Blender object and returns a reference to the latter. The generic Blender object holds information common to all objects, such as position, whereas the Text3d object holds specific information, such as the text font.

Finally, we tell the window manager to refresh any window that needs a refresh due to the addition of a new object.

Integrating a script in Blender's menus

Your own script doesn't have to be a second class citizen. It can be made part of Blender on par with any of the bundled scripts that come with Blender. It can be added to the **Add** menu present in the header at the top of the View3D window.

 Actually, the **Add** menu is present in the header at the bottom of the user preferences window but as this window is situated above the View3D window, and is by default minimized to just the header, it looks as if it's a header at the top of the View3D window. Many users are so accustomed to it that they see it as part of the View3D window.

It may supply information to Blender's help system just like any other script. The following few lines of code make that possible:

```
"""
Name: 'HelloWorld'
Blender: 249
Group: 'AddMesh'
Tip: 'Create a Hello World text object'
"""
```

We start the script with a standalone string containing several lines.

 Each line starts with a label followed by a colon and a value. The colon should follow the label immediately. There should not be any intervening space, otherwise our script will *not* show up in any menu.

The labels at the beginning of each line serve the following purpose:

- `Name` (a string) defines the name of the scripts as it appears in the menu
- `Blender` (a number) defines the minimum version of Blender needed to use the script
- `Group` (a string) is the submenu of the scripts menu under which this script should be grouped

  If our scripts are to appear under the **Add | Mesh** menu in the View3D window (also accessible by pressing *Space*) this should read `AddMesh`. If it should be under a different submenu of the script's menu, it could read, for example, `Wizards` or `Object`. Besides the necessary labels the following optional labels might be added:

- `Version` (a string) is the version of the script in any format you like.

- `Tip` (a string) is the information shown in the tooltip when hovering over the menu item in the **Scripts** menu. If the script belongs to the group `AddMesh`, no tooltip will be shown even if we define one here.

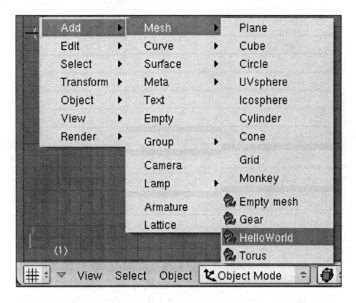

Integrating a script in Blender's help system

Blender has an integrated help system that is accessible from the **Help** menu at the top of the screen. It gives access to online resources and to information on registered scripts via the **Scripts Help Browser** entry. Once selected, it shows a collection of drop-down menus, one for each group, where you can select a script and view its help information.

If we want to enter our script in the integrated help system we need to define some additional global variables:

```
__author__      = "Michel Anders (varkenvarken)"
__version__     = "1.00 2009/08/01"
__copyright__   = "(c) 2009"
__url__         = ["author's site, http://www.swineworld.org"]
__doc__         = """
A simple script to add a Blender Text object to a scene.
It takes no parameters and initializes the object to contain the
text 'Hello World'
"""
```

These variables should be self-explanatory except for the __url__ variable – this one will take a list of strings where each string consists of a short description, a comma, and a URL. The resulting help screen will look like this:

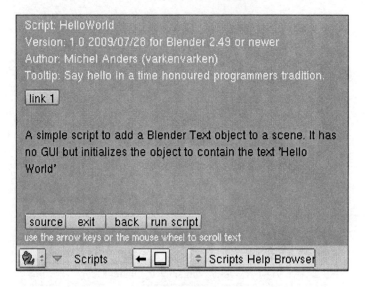

Now all that we have left to do is to test it and then place this script in an appropriate location. We can test the script by pressing *Alt + P*. If no errors are encountered, this will result in our Hello World Text3d object being added to the scene but the script will *not* be appended to the **Add** menu yet.

If a script is to be added to the **Add** menu it has to reside in Blender's script directory. To do this, first save the script in the text buffer to a file with a meaningful name. Next, make sure that this file is located in Blender's script directory. This directory is called scripts and is a subdirectory of .blender, Blender's configuration directory. It is either located in Blender's installation directory or (on Windows) in the Application Data directory. The easiest way to find ours is to simply look at the sys.path variable again to see which listed directory ends in .blender\scripts.

Scripts located in Blender's scripts directory will be automatically executed on startup, so our hello world script will be available anytime we start up Blender. If we want Blender to reexamine the script directory (so that we don't have to restart Blender to see our new addition) we can choose **Scripts | Update menus** in the interactive console.

Don't get confused, stay objective

As you may have noticed the word **object** is used in two different (possibly confusing) ways. In Blender almost anything is referred to as an Object. A `Lamp` for instance is an Object, but so is a `Cube` or a `Camera`. **Objects** are things that can be manipulated by the user and have for example a position and a rotation.

In fact, things are a little bit more structured (or complicated, as some people say): any `Blender` object contains a reference to a more specific object called the **data block**. When you add a `Cube` object to an empty scene you will have a generic object at some location. That object will be called `Cube` and will contain a reference to another object, a `Mesh`. This `Mesh` object is called `Cube` by default as well but this is fine as the namespaces of different kind of objects are separate.

This separation of properties common to all objects (such as position) and properties specific to a single type of object (such as the energy of a `Lamp` or the vertices of a `Mesh`) is a logical way to order sets of properties. It also allows for the instantiation of many copies of an object without consuming a lot of memory; we can have more than one object that points to the same `Mesh` object for example. (The way to achieve that is to create a **linked duplicate**, using *Alt + D*.) The following diagram might help to grasp the concept:

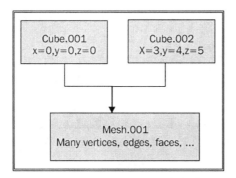

Another way the word **object** is used is in the Python sense. Here we mean an instance of a class. The Blender API is object-oriented and almost every conceivable piece of structured data is represented by an object instanced from a class. Even fairly abstract concepts such as an **Action** or an **IPO** (abstract in the sense that they do not have a position somewhere in your scene) are defined as classes.

How we refer to the Blender or to the Python sense of the word object in this book will mostly be obvious from the context if you keep in mind this distinction. But if not, we tend to write the Blender sense as *Object* and the Python sense as *object* or *object instance*.

Adding different types of object from a script

Adding other types of objects is, in many cases, just as straightforward as adding our text object. If we want our scene to be populated in a way that enabled us to render it, we would have to add a camera and a lamp to make things visible. Adding a camera to the same scene could be done like this (assuming we still have a reference to our active scene in the `scn` variable):

```
from Blender import Camera
cam = Camera.New()            # creates new camera data
ob = scn.objects.new(cam)     # adds a new camera object
scn.setCurrentCamera(ob)      # makes this camera active
```

Note that the `Camera` object is again different from the actual camera data. A `Camera` object holds camera-specific data, such as viewing angle, and a Blender object holds data common to all objects, notably its position and rotation. We will encounter cameras again later and see how we can point them and set the view angle.

Lamps follow pretty much the same pattern:

```
from Blender import Lamp
lamp = Lamp.New()             # create a new lamp
ob = scn.objects.new(lamp)
```

Again, the `Lamp` object holds lamp-specific data such as its type (for example, spot or area) or its energy while the Blender object that encapsulates it defines its position and rotation.

This pattern is similar for a `Mesh` object but the situation is subtly different here because a mesh is a conglomerate of vertices, edges, and faces among other properties.

Adding a mesh object

Like a `Lamp` or a `Camera`, a `Mesh` is a Blender object that encapsulates another object in this case, a `Blender.Mesh` object. But unlike `Blender.Lamp` or `Blender.Camera` objects it does not stop there. A `Blender.Mesh` object itself may contain many other objects. These objects are vertices, edges, and faces. Each of these may have a number of associated properties. They may be selected or hidden and may have a surface normal or an associated UV-texture.

Beside's any associated properties, a single vertex is basically a point in 3D space. In a `Blender.Mesh` object any number of vertices are organized in a list of `Blender.Mesh.MVert` objects. Given a `Mesh` object me, this list may be accessed as `me.verts`. An **edge** is a line connecting two vertices in Blender represented by a `Blender.Mesh.MEdge` object. Its main properties are `v1` and `v2`, which are references to `MVert` objects. The list of edges in a `Mesh` object can be accessed as `me.edges`.

A `MFace` object is a like an edge, basically a list of references to the vertices that define it. If we have a `MFace` object `face`, this list may be accessed as `face.verts`.

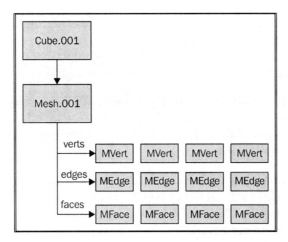

This jumble of objects containing other objects may be confusing, so keep the previous diagram in mind and let's look at some example code to clarify things. We will define a cube. A cube consists of eight vertices connected by twelve edges. The eight vertices also define the six sides (or faces) of the cube.

```
from Blender import Mesh,Scene

corners=[ (-1,-1,-1), (1,-1,-1), (1,1,-1), (-1,1,-1),
          (-1,-1, 1), (1,-1, 1), (1,1, 1), (-1,1, 1) ]
sides= [ (0,1,2,3), (4,5,6,7), (0,1,5,4), (1,2,6,5),
         (2,3,7,6), (3,0,4,7) ]

me = Mesh.New('Cube')
me.verts.extend(corners)
me.faces.extend(sides)
scn = Scene.GetCurrent()
ob = scn.objects.new(me, 'Cube')
Window.RedrawAll()
```

We start by defining a list of corners. Each of the eight corners is represented by a tuple of three numbers, its x, y, and z coordinates. Next we define a list of tuples defining the faces of the cube. The sides of a cube are squares so each tuple holds four integers—each integer is an index to the list of corners. It is important to get the order of these indices right: if we would list the first side as (0,1,3,2) we would get a twisted or a bow-tie face.

Now we can define a `Mesh` object and name it `Cube` (the highlighted part in the preceding code). As noted earlier, the vertices of a `Mesh` object are accessible as a list named `verts`. It has an `extend()` method that may take a list of tuples representing vertex positions to define additional `MVert` objects in our `Mesh`.

Likewise, we can add extra faces to the list of faces of a `Mesh` object by calling the `extend()` method of `faces` with a list of tuples. Because all edges of a cube are edges of the faces there is no need to add any edges separately. This is done automatically when we `extend()` the list of faces.

The `Mesh` object that we have defined so far can now be embedded in a Blender object that can be added to the active scene. Note that it is perfectly acceptable to have a `Mesh` object and a Blender Object with the same name (`Cube` in this case) because different kind of objects in Blender have separate namespaces. In the Blender GUI, names are always prefixed with a two letter prefix to distinguish them. (for example, LA for a lamp, ME for a mesh, or OB for a Blender object)

When creating `Mesh` objects a great deal of attention is needed to get all the vertices, edges, and faces added and correctly numbered. This is just the tip of the iceberg when creating meshes. In *Chapter 2, Creating and Editing Objects*, we will see what hides underwater.

Distributing scripts

In the previous sections, we saw that in order to integrate our script in Blender's menu system and help system we had to place the script in the `.blender\scripts` directory. A fully integrated script can be a big advantage, but this method has a clear drawback: the person who wants to use this script has to put it in the correct directory. This might be a problem if this person does not know how to locate this directory or does not have the permission to place scripts in that directory. That last problem may be overcome by setting an alternative script directory in the `User Preferences`, but not everybody might be that tech oriented.

A viable alternative is distributing a script as a text within a .blend file. A .blend file can be saved with the script clearly visible in the main window and one of the first comment lines of the script might read `Press ALT-P to start this script`. This way, the script can be used by anybody who knows how to open a .blend file.

An additional advantage is that it is easy to bundle extra resources in the same `.blend` file. For example, a script might use certain materials or textures or you might want to include sample output from your script. The only thing that is very difficult to do is distribute Python modules this way. You can use the `import` statement to access other text files but this may pose problems (see *Appendix B*). If you have a lot of code and it is organized in modules, you and your users are probably still better off if you distribute it as a ZIP file with clear instructions on where to unpack this ZIP file.

For Pynodes (or dynamic nodes, see *Chapter 7*) you don't have a choice. **Pynodes** can refer to only the Python code contained in text files within a `.blend` file. This is not really a limitation though as these Pynodes are an integral part of a material, and Blender materials can be distributed only within a `.blend` file. When these materials are linked to or appended their associated nodes and any texts associated with Pynodes are linked to or appended as well, completely hiding from the end user the way a material is actually implemented.

The Blender API

When developing Python programs in Blender it is important to understand what functionality is provided by the API and even more so, what not. The API basically exposes all data and provides functions for manipulating that data. Additionally, the API provides the developer with functions to draw on the screen and to interact with the user interface and windowing system. What the Blender API does not provide is object-specific functionality besides setting simple properties, especially lacking any functions to manipulate meshes on the level of vertices, edges, or faces other than adding or removing them.

This means that very high-level or complex tasks such as adding a subsurface modifier to a `Mesh` object or displaying a file selector dialog are as simple as writing a single line of code, while functions as essential and seemingly simple as subdividing an edge or selecting an edge loop are not available. That doesn't mean these tasks cannot be accomplished, but we will have to code them ourselves. So many examples in this book will refer to a module called `Tools` that we will develop in the next chapters and that will contain useful tools from extruding faces to bridging face loops. Where appropriate and interesting we will highlight the code in this module as well but mainly it is a device to squirrel away any code that might detract us from our goals.

The following sections give a short and very high-level overview of what is available in the Blender API. Many modules and utilities will feature prominently in the next chapters as we will develop practical examples. This overview is meant as a way to help you get started if you want to find out about some functionality and do not know where to look first. It is nowhere near a full documentation of the Blender API. For that, check the most recent version of the API documentation online. You can find the link in the *Appendix A Links and Resources*.

The Blender module

The Blender module serves as a container for most other modules and provides functionality to access system information and perform general tasks.

For example, information such as the Blender version that you are using can be retrieved with the `Get()` function:

```
import Blender
version = Blender.Get('version')
```

Incorporating all externally referred files in a `.blend` file (called **packing** in Blender) or saving your current Blender session to a `.blend` file are other examples of functionality implemented in the top-level Blender module:

```
import Blender
Blender.PackAll()
Blender.Save('myfile.blend')
```

Blender objects

Each Blender object type (`Object`, `Mesh`, `Armature`, `Lamp`, `Scene`, and so on) has an associated module which is a submodule of the top-level `Blender` module. Each module supplies functions to create new objects and find objects of a given type by name. Each module also defines a class with the same name that implements the functionality associated with the Blender object.

Note that in Blender, not only the things directly visible in your scene, such as meshes, lamps, or cameras are objects, but also materials, textures, particle systems, and even IPOs, actions, worlds, and scenes.

Many other data items in Blender are not Objects in the Blender sense (you cannot append them from another `.blend` file or move them about in your scene) but are objects in the Python sense. For example, vertices, edges, and faces within a mesh are implemented as classes: `Blender.Mesh.MVert`, `Blender.Mesh.MEdge`, and `Blender.Mesh.MFace` respectively.

Many modules also have submodules of their own; for example the `Blender.Scene` module provides access to the rendering context by way of the `Blender.Scene.Render` module. Among other things, this module defines a `RenderData` class that allows you to render a still image or animation.

So with what we know now it is possible to draw two slightly different family trees of Blender objects.

The first one illustrates what kind of Blender objects may be contained within or referred to by another Blender object where we limit ourselves to the less abstract objects:

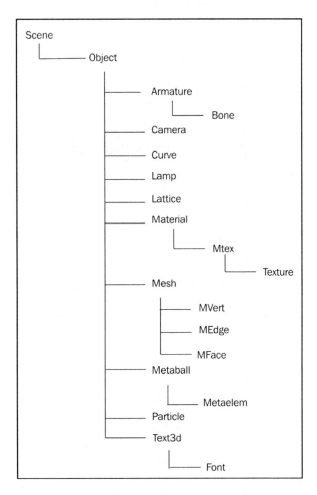

Of course, the diagram above is greatly simplified as we left out some less relevant objects and as it only illustrates a single kind of relationship. There are of course many more types of relationship in a scene, such as parent-child relationships or constraints.

We may contrast the previous diagram with the one that shows in which module a type of object (a class) is defined:

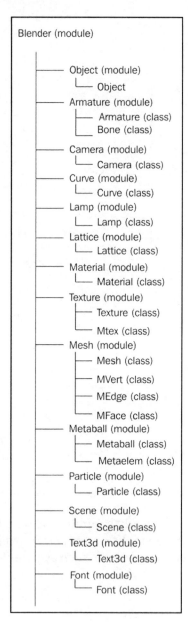

The differences are quite noticeable and are important to keep in mind, especially when looking for specific information in the Blender API documentation. Don't expect to find information on a `Curve` object in the documentation for the `Blender.Object` module because a Blender Curve is a specific Blender Object; the `Curve` class is defined and documented in the `Blender.Curve` module. In general you can expect the documentation of a class to be in the module of same name.

The bpy module

Besides the Blender module, there is another top-level module called `bpy` that provides a unified way to access data. It is considered experimental, but it is stable and might be used as a more intuitive way of accessing objects. For example, if we want to access an object called `MyObject` we normally would do something like this:

```
import Blender
ob = Blender.Object.Get(name='MyObject')
```

With the `bpy` module we might rephrase this:

```
import bpy
ob = bpy.data.objects['MyObject']
```

Likewise, to get access to the active `scene` object we might write this:

```
import Blender
scene = Blender.Scene.GetCurrent()
```

Which can be written in an alternative way:

```
import bpy
scene = bpy.data.scenes.active
```

Which one to prefer is a matter of taste. The `bpy` module will be the only way to access data in the upcoming Blender 2.5 but the changes in Blender 2.5 go deeper than just this data access so don't be fooled by the superficial similarity of the module name!

Drawing on the screen

Access to Blender's windowing system is provided by the `Blender.Draw` module. Here you will find classes and functions to define buttons and pop-up menus and ways to interact with the user. The types of graphical elements that you can display using the `Draw` module are limited to the commonly used ones and customization is not an option.

More advanced functions are provided in the `Blender.BGL` module that gives you access to virtually all OpenGL functions and constants, allowing you to draw almost anything on screen and to let the user interact in many different ways.

Utilities

Finally, there are a number of modules that encapsulate various functionality that do not fit in any of the previous categories:

- `Blender.Library`: Blender allows you to append (that is, import) or link (refer to) objects in another `.blend` file. Another way to look at this is that a `.blend` file can act as a library where you can store your assets. And because almost anything is an object in Blender, almost any asset can be stored in such a library, be it models, lamps, textures, or even complete scenes. The `Blender.Library` module provides script authors the means to access those libraries.

- `Blender.Mathutils` and `Blender.Geometry`: These modules contain among other things, the `Vector` and `Matrix` classes with associated functions to apply all sorts of vector algebra to Blender objects. With the functions provided in these modules you will be able to rotate or shear your object's co-ordinates or calculate the angle between two vectors. Many more convenience functions are provided and these will make many surprise appearances in the examples in this book. Don't worry, we will provide explanations where necessary for people not so at home with vector math.

- `Blender.Noise`: Noise is used in generating all the (apparently) random patterns that form the basis of many of the procedural textures in Blender. This module gives access to the same routines that provide the noise for those textures. This might not only be useful in generating your own textures but might for instance be used in the random placement of objects or implementing a slightly shaky camera path to add realism to your animation.

- `Blender.Registry`: The data inside scripts, whether local or global, is not stored once a script exits. This can be very inconvenient, for example if you want to save the user preferences for your custom script. The `Blender.Registry` module provides ways to store and retrieve persistent data. It does not, however, provide any means to store this data on disk, so the persistence is only for the duration of a Blender session.

- `Blender.Sys`: To quote this module's documentation:

This module provides a minimal set of helper functions and data. Its purpose is to avoid the need for the standard Python module os *in special* os.path, *though it is only meant for the simplest cases.*

As we argued earlier, it is generally advisable to install a full Python distribution which among other things includes the os and os.path modules that give you access to a far wider range of functionality. Therefore, we will not use the Blender.sys module in this book.

- Blender.Types: This module provides constants that can be used for the type checking of objects. Python's built-in function type() returns the type of its argument. This makes it quite easy to check whether an object has a given type when compared to one of the constants in this module.

If we would want to make sure an Object is a Curve object we could, for example, do it like this:

```
...
if type(someobject) == Blender.Types.CurveType :
    ... do things only allowed for Curve objects ...
```

Summary

In this chapter, we have seen how to extend Blender with a full Python distribution and familiarized ourselves with the built-in editor. This enabled us to write scripts that, although simple, were fully integrated in Blenders scripting menu and help system. We covered many subjects in detail including:

- What can and cannot be accomplished with Python in Blender
- How to install a full Python distribution
- How to use to the built-in editor
- How to run a Python script
- How to explore built-in modules
- How to write a simple script that adds an object to a Blender scene
- How to register a script in the Blender scripts menu
- How to document your script in a user-friendly way
- How to distribute a script

In the next chapter, we take this knowledge a step further to create and edit complex objects and we will see how to define a graphical user interface.

2
Creating and Editing Objects

In a way, meshes are the most essential type of objects in a 3D application. They form the basis of most visible objects and are the raw material that might get rigged and animated further down the line. This chapter deals with the creation of meshes and with ways to manipulate a mesh object, both as a whole and as the individual entities it consists of—the vertices, edges, and faces.

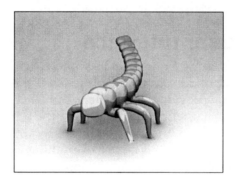

In this chapter, you will learn:

- How to create configurable mesh objects
- How to design a graphical user interface
- How to make your script store user choices for later reuse
- How to select vertices and faces in a mesh
- How to parent an object to another
- How to create groups
- How to modify meshes
- How to run Blender from the command line and render in the background
- How to process command-line parameters

Creepy crawlies—a GUI to configure objects

Instantiating a single copy of a one-off Blender object (like we did in the "hello world" example in *Chapter 1, Extending Blender with Python*) might be a good programming exercise, but an object creation script really comes into its own when built-in methods such as copying objects, or modifiers such as the array modifier, are not sufficient.

A good example is where we want to create one or many object variants and these variants need to be easy to configure for the end user. For example, nuts and bolts come in many shapes and sizes so Blender comes included with a script to create them. Many more scripts are available on the Web to create anything from mechanical gears to stairs, from trees to church domes.

In this section, we show how to build a small application that can create all sorts of bug-like creatures and comes with a simple but effective GUI to set the many configurable parameters. This application also stores the user preferences for later reuse.

Building the user interface

Designing, building, and testing a graphical user interface can be a formidable task, but the Blender API provides us with tools to make this task a lot easier. The `Blender.Draw` module provides simple, but often used and easy to configure components to quickly put a user interface together. The `Blender.BGL` module gives access to all the nuts and bolts to design a graphical user interface from scratch. We will mostly use the former because it is almost everything we need but we give an example of the latter as well to design a simple error pop up. Our main user interface will look like this:

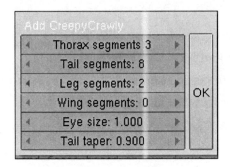

When we invoke our script from the **Add** Menu (normally accessible from the menu bar at the top of the screen or by pressing the spacebar in the 3D view), the previous menu will pop up and the user can tweak the parameters to his or her liking. When the **OK** button is pressed the script generates an insect-like mesh. The pop up can also be exited by pressing *Esc,* in which case the script terminates without generating a mesh.

Creating bugs—some assembly required

Our mission is to create simple creatures from a small sample of building blocks that may be chained together. The outline for our script is this:

1. Import the building blocks for our creatures.

2. Draw a user interface.

3. Assemble the creature mesh from building blocks as defined by the user.

4. Insert the mesh as an object into the scene.

We go through the script step-by-step showing the relevant parts in detail. (The full script is available as `creepycrawlies.py`.) The first step involves creating body parts that are suitable for assembling together. This means we have to model these parts in Blender, defining suitable joints and marking those joints as vertex groups. Then we export these meshes as Python code by using a script that we encounter again in the next chapter as it deals with vertex groups.

For now, we use this generated Python code simply as a module containing several lists of vertices defining each body part. We have to make sure that this module is somewhere in the Python path, for example, `.blender\scripts\bpymodules` would be a logical choice or alternatively the user `scriptdir`. The Python file with the mesh building blocks is called `mymesh.py` so the first part of our code contains the following `import` statement:

```
import mymesh
```

Creating a user interface

Drawing a simple user interface is a matter of using `Draw.Create()` to create the required buttons and assembling and initializing these buttons with `Draw.PupBlock()`

This is somewhat limited compared to full-fledged libraries available for some programming languages, but very easy to use. The basic idea is to create interactive objects, such as buttons, and then assemble them in a dialog box to display to the user. At the same time, the dialog box states some of the limitations on the values the button may produce. The dialog or pop up will be shown at the position of the cursor. Blender is capable of producing a more sophisticated user interface, but for now we stick to the basics.

Although `Draw.Create()` can produce toggle buttons and input buttons for strings as well, for our application we need input buttons only for integer values and floating point values. The type of the variable (for example a floating point value or an integer) is determined by the type of the default value given to `Draw.Create()`. The **OK** button is automatically displayed by `Draw.PupBlock()`. This function takes a list of tuples as an argument with each tuple defining a button to display. Each tuple consists of a text to display on the button, a button object created with `Draw.Create()`, minimum and maximum allowable values, and a tooltip text to show when hovering above the button.

```
Draw = Blender.Draw
THORAXSEGMENTS = Draw.Create(3)
TAILSEGMENTS = Draw.Create(5)
LEGSEGMENTS = Draw.Create(2)
WINGSEGMENTS = Draw.Create(2)
EYESIZE = Draw.Create(1.0)
TAILTAPER = Draw.Create(0.9)

if not Draw.PupBlock('Add CreepyCrawly', [
('Thorax segments:' , THORAXSEGMENTS, 2, 50,
   'Number of thorax segments'),
('Tail segments:' , TAILSEGMENTS, 0, 50, 'Number of tail segments'),
('Leg segments:' , LEGSEGMENTS, 2, 10,
  'Number of thorax segments with legs'),
('Wing segments:' , WINGSEGMENTS, 0, 10,
  'Number of thorax segments with wings'),
('Eye size:' , EYESIZE, 0.1,10, 'Size of the eyes'),
('Tail taper:' , TAILTAPER, 0.1,10,
   'Taper fraction of each tail segment'),]):
   return
```

As you can see, we limit the possible values of our input buttons to a reasonable range (up to 50 for the thorax and tail segments) to prevent unwanted results (huge values might cripple your system if memory or processing power is scarce).

Remembering choices

It would be very convenient if we could remember the user's choices so that we could present the last settings when the script is run again, but in Blender each script is run in isolation and all information within the script is lost once the script ends. Therefore, we need some mechanism to store information in a persistent way. For this purpose, the Blender API has the `Registry` module that allows us to keep values in memory (and on disk as well) indexed by an arbitrary key.

Our GUI initialization code changes little in itself if we want to add this functionality, but is prepended by code retrieving remembered values (if they are present) and followed by code saving the user's choices:

```
reg = Blender.Registry.GetKey('CreepyCrawlies',True)
try:
    nthorax=reg['ThoraxSegments']
except:
    nthorax=3
try:
    ntail=reg['TailSegments']
except:
    ntail=5
... <similar code for other parameters> ...

Draw = Blender.Draw
THORAXSEGMENTS = Draw.Create(nthorax)
TAILSEGMENTS = Draw.Create(ntail)
LEGSEGMENTS = Draw.Create(nleg)
WINGSEGMENTS = Draw.Create(nwing)
EYESIZE = Draw.Create(eye)
TAILTAPER = Draw.Create(taper)

if not Draw.PupBlock('Add CreepyCrawly', [\
... <identical code as in previous example> ...
return
reg={'ThoraxSegments':THORAXSEGMENTS.val,
     'TailSegments' :TAILSEGMENTS.val,
     'LegSegments' :LEGSEGMENTS.val,
     'WingSegments' :WINGSEGMENTS.val,
     'EyeSize' :EYESIZE.val,
     'TailTaper':TAILTAPER.val}
Blender.Registry.SetKey('CreepyCrawlies',reg,True)
```

The actual reading and writing of our registry entry is highlighted. The `True` argument indicates that we want to retrieve our data from disk if it is not available in memory, or write it to disk as well when saving so that our script can access this saved information even if we stop Blender and restart it later. The actual registry entry received or written is a dictionary that can hold whatever data we want. Of course, there might not yet be a registry entry present, in which case we get a `None` value—a situation taken care of by the `try ... except ...` statements.

The full power of Blender graphics

A pop-up dialog is sufficient for many applications but if it does not fit your requirements, Blender's `Draw` module has many more building blocks to create a user interface but these building blocks require a little bit more effort to glue them together in a working application.

We will use these building blocks to create an error pop up. This pop up merely shows a message on an alarmingly colored background but illustrates nicely how user actions (such as key presses or button clicks) are linked to the graphical elements.

```
from Blender import Window,Draw,BGL

def event(evt, val):
    if evt == Draw.ESCKEY:
        Draw.Exit() # exit when user presses ESC
    return

def button_event(evt):
    if evt == 1:
        Draw.Exit()
    return

def msg(text):
    w = Draw.GetStringWidth(text)+20
    wb= Draw.GetStringWidth('Ok')+8
    BGL.glClearColor(0.6, 0.6, 0.6, 1.0)
    BGL.glClear(BGL.GL_COLOR_BUFFER_BIT)
    BGL.glColor3f(0.75, 0.75, 0.75)
    BGL.glRecti(3,30,w+wb,3)
    Draw.Button("Ok",1,4,4,wb,28)
    Draw.Label(text,4+wb,4,w,28)

def error(text):
    Draw.Register(lambda:msg(text), event, button_event)
```

The `error()` function is where it all starts and ends for the user; it tells Blender what to draw, where to send events such as button clicks, where to send key presses, and starts the interaction. The `lambda` function is necessary as the function that we pass to `Draw.Register()` to draw things cannot take an argument, yet we want to pass a different text argument every time we call `error()`. The `lambda` function basically defines a new function without arguments but with the text enclosed.

The `msg()` function is responsible for drawing all of the elements on the screen. It draws a colored backdrop with the `BGL.glRecti()` function, a label with the text to display (with `Draw.Label()`), and an OK button that is assigned an event number of `1` (with `Draw.Button()`). When the user clicks the OK button, this event number is sent to the event handler—the `button_event()` function that we passed to `Draw.Register()`. All that the event handler does when it is called with this event number of `1` is to terminate the `Draw.Register()` function by calling `Draw.Exit()`, so our `error()` function may return.

Creating a new Mesh object

Once we have retrieved our lists of vertex co-ordinates and face indices from the `mymesh` module, we need some manner to create a new `Mesh` object in our scene and add `MVert` and `MFace` objects to this mesh. This might be implemented like this:

```
me=Blender.Mesh.New('Bug')
me.verts.extend(verts)
me.faces.extend(faces)
scn=Blender.Scene.GetCurrent()
ob=scn.objects.new(me, 'Bug')
scn.objects.active=ob

me.remDoubles(0.001)
me.recalcNormals()
```

The first line creates a new `Mesh` object with the name `Bug`. It will contain no vertices, edges, or faces and will not be embedded in a Blender object nor connected to any `Scene` yet. If the name of the mesh already exists, it is appended with a unique numerical suffix (for example, `Bug.001`).

The next two lines actually create geometry inside the mesh. The `verts` attribute is where our list of `MVert` objects is referenced. It has a method `extend()` that will take a list of tuples, each containing the x, y, and z coordinates of the vertices to create. Likewise, the `extend()` method of the `faces` attribute will take a list of tuples, each containing three or more indices into the vertex list that together define a face. Order is important here: we need to add new vertices first; otherwise newly-created faces cannot refer to them. It is not necessary to define any edges, as adding faces will also create implied edges that are not already present.

A mesh in itself is not yet an object that can be manipulated by the user, so in the next few lines (highlighted) we retrieve the current scene and add a new object to the scene. The arguments to `new()` are the `Mesh` object that we created earlier and the name we want to give to the object. The name given to the object might be the same as the one given to the mesh, as mesh names and object names live in different namespaces. As with meshes, an existing name will be made unique by adding a suffix. If the name is left out, the new object will have the type of its argument as a default name (`Mesh` in this case).

A newly-created object will be selected but not active so we correct that by assigning our object to `scene.objects.active` .

As we add together our mesh from various collections of vertices the result might not be as clean as we would like and therefore, the final two actions make sure we do not have any vertices that occupy almost the same location in space and that all face normals consistently point outward.

Transforming mesh topology

Creating the creature from building blocks requires that we duplicate, scale, and mirror those building blocks before we stick them together. In Blender 2.49, this means we have to define some utility functions to perform those actions as they are not present in the API. We define these utility functions in the **Tools** module, but we highlight some of them here as they show some interesting methods.

Some actions such as scaling around a median point or translation of vertices are straightforward but connecting a group of vertices to another one is tricky, as we would like to prevent edges from crossing each other and keep faces flat and undistorted. We cannot simply connect two sets of vertices (or edge loops) together. But by trying different starting points on an edge loop and checking if such a choice minimizes the distance between all vertex pairs we insure that no edges cross and distortion is minimal (although we can't prevent faces to distort if the edge loops are very dissimilar in shape).

Code outline bridging edge loops

In the function that creates the new faces we have to perform the following steps:

1. Check that both edge loops are equally long and nonzero.
2. For every edge in loop 1:
    1. Find the edge in loop 2 that is closest.
    2. Create a face connecting these two edges.

The function that implements this outline looks fairly complicated:

```
def bridge_edgeloops(e1,e2,verts):

    e1 = e1[:]
    e2 = e2[:]
    faces=[]

    if len(e1) == len(e2) and len(e1) > 0 :
```

The function takes two lists of edges as an argument and a list of vertices. The edges are represented as tuples of two integers (indices into the `verts` list) and the vertices are tuples of x, y, and z co-ordinates.

The first thing we do is make copies of the two edge lists because we do not want to mangle the lists in their original context. The list of faces that we will be constructing is initialized to an empty list and we do a sanity check on the length of both edge lists. If that checks out we proceed to the next bit:

```
for a in e1:
    distance = None
    best = None
    enot = []
```

We iterate over every edge in the first list, referring to this edge as a. The `distance` parameter will hold the distance to the closest edge in the second edge list and `best` will be a reference to that edge. `enot` is a list that will accumulate all edges from the second list that are at a greater distance than `best`.

At the end of each iteration, `enot` will hold all edges from the second list minus one — the one we consider the closest. We then reassign `enot` to the second list so the second list will shrink by one edge over each iteration. We are done once the second list of edges is exhausted:

```
while len(e2):
    b = e2.pop(0)
```

The current edge from the second list that we are considering is referred to as b. For our purposes, we define the distance between a and b as the sum of the distance between corresponding vertices in a and b. If that one is shorter, we define it as the sum of the distance to the flipped vertices of b. If the last situation applies, we swap the vertices in edge b. This may seem a complicated way to do things, but by summing the two distances we assure that edges which are relatively co-linear are favored thereby diminishing the number of non-flat faces that will be constructed. By checking whether flipping the second edge will result in a shorter distance, we prevent the formation of warped or bow-tie quads as illustrated in the following figure:

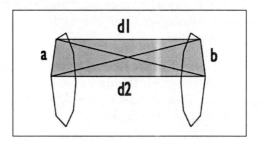

The implementation will look like the previous figure where the highlighted vec are aliases to Mathutil.Vector, converting our tuples of x, y, and z co-ordinates to proper vectors that we can subtract, add, and take the length of.

First we calculate the distance:

```
d1 = (vec(verts[a[0]]) - vec(verts[b[0]])).length + \
(vec(verts[a[1]]) - vec(verts[b[1]])).length
```

Then we check whether flipping the b edge results in a shorter distance:

```
d2 = (vec(verts[a[0]]) - vec(verts[b[1]])).length + \
(vec(verts[a[1]]) - vec(verts[b[0]])).length
if d2<d1 :
    b =(b[1],b[0])
    d1 = d2
```

If the calculated distance is not the shortest, we set aside the edge for the next iteration, unless it is the first we encounter:

```
if distance == None or d1<distance :
    if best != None:
        enot.append(best)
        best = b
        distance = d1
    else:
        enot.append(b)
        e2 = enot
        faces.append((a,best))
```

Finally, we convert our list of faces, consisting of tuples of two edges, to a list of tuples of four indices:

```
return [(a[0],b[0],b[1],a[1]) for a,b in faces]
```

There is much more to this script and we will revisit `creepycrawlies.py` in the following chapter as we add modifiers and vertex groups and rig our model. The illustration shows a sample of the bestiary that can be created by the script.

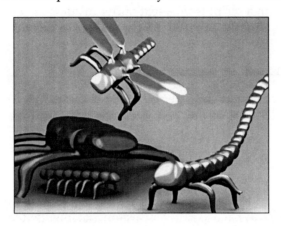

Dazzle your boss—bar charts in Blender style

To prove that Blender is adaptable to many tasks besides the interactive creation of 3D graphics, we will show you how to import external data (a spreadsheet in CSV format) and automate the task of creating and rendering the 3D representation of a bar chart.

The idea is to run Blender with arguments directing it to run a script that reads a `.csv` file, renders an image, and saves that image when finished. For this to be possible we need a way to call Blender with the correct parameters. We get to that script shortly, but first let's see how to pass parameters to Blender to make it run a Python script:

```
blender -P /full/path/to/barchart.py
```

It is also possible to run a script from a text buffer inside a `.blend` file by naming that text buffer instead. Notice the order of the parameters in this case—the `.blend` file comes first:

```
blender barchart.blend -P barchart.py
```

We also need a way to specify arguments to pass to our script. In contrast to what is described in the API docs, we can just access the command-line arguments from Python like this:

```
import sys
print sys.argv
```

This last snippet will print all arguments, including the name of the Blender executable as the first. Our script will have to skip any arguments intended for Blender itself when using this list. Any arguments intended only for our script that shouldn't be interpreted by Blender itself should come after an **end-of-options argument**, the double minus (`--`).

Finally, we don't want Blender to pop up and show an interactive GUI. Instead, we will instruct it to run in the background and exit when done. This is done by passing the `-b` option. Putting all this together, the command line will look like this:

```
blender -b barchart.blend -P barchart.py -- data.csv
```

If Blender is run in background mode you *must* specify a `.blend` file, otherwise Blender will crash. If we have to specify a `.blend` file we can use an internal text as our Python script just as well, otherwise we'd have to keep two files together instead of one.

The bar chart script

Here, we show the relevant parts of the code in chunks (the complete file is available as `barchart.blend` that has `barchart.py` as an embedded text). We start by creating a new `World` object and set its zenith and horizon colors to a neutral all white (highlighted part of the following code):

```
if __name__ == '__main__':
    w=World.New('BarWorld')
```

```
w.setHor([1,1,1])
w.setZen([1,1,1])
```

Next, we retrieve the last argument passed to Blender and check whether the extension is that of a `.csv` file. Real world production code would have more sophisticated error checking of course:

```
csv = sys.argv[-1]
if csv.endswith('.csv'):
```

If it has the correct extension we create a new `Scene` named `BarScene` and set its `world` attribute to our newly created world (This was inspired by a much more elaborate script by *jessethemid* on Blender Artists `http://blenderartists.org/forum/showthread.php?t=79285`). The background mode does not load any default `.blend` file so the default scene will not contain any objects. However, just to make sure, we create a new empty scene with a meaningful name that will hold our objects:

```
sc=Scene.New('BarScene')
sc.world=w
sc.makeCurrent()
```

Then, we pass the filename to a function that adds the `barchart` objects to the current scene and returns the center of the chart so that our `addcamera()` function can use it to aim the camera. We also add a lamp to make rendering possible (otherwise our render would be all black).

```
center = barchart(sys.argv[-1])
addcamera(center)
addlamp()
```

The rendering itself is straightforward (we will encounter more elaborate examples in *Chapter 8, Rendering and Image Manipulation*). We retrieve the rendering context that holds all information about how to render, for example which frame, what output type, the size of the render, and so on. And, because most attributes have sensible defaults, we just set the format to PNG and render.

```
context=sc.getRenderingContext()
context.setImageType(Scene.Render.PNG)
context.render()
```

Finally, we set the output directory to an empty string to make our output go to the current working directory (the directory we were in when we called Blender) and save our rendered image. The image will have the same basename as the `.csv` file that we passed as the first argument but will have a `.png` extension. We checked that the filename ends in `.csv` so it's safe to bluntly strip the last four characters from the filename and add `.png`

```
context.setRenderPath('')
context.saveRenderedImage(csv[:-4]+'.png')
```

Adding a lamp is not much different from adding any other object and is very similar to the "hello world" example. We create a new `Lamp` object, add it to the current scene, and set its location. A `Lamp` object has of course many configurable options but we settle for a default non-directional lamp in this example. The highlighted code shows some typical Python idiom: `loc` is a tuple of three values but `setLocation()` takes three separate arguments so we indicate we want to unpack the tuple as separate values with the * notation:

```
def addlamp(loc=(0.0,0.0,10.0)):
    sc = Scene.GetCurrent()
    la = Lamp.New('Lamp')
    ob = sc.objects.new(la)
    ob.setLocation(*loc)
```

Adding a camera is a little more intricate as we have to point it to our bar chart and make sure that the view angle is wide enough to see everything. We define a perspective camera here and set a fairly wide angle. Because the default camera is already oriented along the z-axis we do not have to set any rotation, just set the location 12 units removed from the center along the z-axis as highlighted in the second last line of the following code:

```
def addcamera(center):
    sc = Scene.GetCurrent()
    ca = Camera.New('persp','Camera')
    ca.angle=75.0
    ob = sc.objects.new(ca)
    ob.setLocation(center[0],center[1],center[2]+12.0)
    sc.objects.camera=ob
```

The `barchart` function itself is not much of a surprise. We open the passed-in filename and use the standard `csv` module from Python to read the data from the file. We store all column headers in `xlabel` and other data in `rows`.

```
from csv import DictReader

def barchart(filename):
    csv = open(filename)
    data = DictReader(csv)
    xlabel = data.fieldnames[0]
    rows = [d for d in data]
```

In order to scale our bar chart to reasonable values we have to determine the extremes of the data. The first column of each record holds the x-value (or label) so we exclude that from our calculation. As each value is stored as a string we have to convert it to a floating point value for comparisons.

```
maximum = max([float(r[n]) for n in data.fieldnames[1:]
                for r in rows])
minimum = min([float(r[n]) for n in data.fieldnames[1:]
                for r in rows])
```

To create the actual bars we iterate over all rows. Because the x-value might be a textual label (such as the name of a month for example), we keep a separate numerical x-value in order to position the bars. The x-value itself is added to the scene as a `Text3d` object by the `label()` function, whereas the y-values are visualized by appropriately scaled `Cube` objects added by the `bar()` function. Neither the `label()` nor the `bar()` function are shown here.

```
for x,row in enumerate(rows):
    lastx=x
    label(row[xlabel],(x,10,0))
    for y,ylabel in enumerate(data.fieldnames[1:]):
        bar(10.0*(float(row[ylabel])-minimum)/maximum,(x,0,y+1))
    x = lastx+1
```

Finally, we label each column (that is, each set of data) with its own column header as a label. We stored the number of x-values so we can return the center of our bar chart by dividing it by two (the y component is set to 5.0 as we scaled all y-values to lie within the range 0-10).

```
for y,ylabel in enumerate(data.fieldnames[1:]):
    label(ylabel,(x,0,y+0.5),'x')
    return (lastx/2.0,5.0,0.0)
```

A Windows trick: SendTo

Once you have your `.blend` file containing a correct Python script and you have figured out the correct way to invoke it from the command line, you can integrate this more closely with Windows XP by creating a `SendTo` program. A `SendTo` program (a `.BAT` file in this case) is any program that will take a single filename as an argument and acts upon it. It has to reside in the `SendTo` directory—which may be located in different places depending on your system configuration. It is simple to find by clicking on the **Start** button, selecting **Run**, and typing **sendto** instead of a command. This will open the correct directory. In this directory you can place the `.BAT` file, in our case we call it `BarChart.BAT`, and it will contain a single command: `/full/path/to/blender.exe /path/to/barchart.blend -P barchart.py -- %1` (note the percent sign). Now we can simply right-click any `.csv` file we encounter and we can then select `BarChart.BAT` from the `SendTo` menu and hey presto, a `.png` file will appear alongside our `.csv`.

Weird faces—selecting and editing faces in meshes

Blender already provides a host of options to select and manipulate the faces, edges, and vertices of a mesh, either via built-in methods or via Python extension scripts. But if you want to select some elements based on your unique requirements, this section shows how to implement that. We build a few small scripts that illustrate how to access faces, edges, and vertices and how to work with the various properties of these objects.

Selecting warped (non-planar) quads

Warped quads, also known as **bow-tie quads,** are sometimes formed when accidentally mixing up the vertex order during face creation. In a less extreme case they might be formed when moving a single vertex of a planar quad. This small illustration shows how these may look in the 3D-view:

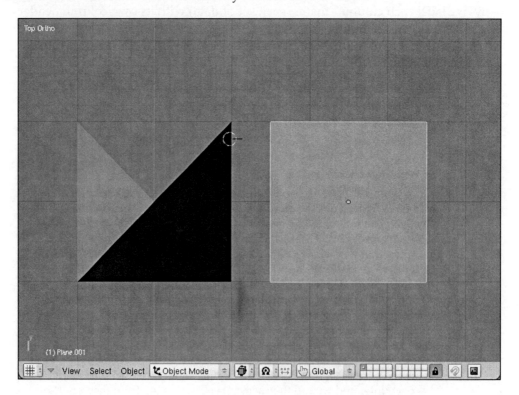

In the 3D view, the warped face on the right didn't seem out of the ordinary but when rendered it does not show uniform shading:

Both objects are planes and consist of a single face with four vertices. The one on the left is a bow-tie quad. Its right edge is rotated a full 180 degrees resulting in an ugly, black triangle where we see the back of the warped face. The plane on the right shows no noticeable distortion in the 3D view even though its upper-right vertex is moved a considerable distance along the z-axis (our line of sight). When rendered however, the distortion of the right plane is clearly visible. The visible distortion of slightly warped quads may be overcome by setting the smooth attribute of a face that will interpolate the vertex normals along the face resulting in a smooth appearance. Slightly warped quads are almost inevitable when modeling or deforming a mesh by an armature and whether they result in visible problems depends on the situation. Often it is helpful if you can identify and select them to make your own judgment.

Warped quads can be identified by checking whether the normals of the triangles that form the quad are pointing in the same direction. A flat quad will have its triangle normals pointing in the same direction as shown in the following figure:

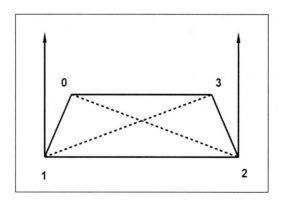

Whereas in a warped quad these normals are not parallel:

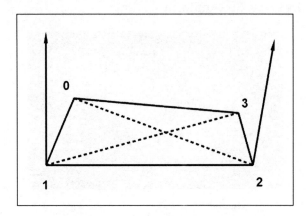

These triangle normals are not the same as vertex normals: those are defined as the average of all face normals of the faces sharing a vertex so we will have to calculate these triangle normals ourselves. This can be done by taking the cross product of the edge vectors, that is, the vectors defined by the two vertices at the end of each edge. In the examples shown we have the left triangle normal formed by taking the cross product of the edge vectors $1 \rightarrow 0$ and $1 \rightarrow 2$ and the right triangle by taking the cross product of the edge vectors $2 \rightarrow 1$ and $2 \rightarrow 3$.

It does not matter whether we traverse our edges clockwise or counterclockwise but we have to be careful to be consistent in ordering edges when calculating the cross products because the sign will be reversed. Once we have our triangle normals we can check whether they point in exactly the same direction by verifying that all components (x, y, and z) of one vector are scaled by the same factor when compared to the corresponding components of the second vector. To give us somewhat more flexibility however, we would like to calculate the angle between the triangle normals and select a face only if that angle exceeds some minimum. We do not have to devise such a function ourselves because the `Blender.Mathutils` module provides the `AngleBetweenVecs()` function.

It is possible to construct four different triangles within a quad but is not necessary to compare all triangle normals—any two normals will suffice because moving a single vertex of a quad will alter three of the possible four triangle normals.

Code outline warp select

Armed with all this information, the outline for our tool will look like this:

1. Show pop up for minimum angle.
2. Verify that the active object is a mesh and in *edit* mode.
3. Enable *face select* mode.
4. For all faces, check if the face is a quad and if so:
   ° Calculate the triangle normal defined by vertex 0, 1, and 2
   ° Calculate the triangle normal defined by vertex 1, 2, and 3
   ° Calculate the angle between normals
   ° If angle > minimum angle, select the face

This translates in the following code for the actual detection and selection (the full script is provided as `warpselect.py`):

```
def warpselect(me,maxangle=5.0):
    for face in me.faces:
        if len(face.verts) == 4:
            n1 = ( face.verts[0].co - face.verts[1].co ).cross(
            face.verts[2].co - face.verts[1].co )
            n2 = ( face.verts[1].co - face.verts[2].co ).cross(
            face.verts[3].co - face.verts[2].co )
            a = AngleBetweenVecs(n1,n2)
            if a > maxangle :
                face.sel = 1
```

As you can see, our outline corresponds almost one-to-one to the code. Note that `AngleBetweenVecs()` returns the angle in degrees so we can directly compare it to `maxangle` which is also in degrees. Also, there is no need to implement the cross product of two vectors ourselves as Blender's `Vector` class is well stocked with all sorts of operators. Before we can call this function we have to take care of an important detail: in order to select faces, *face selection* mode should be enabled. This can be done as follows:

```
selectmode = Blender.Mesh.Mode()
Blender.Mesh.Mode(selectmode | Blender.Mesh.SelectModes.FACE)
```

To illustrate the less well-known fact that select modes are *not* mutually exclusive we set the *face select* mode in addition to any mode already selected by combining values with a binary or operator (|). At the end of the script we restore the mode that was active.

Selecting ultra sharp faces

Many tools exist to select faces that are in some sense unwieldy to work with. Blender has built-in tools to select faces that have an area that is too small or that have a perimeter that is too short. However, it lacks a tool to select faces with edges that form angles that are sharper than some limit. In some modeling tasks it would be very convenient if we could select such faces, as they are generally difficult to manipulate and may give rise to ugly artifacts when applying a subsurface modifier or deforming a mesh.

Note that Blender's *select sharp edges* tool (*Ctrl + Alt + Shift + S*) does something different despite its name; it selects those edges that are shared by exactly two faces whose angle of contact is less than some minimum value or, to put it in another way, selects edges between faces that are relatively flat.

We already have seen that Blender's `Mathutils` module has a function to calculate the angle so our code is very brief as the real work is done by a single function shown below. (The full script is provided as `sharpfaces.py`.)

```
def sharpfaces(me,minimum_angle):
    for face in me.faces:
        n = len(face.verts)
        edges = [face.verts[(i+1)%n].co - face.verts[i].co
                for i in range(n)]
        for i in range(n):
            a = AngleBetweenVecs(-edges[i],edges[(i+1)%n])
            if a < minimum_angle :
                face.sel = 1
                break
```

Note that we do not distinguish between tris or quads as both may have edges that are joined by a sharp angle. The highlighted part in the preceding code shows one subtle detail; each time we calculate the angle between our two edge vectors, we invert one of them because to calculate the correct angle, each of the vectors should originate in the same vertex whereas we calculated them all as pointing from one vertex to the next.

The distinction is illustrated in the following figure:

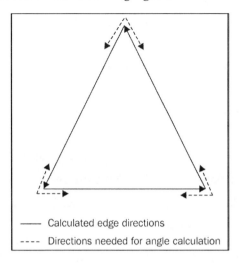

—— Calculated edge directions

---- Directions needed for angle calculation

Selecting vertices with many edges

Ideally, a mesh will contain faces that consist of only four vertices (these faces are generally referred to as **quads**) and are fairly even sized. Such a configuration is optimal when deforming the mesh, as is often necessary with animations. Of course, there is nothing intrinsically wrong with three-sided faces (**tris**) but in general it is better to avoid them because small triangular faces wreck havoc with subsurface modifiers, causing them to show unsightly ripples.

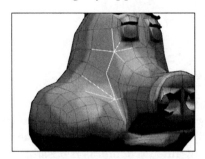

Now even when you have a mesh that consists only of quads, some vertices are the center of more than four edges. These vertices are sometimes called **poles**, hence the name of the scripts in the following sections. If the number of edges is excessive, say six or more (as shown in the previous screenshot), such an area might become difficult to deform and difficult to manipulate for the modeler. In a large and complex mesh these vertices might be difficult to pinpoint and therefore we need a selection tool that selects those vertices.

Selecting poles

In order to select vertices with a certain number of steps we may perform the following steps:

1. Check whether the active object is a `Mesh`.
2. Check whether we are in *object* mode.
3. Show a pop-up menu to input the minimum number of edges.
4. For every vertex:
    ◦ Iterate over all edges, counting occurrences of the vertex
    ◦ If count is larger or equal to the minimum, select the vertex

This approach is straightforward and simple. The function that is responsible for the actual work is shown below (the full script is called `poleselect1.py`). It follows our outline closely. The actual selection of a vertex is effected by assigning to the `sel` attribute of the vertex. Note also that the `v1` and `v2` attributes of an `edge` object are not indices into the `verts` attribute of our mesh but refer to `MVert` objects. That is why we need to retrieve the `index` attributes to compare.

```
def poleselect1(me,n=5):
    for v in me.verts:
        n_edges=0
        for e in me.edges:
            if e.v1.index == v.index or e.v2.index == v.index:
                n_edges+=1
                if n_edges >= n:
                    v.sel = 1
                    break
```

Selecting poles, again

You probably noticed that we iterated over the list of edges for each and every vertex (highlighted in the previous code). This might be costly in terms of performance and this cost is even compounded by the need to compare indices which have to be retrieved again and again. Is it possible to write more efficient code that stays readable nonetheless? It is if we follow this strategy:

1. Check whether the active object is a `Mesh`.
2. Check whether we are in *object* mode.
3. Show a pop-up menu to input the minimum number of edges.

4. Initialize a dictionary, indexed by vertex index that will contain edge counts.
5. Iterate over all edges (update the count for both referred vertices).
6. Iterate over the items in the dictionary (if count is larger or equal to the minimum, select the vertex).

By using this strategy we perform just two possibly lengthy iterations at the cost of needing the memory to store the dictionary (nothing is free). The speed increase is negligible for small meshes but might be considerable (I clocked a 1,000-fold speed boost on a smallish mesh of 3,000 vertices) for large meshes, and those are just the kind of meshes where someone might need a tool like this.

Our revised selection function is shown below (the full script is called `poleselect.py`). First note the `import` statement. The dictionary that we will be using is called a default dictionary and is provided by Python's collections module. A **default dictionary** is a dictionary that initializes missing items the first time they are referred to. As we want to increment the count for every vertex that is referred to by an edge, we should either initialize our dictionary with a zero value for every vertex in the mesh beforehand or check if a vertex is already indexed every time we want to increment the count and, if not, initialize it. A default dictionary does away with the need to initialize everything in advance and allows for a very readable idiom.

We create our dictionary by calling the `defaultdictionary()` function (a function returning a new object whose behavior is configured by some argument to the function is called a factory in object-oriented circles) with an `int` argument. The argument should be a function taking no arguments. The built-in function `int()` that we use here will return an integer value of zero when called without arguments. Every time we access our dictionary with a non-existing key, a new item is created and its value will be the return value of our `int()` function, that is, zero. The essential lines are the two where we increment the `edgecount` (highlighted part of the following code). We could have written that expression in a slightly different way to illustrate why we need a default dictionary:

```
edgecount[edge.v1.index] = edgecount[edge.v1.index] + 1
```

The dictionary item we refer to on the right-hand side of the expression might not yet exist every time we refer to a vertex index that we encounter for the first time. Of course, we could check beforehand but that would render the code a whole lot less readable.

```
from collections import defaultdict

def poleselect(me,n=5):
    n_edges = defaultdict(int)
    for e in me.edges:
```

```
        n_edges[e.v1.index]+=1
        n_edges[e.v2.index]+=1
    for v in (v for v,c in n_edges.items() if c>=n ):
        me.verts[v].sel=1
```

Determining the volume of a mesh

Although Blender is not really a CAD program, many people use it for CAD-like issues such as architectural visualization. Blender is capable of importing many types of files including those of major CAD programs, so including technical models drawn to precise measurements is never a problem.

These CAD programs often offer all kinds of tools to measure the dimensions of (parts of) your model, yet Blender, by its nature, provides very few of those tools. It is possible to inspect the size and location of an object by pressing the *N* key in the 3D view window. In *edit* mode you may enable the display of edge lengths, edge angles, and face areas (see the panel **Mesh tools more** in the editing context (*F9*) of the Buttons window) but that is about as far as it gets.

Python may overcome those limitations in situations where we need some specific measurement and exporting our model to a CAD tool is not an option. A practical example is the calculation of the volume of a mesh. Nowadays, a number of companies offer possibilities to re-create your digital model as real world objects by way of 3D printing techniques. I have to say it is a rather special feeling to hold a plastic or even metal replica of your Blender model in your hands, it really adds a whole new dimension to 3D.

Now a major component of the price of 3D-printing a model is the amount of material that will be used. Often, it will be possible to design your model as a hollow object that takes less material to produce, but it is quite inconvenient to upload intermediate versions of your model again and again to let the manufacturer's software calculate the volume and give you a price quote. So what we would like to have is a script that can calculate the volume of a mesh in a fairly accurate manner.

A common method to calculate the volume of a mesh is sometimes referred to as the **Surveyor's Formula** as it is related to the way surveyors may calculate the volume of a hill or mountain by triangulating its surface.

The central idea is to split a triangulated mesh into many columns that have their base on the xy-plane.

The surface area of the triangle projected onto the xy-plane times the average z-position of the three vertices then gives the volume of such a column. Summing these volumes finally gives the volume of the complete mesh (see the next figure).

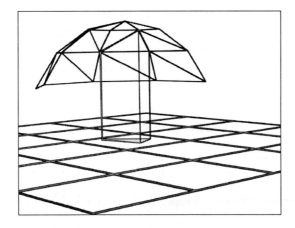

There are a couple of things that have to be taken into account. First, a mesh may extend below the xy-plane. If we construct a column from a face that lies below the xy-plane, the product of the projected area and the average of the z-coordinates will be a negative number, so we have to negate its value to get a volume.

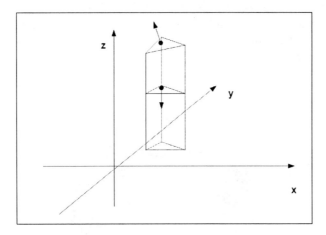

Second, a mesh may lie completely or partially above the xy-plane. If we take a look at the example in the previous diagram we see that the object has two triangles that contribute to the volume of the object, the top and bottom ones (the vertical triangles have a projected area of zero, so will contribute nothing). As the top and bottom faces both lie above the xy-plane, we have to subtract the volume of the column constructed from the bottom face from the one constructed from the top face. If the object was completely below the xy-plane it would be the other way around, and we would have to subtract the volume of the top column from the volume of the bottom column.

How we can tell what to do is determined by the direction of the face normal of our triangles. If, for example, a triangle is above the xy-plane but its face normal is pointing downward (it has a negative z-component), then we have to subtract the calculated volume. It is therefore vital that all face normals point consistently outward (in *edit* mode, select all faces and press *Ctrl + N*).

If we take into account all four possibilities (face normal up or down, face above or below the xy-plane) we can write the following outline for our function:

1. Make sure all face normals consistently point outward.
2. For all faces:
   - Calculate the z-component of face normal vector **Nz**
   - Calculate the product **P** of the average z-coordinates and the projected surface area.
   - If Nz is positive: add P
   - If Nz is negative: subtract P

This nifty algorithm works for simple objects without holes and just as well for objects containing holes (such as a torus), or even hollow ones (that is, containing an object completely enclosed in another object) like the examples shown in the following screenshot:

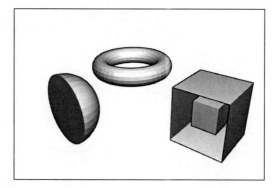

Because we allow the product of area and z-coordinates to be negative, we have to check only for the direction of the face normal to cover all situations.

Note that it is necessary for the mesh to be closed and manifold: There shouldn't be any missing faces nor should there be any edges that do not share exactly two faces, such as interior faces.

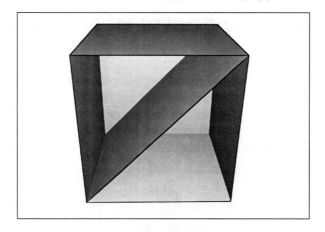

The important part of the code is shown here (the complete script is called `volume.py`):

```
def meshvolume(me):
    volume = 0.0
    for f in me.faces:
        xy_area = Mathutils.TriangleArea(vec(f.v[0].co[:2]),
                    vec(f.v[1].co[:2]),vec(f.v[2].co[:2]))
        Nz = f.no[2]
        avg_z = sum([f.v[i].co[2] for i in range(3)])/3.0
        partial_volume = avg_z * xy_area
        if Nz < 0: volume -= partial_volume
        if Nz > 0: volume += partial_volume
    return volume
```

The highlighted code shows how we calculate the area of the triangle projected on the xy-plane. `TriangleArea()` will calculate the area of a two-dimensional triangle when given two dimensional points (points in the xy-plane). So we pass not the full coordinate vectors of the vertices, but truncate them (that is, we drop the z-coordinate) into two component vectors.

After running the script from the text editor, or from the **Scripts** menu when in *object* mode, a pop up is displayed showing the volume in Blender units. Before running the script make sure that all modifiers are applied, scale and rotation are applied (*Ctrl + A* in *object* mode), the mesh is fully triangulated (*Ctrl + T* in *edit* mode), and that the mesh is manifold (closed or water-tight) by checking for non-manifold edges (*Ctrl + Alt + Shift +M* in *edge selection* mode). **Manifold edges** are edges that are shared by exactly two faces. Also make sure that all normals are pointing in the right direction. The application of modifiers is necessary to make the mesh closed (if it is a mirror modifier) and to make the calculation of the volume accurate (if it is a subsurface modifier).

Determining the centre of mass of a mesh

When printing a three-dimensional object in plastic or metal, a seemingly innocent question might pop up once we create our first toy based on a mesh we created; what is its center of mass? If our model has legs but we don't want it to keel over, its center of mass better be somewhere over its feet and, preferably, as low as possible to keep it stable. This figure shows this schematically:

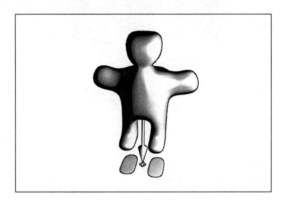

Once we know how to determine the volume of a mesh we can reuse many of the concepts to devise a script to determine the center of mass. Two additional bits of knowledge are needed to compute the position of the center of mass:

- The centers of mass of the projected volumes we construct when calculating the volume of the mesh
- How to add up the calculated centers of mass of all these individual volumes

All of this assumes that solid sections of our mesh have a uniform density. A mesh may have any form or even be hollow but the solid parts are assumed to be of a uniform density. This is valid assumption for the materials deposited by 3D printers.

The first issue is a bit of geometry: the projected volume is essentially a triangular column (or triangular prism) capped by a possibly slanted triangular face. Calculating the center of mass might be done as follows: the x and y coordinates of the center of mass are the x and y coordinates of the center of the projected triangle on the xy-plane—those are simply the averages of the x and y coordinates respectively of the three points defining the triangular face. The z-coordinate of the center of mass is halfway along the average height of our projected column. This is the average of the z-coordinates of the three points of the triangular face divided by two.

The second issue is mainly common sense: given two masses m1 and m2 with their centers of mass at v1 and v2 respectively, their combined center of mass is the weighted average. That is to say, the center of mass is proportionally closer to the center of the mass of the heaviest component.

Of course it is common sense to us now, but it took someone like Archimedes to see that it actually was common sense. After finding out about this 'law of levers' (as he called it), he didn't shout 'eureka' or went running around naked, so it took somewhat longer to attract attention.

Let's put all this information into a recipe that we can follow:

1. Make sure all face normals consistently point outward.
2. For all faces:
   - Calculate the z-component of face normal vector Nz
   - Calculate the product P of the average z-coordinates and the projected surface area
   - Calculate CM(x, y, z) with x, y the average of the projected x, y coordinates of the face and z (the average of the z-coordinates of the face)/2
   - If Nz is positive: add P times CM
   - If Nz is negative: subtract P times CM

From the outline above, it is clear that calculating the center of mass goes hand in hand with the calculation of the partial volumes, so it makes sense to redefine the `meshvolume()` function to the following:

```
def meshvolume(me):
    volume = 0.0
    cm = vec((0,0,0))
    for f in me.faces:
        xy_area = Mathutils.TriangleArea(vec(f.v[0].co[:2]),
                vec(f.v[1].co[:2]),vec(f.v[2].co[:2]))
        Nz = f.no[2]
        avg_z = sum([f.v[i].co[2] for i in range(3)])/3.0
        partial_volume = avg_z * xy_area
        if Nz < 0: volume -= partial_volume
        if Nz > 0: volume += partial_volume
```

```
        avg_x = sum([f.v[i].co[0] for i in range(3)])/3.0
        avg_y = sum([f.v[i].co[1] for i in range(3)])/3.0
        centroid = vec((avg_x,avg_y,avg_z/2))
        if Nz < 0: cm -= partial_volume * centroid
        if Nz > 0: cm += partial_volume * centroid
    return volume,cm/volume
```

The added or changed lines of code are highlighted.

Some remarks about accuracy

Although most of us are artists and not engineers, we still may ask how accurate the number is that we calculate for our mesh volume or center of mass. There are two things to consider—intrinsic accuracy and computational accuracy of our algorithm.

Intrinsic accuracy is what we refer to when we consider the fact that our model is made out of small polygons that approximate some imagined shape. When doing organic modeling this hardly matters; if our model looks good, it is good. However, if we try to approximate some ideal form, for example a sphere, by a polygonal model (a uv-sphere say, or an icosphere) there will be a difference between the calculated volume and the known volume of the ideal sphere. We can improve this approximation by increasing the number of subdivisions (or equivalent the size of the polygons) but we will never be able to completely eliminate this difference and the algorithm used to calculate the volume cannot change that.

Computational accuracy has several aspects. First, there is the precision of the numbers we calculate with. On most platforms that Blender runs on, calculations are performed using double precision floating point numbers. This amounts to about 17 digits of precision and there is nothing we can do to improve that. Luckily, that is ample precision to work with.

Then there is the accuracy of our algorithm. When you look at the code you will see that we are adding and multiplying a potentially huge amount of values, as a typical high-resolution model may well contain over a hundred thousand faces or even a million. For each face we calculate the volume of the projected column and all of these volumes are added (or subtracted) together. The problem is that these volumes may differ considerably in size, not only because the areas of the faces may differ but especially because the projected area of a near vertical face is very small compared to a near horizontal one.

Now if we add a very large and a very small number with limited precision calculations we will *lose* the small number. For example, if our precision would be limited to three significant digits, adding 0.001 and 0.0001 would end up as 0.001, losing the effect of the small number. Now our precision is a lot better (about 17 digits) but we add a lot more than two numbers. If we implement the volume() function by using one of the cited algorithms however, the difference never adds up to more than one in million, so as long as we don't aim to do nuclear science with Blender there is no need to bother. (For those who do, an alternative is provided in the script as the function volume2(). Still, be careful that you know what you are doing).

Python is able to work with numbers of potentially infinite size and precision but this is much slower than doing normal floating point calculations. The functions and classes provided in Mathutils are primarily coded in C for speed and limited to double precision floats. See http://code.activestate.com/recipes/393090/ http://code.activestate.com/recipes/298339/ or Section 18.5 of Python Cookbook, 2nd edition, by O'Reilly for some other techniques and mathematical background.

Growing sunflowers—parenting and grouping objects

Creating elaborate assemblies of objects is automated easily enough, but we would like to provide the end user with ways to select all of these related objects and to move them together. This section shows how we can achieve that by creating groups and by parenting objects to each other. You will end up with a bunch of nice sunflowers as a result.

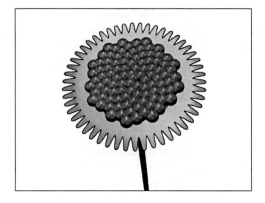

Groups

Groups are devised to make it easier to select, or manipulate, more than one object at the same time. Sometimes this behavior is part of a larger scheme. An armature for example, is a collection of bones, but then these collections have very specific relations (bones in an armature have precisely defined relations to each other).

There are many situations where we would like to identify a bunch of objects as belonging together without there being a specific relationship. Blender provides two kinds of groups to help us define their loose relations: **object groups** (or simply groups) for named collections of objects, and **vertex groups** for named collections of vertices within mesh objects.

Object groups allow us to select an otherwise unrelated set of objects we added to a group (we could group a mesh, an armature, and a bunch of empties together for example). A group relationship is different from a parent-child relationship. Groups merely allow us to select objects but parented objects move along when their parent is moved. The functionality to define and manipulate groups is provided in the `Group` module and its identically named class (a group is just like another Blender object, but one containing a list of references to other objects, but not to other groups unfortunately). You might, for example, append a group from an external `.blend` file just like you would a `Lamp` or a `Mesh`. The following table lists some often used group operations (see the `Blender.Group` module in the Blender API documentation for additional functionality):

Operation	Action
`group=Group.New(name='aGroupName')`	Creates a new group
`group=Group.Get(name='aGroupName')`	Gets a reference to a group by name

Vertex groups are a convenient way to identify groups of related vertices (such as an ear or a leg in a model of a toy for example) but they have their uses beyond mere selecting. They can be used to determine the influence of bone deformations or to identify emitter regions of particle systems to name a few. Vertex groups will be our focus in the next chapter.

Parenting

Parenting in real life might be difficult at times, but in Blender it is rather easy although there is a sometimes bewildering array of options to choose from. It is possible to parent an object to another object, to a single bone in an armature, or to one or three vertices in a `Mesh` object. The following table shows the relevant methods (Refer to `Blender.Object` in the Blender API for additional functionality):

Operator	Action
parent.makeParent([child1, child2, child3])	parent-children to a parent object
parentmesh.makeParentVertex([child1,child2,child3], vertexindex1)	parent-children to a vertex
parentmesh.makeParentVertex([child1,child2,child3], vertexindex1,vertexindex2,vertexindex3)	parent-children to three vertices

Growing a sunflower from a seed

We can put all this information to good use when we write a script that will create a model of a sunflower (Van Gogh would probably have cut off his other ear as well if he saw this "sunflower" but then again, his was another way of looking altogether). The single sunflower that we will be creating consists of a stalk and a flower head. The head of a sunflower consists of tiny flowers that will become the seeds once fertilized and a rim of large petals. (I know, any botanist will cringe at my language. The tiny flowers are called "disc florets" — but floret is just a "little flower" right? And the ones on the edge are "ray florets".) Our head will have seeds and each seed is a separate Mesh object that will be vertex-parented to our head mesh.

We would like our seeds to not just move along with our seed head, but to follow any local curvature and orient themselves perpendicular to the head surface so we can, for example, distort the head mesh with proportional editing and all attached seeds will follow. To accomplish that we use the three vertex variant of vertex parenting.

By parenting an object to three different vertices of a mesh, that object will follow the position of those vertices and orient itself relative to the normal (see the following illustrations):

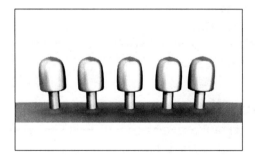

We do not need to connect all those triplets of vertices as the head mesh itself will not be rendered (it will be fully covered by seeds). We do define a face between each triplet of vertices though; otherwise it would be difficult for a modeler to see the head mesh in *edit* mode.

The petals are separate objects parented in the normal way to the head mesh as they need not follow any curvature of the head mesh, just its location and rotation. The head in turn is parented to the stalk so we can move the whole assembly around by moving the stalk.

Finally, we assign all individual objects to a single group. That way it will be easy to select everything in one go and it enables us to link or append one or more sunflowers from an external file as a single entity.

Duplication versus instantiation

We said that all our seeds and petals are separate objects but it might make more sense to instantiate them instead (called **making a linked copy** in Blender). As all seeds and all petals as we have modeled them are identical, we can refer to the same mesh data and just change the location, rotation, or scale of the object as needed — saving possibly a fair amount of memory. When using Blender interactively we can instantiate an object by pressing *Alt + D* (instead of *Shift + D* for a regular copy). In our script, we simply define a new object and point it to the same Mesh object by passing a reference to the same mesh when calling Object.New().

Growing a sunflower

Let's look at the main part of the script that will create the sunflower (the full script is available as sunflower.py). The first step is to calculate the position of the seeds:

```
def sunflower(scene,nseeds=100,npetals=50):
    pos = kernelpositions(nseeds)
```

From these positions we create the head, vertices, and faces that we can parent the kernels to and assemble these into the head mesh (highlighted part of the following code):

```
headverts=pos2verts(pos)
faces=[(v,v+1,v+2) for v in range(0,len(headverts),3)]
head=Tools.addmeshobject(scene,headverts,faces,name='head')
```

The next step is to create the base mesh for the kernel and create objects that reference this mesh (highlighted part of the following code):

```
kernelverts,kernelfaces=kernel(radius=1.5,scale=(1.0,1.0,0.3))
kernelmesh = Tools.newmesh(kernelverts,kernelfaces,name='kernel')
kernels = [Tools.addmeshduplicate(scene,kernelmesh,name='kernel')
   for i in range(nseeds)]
```

Each kernel is then assigned a suitable location and parented to the appropriate vertices in the flower head mesh (highlighted part of the following code):

```
for i in range(nseeds):
   loc = Tools.center(head.data.verts[i*3:(i+1)*3])
   kernels[i].setLocation(loc)
   head.makeParentVertex([kernels[i]],
      tuple([v.index for v in head.data.verts[i*3:(i+1)*3]]))
```

Next, we create a petal mesh and arrange duplicates of this mesh along the rim of the flower head (highlighted part of the following code):

```
petalverts,petalfaces=petal((2.0,1.0,1.0))
petalmesh = Tools.newmesh(petalverts,petalfaces,name='petal')
r = sqrt(nseeds)
petals = [Tools.addmeshduplicate(scene,petalmesh,name='petal')
   for i in range(npetals)]
```

Each petal is positioned and rotated along the rim and parented to the head (highlighted part of the following code):

```
for i,p in enumerate(petals):
   a=float(i)*2*pi/npetals
   p.setLocation(r*cos(a),r*sin(a),0)
   e=p.getEuler('localspace')
   e.z=a
   p.setEuler(e)
   head.makeParent(petals)
```

Finally, we create a stalk mesh and object and parent the head to the stalk. This way the entire flower may be moved by moving the stalk:

```
# add stalk (parent head to stalk)
stalkverts,stalkfaces=stalk()
stalkob = Tools.addmeshobject(scene,stalkverts,stalkfaces,
                              name='stalk')
stalkob.makeParent([head])
```

All that is left to do is to group the kernels and petals in separate groups (highlighted) and then all parts in an overall sunflower group for easy reference:

```
kernelgroup = Blender.Group.New('kernels')
kernelgroup.objects=kernels
petalgroup = Blender.Group.New('petals')
petalgroup.objects=petals
all = Blender.Group.New('sunflower')
all.objects=sum([kernels,petals],[head,stalkob])
```

The addmeshduplicate() function used in the code is implemented in the Tools module in the following manner:

```
def addmeshduplicate(scn,me,name=None):
    ob=scn.objects.new(me)
    if name : ob.setName(name)
    scn.objects.active=ob
    me.remDoubles(0.001)
    me.recalcNormals()
    for f in me.faces: f.smooth = 1
        me.update()
    Blender.Window.RedrawAll()
    return ob
```

Given a scene, a mesh, and a name (optional) for the object, it adds a new object to the scene. The Mesh object passed as an argument might be used again and again to create new objects that refer to the same mesh.

Newly created objects will be selected automatically but not be made active, so the next step is to make the newly-created object active (highlighted in the preceding code). This is not necessary but might be convenient to the user as are the next two actions: ensuring that all face normals point consistently outward and removing any vertices that are very close together. These last two actions can only be performed on a mesh that is embedded in an object.

Also, as a convenience, we set the smooth attribute for all faces, to get smoother images when rendering. Finally, we update the display list for this mesh and notify all Blender windows that there has been a change.

A slight digression, or why rabbits are related to sunflowers.

One of the things you may notice is that we have arranged the seeds in a peculiar spiral. This type of spiral, where subsequent positions along the spiral are spaced by following the so-called *Golden ratio* is called **Fermat's spiral**. Such a spiral results naturally in many seed heads when the florets or seeds are formed in the middle and pushed outward, resulting in a highly efficient packing.

When seen from above, the arrangement of seeds also seem to follow both left and right turning curves. The numbers of these curves usually are a pair from the *Fibonacci sequence [1 1 2 3 5 8 13 21 ...]* and the ratio of such a pair of numbers tends to converge on the *Golden ratio* when they get bigger. (In the two illustrations of our seed head below we can discern 13 counterclockwise spirals and 21 clockwise spirals.) Fibonacci invented this series in an attempt to model the population growth of rabbits. More about sunflowers (and possibly rabbits) may be found here: http://en.wikipedia.org/wiki/Sunflower.

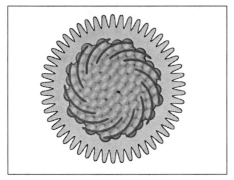

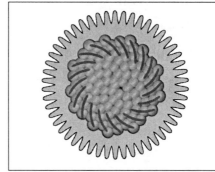

Summary

In this chapter, we have seen how to create complex objects and how to make the task of configuring those objects on easy one for the end user by providing a graphical user interface that remembers previous choices. We saw that it was also possible to recruit Blender as a command-line tool to automate common tasks.

We also learned how to create a parent relation between objects and made a first step in editing meshes. Specifically, we saw how to:

- Create configurable mesh objects
- Design a graphical user interface
- Make your script store user choices for later reuse
- Select vertices and faces in a mesh
- Parent an object to another
- Create groups
- Modify meshes
- Run Blender from the command line and render in the background
- Process command-line parameters

In the next chapter, we will see how we can assign vertex groups and materials to our meshes.

Vertex Groups and Materials

3

Complex meshes might be difficult to handle when the number of vertices is large. In this chapter we will look at how we can make life easier for the end user by defining vertex groups to label collections of vertices. We will also explore some of the many uses of vertex groups including their use in armatures and modifiers, and we will look into methods to apply different materials to different parts of mesh.

In this chapter, we will learn how to:

- Define vertex groups
- Assign vertices to a vertex group
- Assign materials to faces
- Assign vertex colors to vertices
- Set edge properties
- Add modifiers
- Skin bones

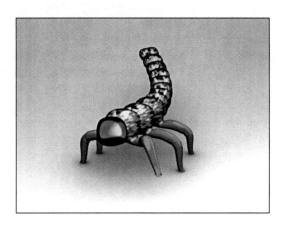

Vertex groups

Vertex groups are a way to organize collections of vertices within a mesh. A mesh may have any number of vertex groups and any vertex within a mesh may be a member of more than one vertex group or may belong to no vertex group at all. A newly created `Mesh` object does not have any vertex groups defined.

In their basic form, vertex groups are a valuable tool in identifying distinct parts of a complex mesh. By assigning vertices to vertex groups, the modeler eventually provides people, such as the rigger or the people who texture a model, with the means to easily identify and select the parts of the model they want to work on.

The use of vertex groups goes far beyond simple identification though. Many mesh modifiers restrict their influence to a designated vertex group and an armature can be configured to deform a mesh by linking the influence of each bone to a single vertex group. We will see examples of that later.

A vertex group is not merely a collection of vertices. Each vertex of a vertex group may have an associated *weight* (between zero and one) that many modifiers use to fine-tune their influence. A vertex may have a different weight associated with it in each vertex group it belongs to.

The bugs we create with `creepycrawlies.py` are an excellent example of a rather complex mesh with many distinct parts that would benefit greatly from defining vertex groups. Not only to make it simpler to select a part by name, for instance the head, but also to make life easier for ourselves if we want to rig the model.

Our primary tools in creating vertex groups are the methods of `Mesh` objects listed in the following table:

Method	Action	Remarks
`addVertGroup(group)`	Adds a new empty vertex group.	
`assignVertsToGroup(group, vertices,weight,mode)`	Adds a list of vertex indices to an existing vertex group with the given weight.	Mode determines what to do when a vertex is already a member of the vertex group. See main text for details.

Method	Action	Remarks
`getVertsFromGroup(group, weightsFlag=0,vertices)`	Returns a list of vertex indices (the default) or a list of (index, weight) tuples (if `weightsFlag = 1`). If the vertices list is specified only those vertices that are in the group and in the given list are returned.	
`removeVertsFromGroup(group, vertices)`	Removes a list of vertices from an existing vertex group. If the list is not specified all vertices are removed.	
`renameVertGroup(groupName, newName)`	Renames a vertex group.	
`getVertGroupNames()`	Returns a list of all vertex group names.	
`removeVertGroup(group)`	Deletes a vertex group.	Will NOT delete the actual vertices.

The important concept to grasp here is that creating a vertex group and assigning vertices to it are two separate actions. Creating a new empty vertex group is done by calling the `addVertGroup()` method of your `Mesh` object. It takes a single string as an argument and that will be the name of the vertex group. If there is already a vertex group with the same name, the name will have a numerical suffix added to prevent a name clash, so for example: `TailSegment` may become `TailSegment.001`.

Adding vertices to an existing vertex group is done by calling the `assignVertsToGroup()` method of your mesh. This method will take four mandatory arguments—the name of the vertex group to assign the vertices to, a list of vertex indices, a weight, and an *assign* mode. If the vertex group does not exist, or one of the vertex indices points to a nonexistent vertex, an exception is raised.

The weight must be a value between 0.0 and 1.0; any weight larger than 1.0 is clamped to 1.0. A weight smaller or equal to 0.0 will remove a vertex from the vertex group. If you want to assign different weights to vertices in the same vertex group, you have to assign them to the group with separate calls to `assignVertsToGroup()`.

The *assign* mode comes in three flavors: ADD, REPLACE, and SUBTRACT. ADD will add new vertices to the vertex group and will associate the given weight with them. If any of the vertices in the list already exist they get the weight added to them. REPLACE will replace the weight associated with the indices in the list if they are members of the vertex group or do nothing otherwise. SUBTRACT will try to subtract the weight from the vertices in the list and again do nothing if they are not members of the vertex group. Most often when adding completely new vertex groups to a mesh you will use the ADD mode.

A weighty issue

For our first example we will add two new vertex groups to an existing mesh object—one that will contain all vertices that have a positive x-coordinate and one that will contain the vertices with a negative x-coordinate. We will name these groups **Right** and **Left** respectively.

Additionally, we will give each vertex in these groups a weight depending on its distance from its object center with larger weights for vertices that are farther away from the center.

Code outline: leftright.py

Schematically we will take the following steps:

1. Get the active object.
2. Verify that it is a mesh and get the mesh data.
3. Add two new vertex groups to the object—Left and Right.
4. For all vertices in the mesh:

    1. Calculate the weight
    2. If the x-coordinate > 0:
    3. Add vertex index and weight to vertex group *right*
    4. If the x-coordinate < 0:
    5. Add vertex index and weight to vertex group *left*

In order to make certain that a new vertex group is empty we check if the group already exists and remove it if that is the case. This checking is highlighted in the code:

```
def leftright(me,maximum=1.0):
    center=vec(0,0,0)
    left =[]
    right=[]
```

```
    for v in me.verts:
        weight = (v.co-center).length/maximum
        if v.co.x > 0.0 :
            right.append((v.index, weight))
        elif v.co.x > 0.0 :
            left.append((v.index, weight))
    return left,right

if __name__ == "__main__":
    try:
        ob = Blender.Scene.GetCurrent().objects.active
        me = ob.getData(mesh=True)

        vgroups = me.getVertGroupNames()
        if 'Left' in vgroups:
            me.removeVertsFromGroup('Left')
        else:
            me.addVertGroup('Left')
        if 'Right' in vgroups:
            me.removeVertsFromGroup('Right')
        else:
            me.addVertGroup('Right')

        left,right = leftright(me,vec(ob.getSize()).length)

        for v,w in left:
            me.assignVertsToGroup('Left',[v],
                              w,Blender.Mesh.AssignModes.ADD)
        for v,w in right:
            me.assignVertsToGroup('Right',[v],w,
                              Blender.Mesh.AssignModes.ADD)

        Blender.Window.Redraw()

    except Exception as e:
        Blender.Draw.PupMenu('Error%t|'+str(e)[:80])
```

The full script is available as `leftright.py`. The formula to calculate the weight may need some explanation: in order to assign a maximum weight of 1.0 to the points lying at the greatest distance from the center of the object we have to scale by the maximum distance possible. We could loop over all vertices to determine that maximum first, but here we choose to approximate this maximum by the root mean square of the size. This will exaggerate the maximum distance so the maximum weight assigned to any vertex will probably be less than 1.0. However, getting the size is much faster than calculating the exact maximum for large meshes. Also, note that we calculate the distance to the object center (the object center from the point of view of the vertices in a mesh is always at $(0, 0, 0)$).

This may be completely different from what may be perceived by the user as the center of the mesh. (The object center is normally displayed as a pink dot in Blender and may be changed to lie at the average position of all vertices by selecting **Object | Transform | Center new**.)

The resulting weights for a mesh might looks like this:

Modifiers

Modifiers are tools that change a mesh in a non-destructive way and that can be adjusted interactively. Other objects may have modifiers as well: Text3d, Metaballs, and Curves for example. These objects may be represented as meshes so they can be modified as well. Not all modifiers can be associated with these objects though. If desired, the effects of modifiers can be made permanent by *applying* them. Blender provides a whole host of modifiers ranging from subsurface modifiers to all sorts of deformation modifiers. The table shows the list of available modifiers:

Modifier	Vertex group influence	Remarks
displacement	yes	
curve	yes	
explode	yes	
lattice	yes	
mask	yes	
meshdeform	yes	
shrinkwrap	yes	
simpledeform	yes	
smooth	yes	
wave	yes	
array	no	

Modifier	Vertex group influence	Remarks
bevel	no	
boolean	no	
build	no	
cast	no	
decimate	no	
edgesplit	no	
mirror	no	
subsurface	no	
uvproject	no	
Particle system	yes	Many parameters influenced by different vertex groups
armature	yes	Each bone may be restricted to influence a single vertex group

Many modifiers can be made to restrict their influence to a specific vertex group and a few modifiers are special. A particle system is considered a modifier although generally particle systems are managed via their own set of tools. Also, its relation to vertex groups is in a way reversed; instead of restricting its influence to the vertices within a vertex group, the weights of the vertices of vertex groups may influence all sorts of parameters of the particle system, such as emission density and velocity of the particles. We will see an example of that in the *Flying sparks* section.

Armature modifiers are also somewhat special as they do not restrict their influence to a single vertex group. However, they may be configured to restrict the influence of each separate bone to a specific vertex group as we will examine in the *Bones* section.

From a Python programmer's point of view the list of modifiers is a property of an object (that is, *not* of the underlying mesh). Objects referring to the same mesh may have different modifiers. This list contains `Modifier` objects and these can be added to and removed from this list, and individual modifiers can be moved up or down in the list. The order of modifiers is important in some cases. For example, adding a subsurface modifier after a mirror modifier may look different from adding the mirror modifier before the subsurface modifier.

A `Modifier` object has a type and a name (initially representing its type but it may be set to something more appropriate). The type is one of the types from the list of constants in `Modifier.Types`. Each modifier object may have many settings indexed by keys that are defined in `Modifier.Settings`. Not all settings are appropriate for all types.

If we had two objects, a mesh object named `Target` and a lattice object named `Deformer`, and we would like to associate the `Deformer` object as a lattice modifier to the `Target` object, the following code snippet would do the trick:

```
import Blender
from Blender import Modifier

target  = Blender.Object.Get('Target')
deformer= Blender.Object.Get('Deformer')

mod = target.modifiers.append(Modifier.Types.LATTICE)
mod[Modifier.Settings.OBJECT] = deformer
target.makeDisplayList()
Blender.Window.RedrawAll()
```

If the `Target` object had a vertex group named `Right` consisting of the vertices in the right half of the `Target` object we could restrict the influence of the modifier by changing the VERTGROUP attribute. Our snippet would change to the following (added line highlighted):

```
import Blender
from Blender import Modifier

target  = Blender.Object.Get('Target')
deformer= Blender.Object.Get('Deformer')

mod = target.modifiers.append(Modifier.Types.LATTICE)
mod[Modifier.Settings.OBJECT] = deformer
mod[Modifier.Settings.VERTGROUP] = 'Right'

target.makeDisplayList()
Blender.Window.RedrawAll()
```

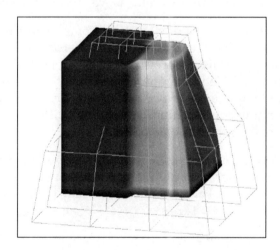

Engraving

Consider the following problem: given some text, we want to render this text as sunken grooves in a surface, just like it was engraved. This is not as simple as it seems. It is simple enough to create a text object, of course, but in order to manipulate this text we would like to convert this text object to a mesh. The Blender GUI offers this possibility in the object menu but strangely enough, the Blender API does not provide an equivalent function. So, our first hurdle would be to convert a text object to a mesh.

The second problem that we have to solve is how to extrude a collection of vertices or edges in order to gauge out a depression in a surface. Again, there is no function in the Blender API for this so we will have to add this to our toolkit ourselves.

The final problem is more subtle. If we have somehow managed to create some sunken grooves we might want to make the edges somewhat less sharp as nothing in real life has perfectly sharp edges. There are various ways to go about this but many involve adding a modifier to our mesh. A **bevel modifier** might be enough to take away just the sharp edges but it is likely we would want to add a subsurface modifier to our mesh as a whole. Here we have a problem, when filling the gaps between the characters of our text it is very likely that we encounter many narrow triangles. These triangles mess up the appearance of our subsurface modifier as can be observed in the following figure:

Two things might help to mitigate this problem. One is to add a crease weight to the edges of our engraved text thereby weighing these edges more than the default when calculating the subsurface. These may help but might also defeat the purpose of the modifier as it makes those edges sharper. The following figure shows the result: better, but still not looking great.

Another approach is to add an extra edge loop just outside the engraved text. This will add a ring of quad faces around the text making the subsurface around the text behave a lot better as can be seen below. In our final implementation we apply both solutions but first we tackle each issue one at a time.

Converting a Text3d object to a mesh

A Text3d object is basically a curve with some additional parameters. The data block it refers to is a Blender Curve object and once we know how to access the individual parts in the curve that make up each character in our text, we can convert these curves to vertices and edges. All relevant functionality can be found in the Blender.Curve and Blender.Geometry modules.

In Blender, the relation between a Text3d object and a Curve object is rather more subtle and confusing than described in the main text. A Text3d object is a specialized version of a Curve object, rather like a subclass in object-oriented parlance. However, in the Blender API, the Text3d object is not a subclass of Curve, nor are the extra attributes available on the same object instance. Sound confusing? It is. How would you retrieve all attributes then? The trick is that you can use the name of the Text3d object to get access to its associated Curve object as this small example shows:

```
txt = ob.getData()
curve = Blender.Curve.Get(txt.getName())
```

Now we can use txt to access Text3d-specific information (for example, txt.setText('foo')) and curve to access Curve-specific information (for example, curve.getNumCurves()).

A Blender Curve object consists of a number of CurNurb objects that represent sections of a curve. A single text character typically consists of one or two curve segments. The small letter *e* for example, consists of an outer curve segment and a small inner curve segment. CurNurb objects in turn consist of a number of **nodes** or **control points** that define the curve segment. These nodes are always BezTriple objects in the case of Text3d objects and Blender's Geometry module provides us with the BezierInterp() function that returns a list of coordinates interpolated between two points. These points and the direction the curve takes at those points (often called a **handle**) can be taken from the `BezTriple` objects. The resulting code looks this (the full code is part of our toolkit in `Tools.py`):

```python
import Blender

from Blender.Geometry import BezierInterp as interpolate
from Blender.Mathutils import Vector as vec

def curve2mesh(c):
    vlists=[]
    for cn in c:
        npoints = len(cn)

        points=[]
        first=True
        for segment in range(npoints-1):
            a=cn[segment].vec
            b=cn[segment+1].vec
            lastpoints = interpolate(vec(a[1]),vec(a[2]),vec(b[0]),
                                     vec(b[1]),6)
            if first:
                first = False
                points.append(lastpoints[0])
            points.extend(lastpoints[1:])
        if cn.isCyclic():
            a=cn[-1].vec
            b=cn[0].vec
            lastpoints=interpolate(vec(a[1]),vec(a[2]),vec(b[0]),
                                   vec(b[1]),6)
            points.extend(lastpoints[:-2])

        vlists.append(points)

    return vlists
```

The highlighted lines show two important aspects. The first one shows the actual interpolation. We have renamed the rather awkwardly name `BezierInterp()` function to `interpolate()` and it takes five arguments. The first four are taken from the two `BezTriple` objects that we are interpolating between. Each `BezTriple` object can be accessed as a list of three vectors — the incoming handle, the position of the point, and the outgoing handle (see the next figure). We pass the position of the first point and its outgoing handle and the position of the second point and its ingoing handle. The fifth argument is the number of points we want the `interpolate()` function to return.

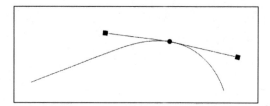

The second highlighted line takes care of **closed curves**, that is curves that have their first and last points connected. This is the case for all curves that form characters in a text. The function returns a list of lists. Each list contains all of the interpolated points (tuples of x, y, z coordinates) for each curve. Note that some characters consist of more than one curve. For example, the small letter *e* in many fonts or the letter *o* consist of two curves, one defining the outline of the letter and one the interior. A `Text3d` object containing the text `Foo` for example will return a list of five lists — the first one will contain the vertices defining the capital letter *F* and the second and third will contain the vertices for the two curves that make up the small letter *o* as will the fourth and fifth.

Extruding an edge loop

Extrusion is the process where we duplicate vertices (and possibly their connecting edges) and move them out in some direction, after which we connect these duplicated vertices to their origins by new edges and finish up the operation by creating a new face between the old and new vertices. We need it in order to sink the outline of our text to create a groove with vertical walls. The function `extrude_selected_edges()` in `Tools.py` takes a mesh and a vector as arguments and will extrude the vertices on selected edges in the mesh in the direction of the vector, adding any necessary new edges and faces. Because the techniques are extensions of things we've seen earlier the code is not shown here.

Expanding an edge loop

If we have a list of edges forming a closed curve (or more than one) defining a character, we would like to surround those edges with an extra edge loop to create a better "flow" in any subsurface modifier that the end user may associate with our mesh. This would be a rather involved process if we would have to calculate this in 3D, but fortunately our converted characters have all their vertices in the xy plane (this is because all of the characters in a newly instantiated `Text3d` object lie in the xy plane).

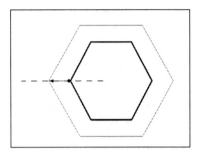

In just two dimensions this is quite a tractable problem. For each point on our edge loop we determine the direction of the vertex normal. The **vertex normal** is the line bisecting the angle between the two edges that share the point we are considering. If the two edges are co-linear (or nearly so), we take the vertex normal to be a line perpendicular to one of the edges. The position of the point to create on the new edge loop will be somewhere on this normal. In order to determine if we have to move outward or inward along this normal, we simply try one direction and check whether the new position is within the outline of our character. If so, we reverse the direction.

One issue needs addressing still, a character may consist of more than one curve. If we want to draw additional edge loops around such a character, such an edge loop should be beyond the outline of a character but inside any interior curve. In other words, if we construct a new edge loop we have to know whether a curve lies within another curve. If so, it is not an outline and the new edge loop should be constructed to lie within the curve. Therefore, our `expand()` function (shown in the next snippet, full code is part of `Tools.py`) takes an extra optional argument `plist`, which is a list of lists containing `MVert` objects defining additional polygons to check against. If the first point of the curve that we want to expand lies within any of these additional curves, we assume that the curve we are expanding is an **interior curve**. (This would be wrong if the interior curve would cross the exterior curve at some point, but for curves defining a character in a font this is never so.)

```
def expand(me,loop,offset=0.05,plist=[]):

    ov = [me.verts[i] for i in verts_from_edgeloop(loop)]

    inside=False
    for polygon in plist:
        if in_polygon(loop[0].v1.co,polygon):
            inside=True
            break    # we don't deal with multiple inclusions

    n=len(ov)
    points=[]
    for i in range(n):
        va = (ov[i].co-ov[(i+1)%n].co).normalize()
        vb = (ov[i].co-ov[(i-1)%n].co).normalize()
        cosa=abs(vec(va).dot(vb))
        if cosa>0.99999 :    # almost colinear
            c = vec(va[1],va[0],va[2])
        else:
            c = va+vb
        l = offset/c.length
        p = ov[i].co+l*c
        if in_polygon(p,ov) != inside:
            p = ov[i].co-l*c
        print i,ov[i].co,va,vb,c,l,cosa,p
        points.append(p)

    return points
```

The highlighted code calls a function (provided in `Tools.py`) that takes a list of edges that form an edge loop and returns a sorted list of vertices. This is necessary because our `in_polygon()` function takes a list of vertices rather than edges and assumes that this list is sorted, that is adjacent vertices form edges that do not cross.

To determine whether a point is inside a closed polygon defined by a list of vertices, we count the number of edges that are crossed by a line (often called a **ray**) that starts at the point and extends to infinity. If the number of edges crossed is odd, the point will lie inside the polygon; if it's even, it lies outside of the polygon. The following figure illustrates the concept:

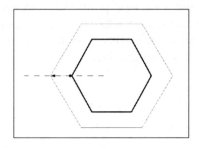

The function `in_polygon()` shown here is part of `Tools.py`. It takes a point (a `Vector`) and a list of vertices (`MVert` objects) and returns either `True` or `False`. Note that any z-coordinate in either the point or the vertices in the polygon is ignored.

```
from Blender.Geometry import LineIntersect2D
from Blender.Mathutils import Vector as vec

def in_polygon(p,polygon):
    intersections = 0
    n = len(polygon)
    if n<3 : return False
    for i in range(n):
        if LineIntersect2D (p,vec(1.0,0.0,0.0),polygon[i].
co,polygon[(i+1)%n].co):
            intersections+=1
    return intersections % 2 == 1
```

The heavy lifting is done in the highlighted line by the `LineIntersect2D()` function available in the `Blender.Geometry` module. The *modulo* (`%`) operation in the `return` statement is a way to determine whether the encountered number of intersections is odd.

Putting it all together: Engrave.py

Armed with all the supporting functions developed in the previous sections, we can make a list of the steps that we'll have to undertake in order to engrave a text:

1. Show a pop up to enter a string to engrave.
2. Check whether the active object is a mesh and has faces selected.
3. Create a `Text3d` object.
4. Convert it to a mesh, with appropriate vertex groups.
5. Add extra edge loops to the characters.
6. Extrude the original characters downward.
7. Fill the bottom of the extruded characters.
8. Add a "cartouche" (a rectangle) around the text.
9. Fill the space between the cartouche and the characters.
10 Add a subsurface modifier.
11. Set a crease value in the edges contained in `TextTop` and `TextBottom` vertex groups.

Our final script follows this outline almost exactly and makes use of the tools that we developed earlier in this chapter. We show the most relevant sections here (the full script is available as `engrave.py`). We start off by converting a `Text3d` object (c in the following code) to a list containing a list of vertex positions for each curve segment in the text and we add a new empty `Mesh` object to the scene with some empty vertex groups:

```
vlist = curve2mesh(c)

me = Blender.Mesh.New('Mesh')
ob = Blender.Scene.GetCurrent().objects.new(me,'Mesh')

me.addVertGroup('TextTop')
me.addVertGroup('TextBottom')
me.addVertGroup('Outline')
```

The next step is to add these vertices to the mesh and create connecting edges. As all curve segments in a character are closed, we have to take care to add an extra edge to bridge the gap between the last and first vertex as shown in the highlighted line. For good measure, we remove any doubles that may be present in the interpolated curve segment. We add the vertices to the `TextTop` vertex group and store the list of new edges for future reference.

```
loop=[]
for v in vlist:
    offset=len(me.verts)
    me.verts.extend(v)
    edgeoffset=len(me.edges)
    me.edges.extend([[(i+offset,i+offset+1)
                        for i in range(len(v)-1)])
    me.edges.extend([[(len(v)-1+offset,offset)])
    me.remDoubles(0.001)

    me.assignVertsToGroup('TextTop', range(offset,len(me.verts)),
                        1.0, Blender.Mesh.AssignModes.ADD)
    loop.append([me.edges[i] for i in range(edgeoffset,
                    len(me.edges) )])
```

For each edge loop that we stored in the previous part we construct a new, and slightly larger, edge loop around it and add these new vertices and edges to our mesh. We want to construct faces between these edge loops as well and that is started at the highlighted line: here we use the Python built-in function `zip()` to pair the edges of the two edge loops. Each edge loop is ordered by a `utility` function (available in `Tools.py`) that sorts edges to lie in the order in which they are connected to each other. For each pair of edges we construct two possible arrangements of vertex indices and calculate which of them forms an untwisted face. This calculation is done by the `least_warped()` function (code not shown) that basically compares the circumference of the faces defined by the two different orderings of vertices. The untwisted face will have the shortest circumference, which is then added to the mesh.

```
for l in range(len(loop)):
    points = expand.expand(me,loop[l],0.02,loop[:l]+loop[l+1:])
    offset=len(me.verts)
    me.verts.extend(points)
    edgeoffset=len(me.edges)
    me.edges.extend([[(i+offset,i+offset+1)
                    for i in range(len(points)-1)]])
    me.edges.extend([[(len(points)-1+offset,offset)]])
    eloop=[me.edges[i] for i in range(edgeoffset,len(me.edges))]
    me.assignVertsToGroup('Outline',
                    range(offset,len(me.verts)),1.0,
                    Blender.Mesh.AssignModes.ADD)
    faces=[]
    for e1,e2 in zip( expand.ordered_edgeloop(loop[l]),
                expand.ordered_edgeloop(eloop)):
        f1=(e1.v1.index,e1.v2.index,e2.v2.index,e2.v1.index)
        f2=(e1.v2.index,e1.v1.index,e2.v2.index,e2.v1.index)
        faces.append(least_warped(me,f1,f2))
    me.faces.extend(faces)
```

We omitted the code to extrude the character edge loop, but the following lines are informative as they show how to fill an edge loop. First, we select all relevant edges by using two utility functions (these are the extruded edges of the characters). Next, we call the `fill()` method. This method will fill any collection of closed edge loops as long as they lie in the same plane. It even takes cares of holes (like the little island in the letter *e*):

```
deselect_all_edges(me)
select_edges(me,'TextBottom')
me.fill()
```

Adding the cartouche is simply a matter of adding a rectangular edge loop around our characters. If this edge loop is selected together with the vertices in the `Outline` vertex group, the `fill()` method can be used again to fill up this cartouche. This is not shown here. We end with some finishing touches: we convert the triangles in our mesh as much as possible to quads by using the `triangleToQuad()` method and then subdivide the mesh. We also add a subsurface modifier, set the `smooth` attribute on all the faces, and recalculate all face normals to point consistently outward.

```
me.triangleToQuad()
me.subdivide()

mod = ob.modifiers.append(Blender.Modifier.Types.SUBSURF)
mod[Blender.Modifier.Settings.LEVELS]=2

select_all_faces(me)
set_smooth(me)
select_all_edges(me)
me.recalcNormals()
```

The hidden Hook modifier:

We have seen that the modifiers available in Blender can be added to an object in Python. There is, however, one modifier that can be added but seems to have no equivalent within the Blender GUI. This is the so-called **Hook modifier**. A Hook in Blender is a way to parent vertices to an object (so it's the reverse of vertex parenting where we parent an object to a vertex) and in the application itself can be accessed through the **Mesh | Vertex | Add Hook** menu in *edit* mode. Once added, it will show up in the list of modifiers. From a programmer's view the Hook modifier is no different from other modifiers but alas neither its type nor the settings needed are documented in the API.

Flying sparks

Sparks and all sorts of glowing effects can readily be created by adding a suitable particle system to an object. Many of the particle systems' parameters can be controlled by the weight of vertices in a vertex group, including the local density of the emitted particles.

In this example we would like to mimic the behavior of the electrical phenomenon called "St Elmo's fire". This is the effect that under certain circumstances, especially in the advance of a thunderstorm, some objects start to glow. This glow is called **corona discharge** (http://en.wikipedia.org/wiki/St._Elmo%27s_fire) and is most prominent at sharp and protruding parts of larger structures, for example, radio antennae or lightning rods where the electric field that causes the effect is strongest.

In order to influence the number of particles emitted from the mesh in a believable manner we need to calculate a quantity named local curvature and store this curvature suitably scaled as weights in a vertex group. Then, we can apply this vertex group to the density parameter in the **extra** panel of the particle's context to control the emission.

A mesh may have any form, and most of the time there is no neat formula that approximates the form. Therefore, we approximate the local curvature in a necessarily crude way (for more details and some heavy math, see http://en.wikipedia. org/wiki/Mean_curvature) by calculating the average of all edge curvatures of the connected edges for every vertex in the mesh. Here we define the **edge curvature** as the dot product of the normalized vertex normal and the edge vector (that is, the vector form the vertex to its neighbor). This product will be negative if the edge curves down relative to the normal and positive if it curves up. We will reverse this sign as we are more accustomed with the notion of a positive curvature for spikes rather than for troughs. Another way to look at this is that in areas of positive curvature, the angle between the vertex normal and an edge starting at the same vertex is larger than 90°.

The following figure illustrates the concept—it depicts a series of vertices linked by edges. Each vertex has an associated vertex normal shown (the arrows). The vertices marked **a** have a positive curvature, the ones marked **b** a negative curvature. Two of the shown vertices labeled with **c** are in an area of zero curvature—that is, at those locations the surface is flat and the vertex normal perpendicular to the edges.

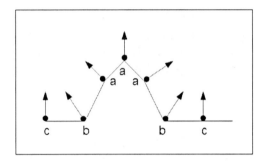

Calculating the local curvature

The function that calculates the local curvature for each vertex in a mesh and returns a list of normalized weights may be implemented as follows:

```
from collections import defaultdict

def localcurvature(me,positive=False):

    end=defaultdict(list)
    for e in me.edges:
        end[e.v1.index].append(e.v2)
        end[e.v2.index].append(e.v1)

    weights=[]
    for v1 in me.verts:
        dvdn = []
```

```
        for v2 in end[v1.index]:
            dv = v1.co-v2.co
            dvdn.append(dv.dot(v1.no.normalize()))
        weights.append((v1.index,sum(dvdn)/max(len(dvdn),1.0)))

    if positive:
        weights = [(v,max(0.0,w)) for v,w in weights]

    minimum = min(w for v,w in weights)
    maximum = max(w for v,w in weights)
    span = maximum - minimum

    if span > 1e-9:
        return [(v,(w-minimum)/span) for v,w in weights]
    return weights
```

The function `localcurvature()` takes a mesh and one optional argument and returns a list of tuples with the vertex index and its weight. If the optional argument is `true` any negative weight calculated is discarded.

The hard work is done in the highlighted lines. Here we loop over all vertices and then, in an inner loop, check each connected edge to retrieve the vertex at the other end from a precomputed dictionary. We then calculate `dv` as the edge vector and append the dot-product of this edge vector and the normalized vertex normal to the list `dvdn`.

```
    weights.append((v1.index,sum(dvdn)/max(len(dvdn),1.0)))
```

The previous line may look strange but it appends a tuple consisting of the vertex index and its average curvature, where the average is computed by summing the list of curvatures and dividing it by the number of values in the list. Because the list may be empty (this happens when the mesh contains unconnected vertices), we safeguard against a divide by zero error by dividing it by the length of the list or by one, whichever is the largest. In this way, we keep our code a little more readable by avoiding `if` statements.

Code outline: curvature.py

With the `localcurvature()` function at our disposal, the actual curvature script becomes quite terse (full script available as `curvature.py`):

```
if __name__ == "__main__":
    try:
        choice = Blender.Draw.PupMenu("Normalization%t|Only
                                       positive|Full range")
```

```
if choice>0:
    ob = Blender.Scene.GetCurrent().objects.active
    me = ob.getData(mesh=True)

    try:
        me.removeVertGroup('Curvature')
    except AttributeError:
        pass

    me.addVertGroup('Curvature')

    for v,w in localcurvature(me,positive=(choice==1)):
        me.assignVertsToGroup('Curvature',[v],w,
                              Blender.Mesh.AssignModes.ADD)

    Blender.Window.Redraw()

except Exception as e:
    Blender.Draw.PupMenu('Error%t|'+str(e)[:80])
```

The highlighted lines show how we remove a possible existing Curvature vertex group from the Mesh object by just trying and catching an AtrributeError that is raised when the group is not present. Next, we add again the group with the same name so it will be completely empty. The last highlighted line shows how we add each vertex separately because any vertex may have a different weight.

All actions are surrounded by a try ... except construct that will catch any errors and that will pop up a nice informational message if anything out of the ordinary occurs. Most likely this will be in situations where the user forgets to select a Mesh object.

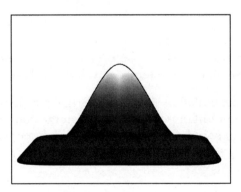

Putting it all together: St. Elmo's fire

The illustration of the discharge from the sharp-tipped rod was made by modeling a simple rod object by hand and then calculating the curvature with `curvature.py`.

Then, a particle system was added and the density parameter in the extra tab was set to the `Curvature` vertex group. The rod and the particle system were given separate materials: a simple gray and white halo respectively. The particles were simulated for 250 frames and frame 250 was rendered for the illustration.

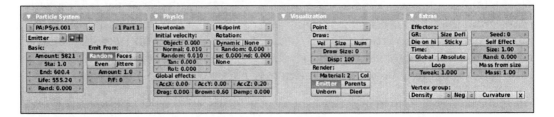

Bones

An armature might be considered the backbone of animation because deforming a mesh in a controllable way, which can be keyed at given frames, is necessary to enable animators to pose their characters in a well-controlled way.

Blender's armature implementation provides the rigger and animator with an overwhelmingly large amount of possibilities, but at the end of the day an armature is foremost a collection of connected bones where each bone will deform part of a mesh. The movements of these bones in respect to each other can be governed by several different constraints.

While bones may be configured to work their influence via an **envelope**, thereby basically deforming any vertex of the target mesh within a certain radius, they may also be configured to deform only those vertices that belong to a vertex group with the same name as the name of the bone. This deformation is further controlled by the weight of the vertices in the vertex group enabling us to fine-tune the bone influence.

Tick-Tock

To illustrate the basic possibilities of an armature we will be rigging a simple clock model. The clock is of a single mesh consisting of three separate, non-connected submeshes — the body, the little hand, and the big hand. The vertices of each clock hand belong to two separate vertex groups — one for the bit of the clock hand connected to the center of the clock, and for the end of the hand itself. This setup allows for a cartoon-like animation where we can make the tip of the hand trail the actual motion for instance.

Code outline: clock.py

We will have to take the following steps to rig our clock in the way we intend:

1. Import mesh data.
2. Create clock mesh.
3. Create vertex groups.
4. Create armature object.
5. Create bones within armature.
6. Associate armature modifier.

The translation from the outline to code is almost one on one and a little repetitive as many instructions are repeated for each bone (full code available as `clock.py`):

```
me=Blender.Mesh.New('Clock')
me.verts.extend(clockmesh.Clock_verts)
me.faces.extend(clockmesh.Clock_faces)

scn=Blender.Scene.GetCurrent()
ob=scn.objects.new(me)
scn.objects.active=ob

me.addVertGroup('BigHand')
me.assignVertsToGroup('BigHand',
                clockmesh.Clock_vertexgroup_BigHand,
                1.0, Blender.Mesh.AssignModes.ADD)

... <similar code for LittleHand, BigArm and LittleArm vertex groups
    omitted> ...

ar = Blender.Armature.New('ClockBones')
ar.envelopes=False
ar.vertexGroups=False
```

```
obbones = scn.objects.new(ar)

mod = ob.modifiers.append(Blender.Modifier.Types.ARMATURE)
mod[Blender.Modifier.Settings.OBJECT]=obbones
mod[Blender.Modifier.Settings.ENVELOPES]=False
mod[Blender.Modifier.Settings.VGROUPS]=True

ar.makeEditable()
bigarm = Blender.Armature.Editbone()
bigarm.head = vec(0.0,0.0 ,0.57)
bigarm.tail = vec(0.0,0.75,0.57)
ar.bones['BigArm'] = bigarm
bighand = Blender.Armature.Editbone()
bighand.head = bigarm.tail
bighand.tail = vec(0.0,1.50,0.57)
bighand.parent = bigarm
ar.bones['BigHand'] = bighand

... <similar code for the little hand omitted> ...

ar.update()

obbones.makeParent([ob])
```

The important things are highlighted. First, we disable the envelopes and the vertexGroups properties on the armature *object*. This may seem strange but these properties are remnants of a time where an armature was not a modifier applied to a mesh, but worked its influence by being parented to the Mesh object (at least as far as I can tell, the available documentation is a bit vague about this). We determine what kind of influence to use by setting properties on the armature *modifier*.

After associating an armature modifier with our Mesh object we construct our armature bone by bone. Before we add any bones to an armature we have to call its makeEditable() method. Note that this **edit mode for armatures** is distinct from the *edit* mode for other objects that can be set with the Blender.Window. editMode() function! Once we are done, we revert to *normal* mode again by calling the update() method.

You may have noticed that when constructing our armature we created instances of Editbone objects. Outside of the *edit* mode, these same bones are referred to as Bone objects. Both refer to the same bone but offer different functionality and attributes appropriate for either *edit* mode or in *object* mode. To accommodate the same sort of approach, Blender also provides PoseBone objects to manipulate bones in **Pose mode**.

The bones are positioned in the armature by specifying their head and tail positions (the blunt and sharp end respectively when representing a bone as an octagon). To connect bones it is not sufficient to make the tail position of one bone equal to the head position of another. In order to let a bone follow the movements of another bone it must be parented to it. Parenting is effected by setting the parent attribute of the child to point to the parent bone object. In our example, we have parented each hand bone to its corresponding arm bone.

Bones within an armature are indexed by their name. If the VGROUPS property of an armature modifier is set, the name of the bone should be identical to the name of the vertex group that it influences.

The final line of our example code is important as well; it is necessary to parent the Mesh object to the armature. This might seem superfluous in situations where the armature and the mesh will stay in the same location and only the individual bones in the armature will move; but failing to do so will result in an erratic display of the mesh when interactively changing a pose (you will have to change the mesh to *edit* mode and back, for example to see the effect of the pose on the armature, which is completely unworkable). The result of our rigging will look like this (we set the display mode of the armature to x-ray to make it visible through the mesh):

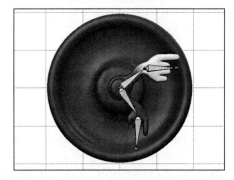

The rendered result may look like this:

We might want to limit the motion of the individual bones to just rotations around the z-axis and this may be accomplished by adding constraints. We will encounter constraints in the next chapter.

Get a bit of backbone boy!

What we have learned so far about rigging can be applied to `creepycrawlies.py` as well. If we want to extend the functionality of the generated model, we may associate an armature modifier with the generated mesh. We have to create an armature object as well, with an appropriate set of bones.

Our task is made light as we already have the vertices grouped by body part in the `mymesh` module, so associating them with a vertex group and a matching bone is trivial. Not so trivial is to create the bones themselves as these might be many and should be positioned and connected in the correct way.

Let's look at how some of the essential elements might be implemented (the full code is in `creepycrawlies.py`). First we have to create an armature and make it editable in order to add bones:

```
ar = Blender.Armature.New('BugBones')
    ar.autoIK = True
    obbones = scn.objects.new(ar)
    ar.makeEditable()
```

We may also set any attributes that alter the behavior of the armature or the way it is displayed. Here we just enable the `autoIK` feature as this will make manipulating the possibly very long tail of our creature a lot simpler for the animator.

The next step is to create a bone for each set of vertices. The `vgroup` list in the following code contains tuples (`vg`,`vlist`,`parent`,`connected`) where `vg` is the name of the vertex group and `vlist` is the list of vertex indices belonging to this group. Each bone that we create may have a parent and it may be physically connected to the parent. These conditions are signaled by the `parent` and `connected` members of the tuple:

```
    for vg,vlist,parent,connected in vgroup:

        bone = Blender.Armature.Editbone()
        bb = bounding_box([verts[i] for i in vlist])
```

For each bone we create we calculate the bounding box of all the vertices in the vertex group that this bone will influence. The next thing will be to position the bone. The way we have set up our creature, all segments of its body will extend along the y-axis except for the wings and legs. These extend along the x-axis. We check this first and set the `axis` variable accordingly:

```
axis=1
if vg.startswith('wing') or vg.startswith('leg'): axis = 0
```

Bones within the armature are indexed by name and the positions of the bone ends are stored in its `head` and `tail` attributes respectively. So, if we have a parent bone and we want to determine its average y-coordinate we can calculate that in the following manner:

```
if parent != None :

    parenty = (ar.bones[parent].head[1] +
               ar.bones[parent].tail[1])/2.0
```

We calculate this position because parts such as legs and wings have parent bones (that is, they move along with the parent bone) but are not connected from head to tail. We will position these bones starting at the center of the parent bone and for that we need the y-position of the parent. The bones of segments lying along the y-axis are positioned along the y-axis themselves and so have zero x and z-coordinates. The x and z-coordinates of leg and wing segments are taken from their bounding boxes. If the bone *is* connected, we simply set its head position to a copy of the position of the tail of the parent (highlighted below).

 The Blender `Vector` class provides the `copy()` function but oddly enough not the `__copy__()` function, so it won't play nice with the functions from Python's copy module.

```
if connected:
    bone.head = ar.bones[parent].tail.copy()
else:
    if axis==1:
        bone.head=Blender.Mathutils.Vector(0,bb[1][0],0)
    else:
        bone.head=Blender.Mathutils.Vector(bb[0][1],
                                           parenty,bb[2][1])
```

```
The tail position of the bone is calculated in a similar manner:
    if axis==1:
        bone.tail=Blender.Mathutils.Vector(0,bb[1][1],0)
    else:
        bone.tail=Blender.Mathutils.Vector(bb[0][0],parenty,
                                           bb[2][0])
```

The final steps in creating a bone are adding it to the armature and setting bone-specific options and any parent relationship.

```
ar.bones[vg] = bone

if parent != None :
    bone.parent=ar.bones[parent]
else:
    bone.clearParent()

if connected: bone.options=Blender.Armature.CONNECTED
```

Note that in the preceding code, the order of the operations is significant: the `parent` attribute may only be cleared on bones that are added to an armature and the `CONNECTED` option may only be set on a bone with a parent.

Again, we should beware of some Blender peculiarity here. A parent may be set on a bone by assigning to its `parent` attribute. If it has no parent, this attribute will return `None`. We cannot *assign* `None` to this attribute however, we must use the `clearParent()` function to remove a parent relationship.

Materials

Materials are what give an object its outward appearance. In Blender, materials are extremely versatile and because of that rather complex. Almost any aspect of the way light behaves when reflecting from an object may be controlled and that not only by simple parameters, but by image maps and node networks as well.

Up to 16 materials can be associated with an object and, within an object, individual parts can refer to one of these 16 materials. In `Text3d` objects, each individual character may refer to a different material and in curves this is true for each control point.

From a developer's point of view, assigning materials to objects is a two-step process. First, we have to define a new material, and then we have to assign a material or materials to an object. The first step may be omitted if we can refer to already existing materials.

If an object like a mesh already has faces defined we then still have to assign a material to each face. Newly created faces will have the active material assigned if the active material is defined.

A small code snippet illustrates how we can assign materials to a Mesh object. Here we assign a material with a white diffuse color to all even numbered faces and one with a black diffuse color to all odd numbered faces in a Mesh object referred to as ob.

```
me=ob.getData(mesh=1)

mats=[ Blender.Material.New(), Blender.Material.New()]
mats[0].rgbCol=[1.0,1.0,1.0]
mats[1].rgbCol=[0.0,0.0,0.0]

ob.setMaterials(mats)
ob.colbits=3

for f in me.faces:
    if f.index%2 == 0 :
        f.mat=0
    else:
        f.mat=1
```

The highlighted line makes sure that the material indices used in each face refer to the materials assigned to the object. (It is also possible to associate materials with the mesh data as we will see in the next section.)

Object materials versus ObData materials

In Blender, both a Mesh object and the top-level Blender object containing the Mesh object may have their own list of 16 materials. This is convenient if we would want to instance many copies of the same mesh but with different materials applied. However, in some situations we might want to apply some or all of the materials to the Mesh instead of to the object. This is controlled by the colbits attribute of the object. This attribute consists of 16 bits, each bit indicating whether to use the material from the Object or that from the Mesh. We saw an example of that already in the previous section.

A `Curve` object may also have its own set of materials, and selecting the actual material obeys the same rules as for a `Mesh` object. Metaballs do have their own set of materials as well and switching between the sets of materials is effected in the same way, but unlike many types of objects that consist of parts (see next section) there is no way to associate different materials with different elements within a Metaball (this is true in the GUI as well: the buttons in the Links and Materials of the Edit context exist to assign material indices to individual metaball elements but they have no effect). Just the first slot of the list of materials is used.

Note that objects that are not rendered themselves, such as armatures and lattices, have no associated materials (that is, any materials associated with the top-level Object containing the armature or lattice is ignored). Some objects that do not have associated materials may have textures associated to them. The `World` and `Lamp` objects for example may have associated textures to control their colors.

Assigning materials to parts of an Object

Within a mesh each face may have its own associated material. This material is identified by its index into the list of materials and stored in the `mat` attribute. Within a `Text3d` object, each character may have its own material, again identified by its index into the list of materials. This time, this index is not stored directly in an attribute but may be set or retrieved by `accessor` methods that take the index of the character in the text as argument.

Sections within a `Curve` (`CurNurb` objects) may be assigned a material index by their `setMatIndex()` method. The index might be retrieved from it by the corresponding `getMatIndex()` method. Note that associating materials with curves that consist of a single line without an extrusion width set or a bevel object associated will have no visible effects as these curves are not rendered.

The following snippet shows how to assign different materials to different characters within a `Text3d` object. The code itself is straightforward but as you may notice we define a list of three materials but use only one. This is wasteful but necessary to work around a peculiarity in `setMaterial()`. Its material index argument should be offset by one, for example, index 2 refers to the second material in the list, however, the largest index may pass is not offset by one. So if we would like to use two materials, we would have to use indices 1 and 2 to access materials 0 and 1, but the actual list of materials should contain three materials, otherwise we can't pass 2 as an argument to `setMaterial()`.

```
mats=[Material.New(),Material.New(),Material.New()]
mats[0].rgbCol=[1.0,1.0,1.0]
mats[1].rgbCol=[0.0,0.0,0.0]
mats[2].rgbCol=[1.0,0.0,0.0]
```

```
ob.setMaterials(mats)
ob.colbits=3
txt=ob.getData()

for i in range(len(txt.getText())):
    txt.setMaterial(i,1+i%2)
```

The highlighted code shows the correction by 1. The full code is provided as `TextColors.py`.

Vertex colors versus face materials

One important aspect of dealing with materials that we have not dealt with so far is **vertex colors**. In meshes, each vertex may have its own vertex color. A vertex color is distinct from a material, but whether vertex colors have any visible effect is controlled by a material's mode flags. For a material to use any vertex colors its `VColPaint` bit should be set by calling its `setMode()` method. When used this way, vertex colors determine the diffuse color of a material while all the materials' regular attributes control the way this diffuse color is rendered. A common use for vertex colors is to *bake* computationally expensive effects such as ambient occlusion. Since vertex colors can be rendered very quickly, ambient occlusion might be approximated this way even in real-time setups such as in the game engine. (Approximated because it will not respond in the same way to changes in lighting.)

Vertex colors are stored as `Mesh`, `MCol` objects (basically RGBA tuples) in the `col` attribute of a face. The `col` attribute is a list containing a reference to an `MCol` object for each vertex in the face. This arrangement makes sense when you consider the fact that materials are associated with faces, not with vertices. When the vertex colors of vertices are different they are linearly interpolated across the face.

It is only possible to assign to the `col` attribute of a face if the mesh has its `vertexColors` attribute set to `True`.

The following example snippet shows how we might set the vertex colors of a mesh. We choose shades of gray depending on the z-coordinate of the vertices (highlighted).

```
import Blender
ob=Blender.Scene.getCurrent().objects.active
me=ob.getData(mesh=1)

me.vertexColors=True
for f in me.faces:
    for i,v in enumerate(f.verts):
        g = int(max(0.0,min(1.0,v.co.z))*255)
        f.col[i].r=g
```

```
            f.col[i].g=g
            f.col[i].b=g

    mats=[Blender.Material.New()]
    mats[0].setMode(Blender.Material.Modes['VCOL_PAINT'])
    ob.setMaterials(mats)
    ob.colbits=1
    ob.makeDisplayList()

    Blender.Window.RedrawAll()
```

The full code is available as `VertexColors.py`.

Adding materials to our engraving

As a finishing touch to our engraving activities we will add two materials. One material index is assigned to the vertices on the surface and another one to the vertices in the chiseled grooves. This way we can, for instance, create the appearance of newly created lettering in a slab of weathered stone.

As we have earlier defined some convenient vertex groups, assigning material indices is a matter of iterating over all faces and assigning to each vertex of a face the appropriate material index depending on which vertex group a vertex is a member of. The function shown below takes a slightly more general approach as it takes a mesh and a list of regular expressions and assigns a material index to each face depending on whether it belongs to a vertex group that has a name that matches one of the regular expressions.

This functions makes it very easy to assign the same material index to all vertex groups that have similar names, for example all tail and thorax segments of the mesh created by `creepycrawlies.py` (these all have names such as `tail.0`, `tail.1`, ..., and so on).

The function is available in `Tools.py`. It depends on Python's `re.search()` function that will match a regular expression against a string. The highlighted line shows that we embed the regular string in so-called anchors (`^` and `$`). This way a regular expression such as `aaaa` will match only a vertex group with the name `aaaa` and not one with the name `aaaa.0` so we can distinguish between them if we want. If we want to match all vertex group names that start with `tail`, we could pass the regular expression `tail.*` for example.

> Regular expressions are an extremely powerful way to match strings. If you are unfamiliar with them you should consult the documentation of the Python module (`http://docs.python.org/library/re.html`). Start with a gentler tutorial, for example, `http://docs.python.org/howto/regex.html`.

Another thing to note in this function is the way we use set operations. These speed up things quite a bit as the Python set operations are extremely fast. We use them here to check efficiently whether the set of vertices (or rather their indices) that comprises a face are all in the set of vertex indices that are in some vertex group. We compute, in advance, both the sets of vertex indices that belong to a vertex group and the sets of vertex indices of each face and store them in dictionaries for easy access. In this way, we create those sets only once for each vertex group and each face respectively instead of recreating each set every time we match against a regular expression. For large meshes, this saves potentially a lot of time (at the expense of storage).

```python
import re

def matindex2vertgroups(me,matgroups):
    if len(matgroups)>16 :
        raise ArgumentError("number of groups larger than number of
                        materials possible (16)")

    groupnames = me.getVertGroupNames()

    vertexgroupset={}
    for name in groupnames:
        vertexgroupset[name]=set(me.getVertsFromGroup(name))
        print name,len(vertexgroupset[name])

    faceset={}
    for f in me.faces:
        faceset[f.index]=set([v.index for v in f.verts])

    for i,matgroup in enumerate(matgroups):
        for name in groupnames:
            if re.search('^'+matgroup+'$',name):
                for f,vset in faceset.items():
                    if vset.issubset(vertexgroupset[name]) :
                        me.faces[f].mat = i
                break
```

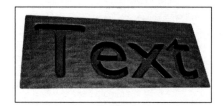

Summary

In this chapter, we saw how to make life easier for our end users by defining vertex groups in meshes to aid in an easy selection of certain features. We also saw how to assign materials to vertices and how to create new materials if needed. First steps were taken to rig a mesh. Specifically, we learned:

- How to define vertex groups
- How to assign vertices to a vertex group
- How to assign materials to faces
- How to assign vertex colors to vertices
- How to set edge properties
- How to add modifiers
- How to skin bones

Next up we go beyond static objects and see how to control the movement of objects.

Pydrivers and Constraints

When designing a complex object with movable parts we'd like to control how these parts move in relation to each other. Sometimes, we might want to try and simulate reality by using a physics engine such as bullet, but often this is either not accurate enough or does not provide an animator with enough control. Most of the time the clever use of multiple constraints will achieve our goals, but sometimes the restrictions and relations cannot be expressed in terms of simple constraints and key-framed motions. In those cases, we can extend Blender's capabilities by defining our own constraints or relations between animated properties by using Python.

In this chapter, we will see how we can associate built-in constraints with Blender objects and how to define complex relationships between animated properties by using the so-called **pydrivers**. We will also define new complex constraints that may be used just like the built-in constraints. We will not yet look into defining key frames for animated properties as we will encounter those in later chapters.

In this chapter, we will see:

- How to drive one **IPO** from another by a Python expression
- How to work around some limitations inherent in **pydrivers**
- How to restrict the motion of objects and bones by adding constraints
- How to write a constraint in Python that will snap an object to the closest vertex on another object

There is a lot to cover here so let's first start off with some definitions to get a clear idea about what we are dealing with.

Getting to grips with animated properties

Blender's system is versatile, yet complex. Before we are able to manipulate animated properties from a Python script it is necessary we understand the concepts involved thoroughly.

IPO

In Blender, almost any property can be animated. Normally this is done by fixing the values of some property such as the position of an Object at certain key frames and interpolating between these values for intermediate frames. Blender groups related animated properties together in so-called IPOs. For instance, all spatial properties such as location, rotation, and scale are grouped as an Object type IPO and may be associated with almost any Blender Object for instance, a `Mesh`, a `Camera`, or a `Lamp`. The many properties of Blender Materials are grouped in the Material type IPO. A Material type IPO may be associated with any object that has associated materials. Likewise, a Lamp type IPO should be associated with a `Lamp` object. An overview of possible IPO types is given in the next table.

> **IPO** sounds like an abbreviation and it probably is, but what it stands for exactly is a bit vague. The Blender wiki states that it stands for InterPOlation system, but InterPolation Object is sometimes encountered as well. Most of the time, IPO is used as a noun by itself however, so this discussion is a bit academical.

Each IPO may be associated with more than one object. It is for example possible to animate the rotation of many objects in the same manner by associating a single appropriate Object type IPO with them. In the Blender Python API, IPOs are represented by IPO objects. An IPO object may be associated with another object by means of the `setIpo()` method. The following table gives an overview of IPO types, typical channels, and the type of objects they can be applied to. Refer to the API documentation for the Blender.IPO module for more details
(`http://www.blender.org/documentation/249PythonDoc/index.html`).

IPO type	IPO channels (some examples, refer to API documentation for a full list)	Relevant to these Blender objects
Object	LocX, LocY, LocZ (location) RotX, RotY, RotZ (rotation) ScaleX, ScaleY, ScaleZ (scale)	All Blender objects that can be positioned, such as Mesh, Lamp, Camera, and so on
Pose	RotX, RotY, RotZ (rotation)	Bone
Material	R,G,B (diffuse color)	Any object that takes a material
Texture	Contrast	Any object with associated textures, such as Mesh, Lamp, World, and so on
Curve	Speed	Curve
Lamp	Energ (energy) R,G,B (color)	Lamp
World	HorR,HorG,HorB (horizon color)	World
Constraint	Inf (Influence)	Constraint
Sequence	Fac (Factor, for example, the volume of an audio strip)	Sequence

IPOchannels and IPOCurves

IPOs of a given type will contain a whole collection of related animated properties. Each of these properties is often referred to as a channel. Examples of channels in an Object type IPO are for example LocX (the x-component of a location) and RotY (the rotation around the y-axis). Each channel is represented by an IPOCurve object that implements the required functionality to return a value interpolated between key frames.

An example of a channel in a Material type IPO would be SpecB — the blue component of the specular color.

IPOCurve objects of a given IPO are accessed as attributes, for example, myipo.LocX will refer to a LocX IPOCurve if myipo is an Object type IPO.

To illustrate these concepts imagine that we want to animate the movement of a simple cube along the x-axis. We want to start the motion at frame number 1 and to end it at frame number 25. Within Blender, this is accomplished by following these steps:

1. Add a simple `Cube` by selecting **Add | Mesh | Cube** and make sure that you are in Object mode again.

2. Go to frame number one (for example, by entering the frame number in the frame number widget below the 3D View window).

3. Insert a location key frame by selecting **Object | Insert keyframe | Loc**. In the `IPOCurve` editing window this location key frame will show up as an Object type IPO (highlighted in the following screenshot).

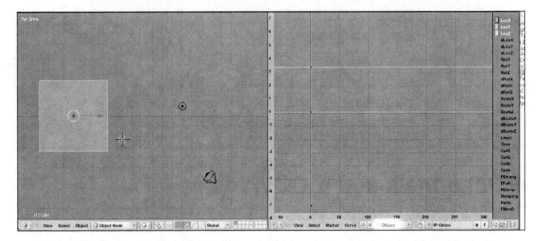

The current frame is visible as a green vertical line. A location IPO holds three distinct channels (for the location along the x-axis, `LocX`, and along the y– and z-axes (`LocY` and `LocZ`). These channels are represented as different colored graphs (they might overlap). These graphs may be manipulated in the `IPOCurve` editor directly, but here we will just add a second key frame in the 3D View window.

1. In the 3D View window, go to frame number 25.

2. Select the Cube and move it along the x-axis to the right.

3. Insert a second location key frame by selecting **Object | Insert keyframe | Loc**. Now we see that each of the graphs representing the three location IPO channels have a second point defined on them. Because we changed the location of the cube only along the x-axis, the graphs of the other channels remain flat, but the `LocX` channel shows how the change of x-position progresses with each frame.

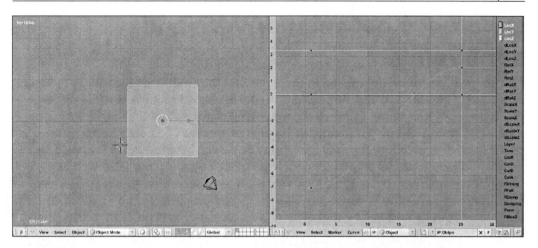

By adding more key frames we can make any motion as complex as we want, but this becomes a lot of work if we want our object to follow a precise precalculated path for example. Later in this chapter we will see how we can manipulate the IPOCurve objects that represent these channels within an IPO programmatically.

Constraints

Constraints in Blender are associated with top-level Blender Objects or Blender Bone objects and represented by Constraint objects. Blender Objects and Bones have a constraints attribute, which is an object implementing a sequence of constraints and methods to add, remove, and alter the order of constraints in this sequence (being able to change the order of constraints is necessary because in some situations the order in which constraints are applied matters).

When a constraint is associated with an object the result will be a mix of the constrained parameters and the calculated parameters. How much this mix will consist of constrained or unconstrained parameters is determined by the influence attribute and this may even be animated.

Difference between drivers and constraints

Drivers and constraints are related in the sense that they influence the way parameters may change but they are also very different: constraints act on objects while drivers determine how IPO curves (animated parameters) change other IPO curves. And where constraints can only influence the spatial properties of an object such as its position, scale or rotation, any IPO curve may be driven by another IPO curve. This means that even material parameters, such as color or a Lamp parameter such as energy, may be driven by another IPO. There is a restriction though: the IPO curves that drive other IPO curves must currently be special properties of an object so you can drive the color of a material by the rotation of some object but you cannot drive that color by the energy of a lamp for instance. Also, the fact that constraints can affect only spatial properties means that there is for instance no way that you can limit the diffuse color of a material. The following table shows some constraints and their relevant attributes. Refer to the API documentation for the Blender.Constraint module for more details.

Constraint type	Typical attributes
TrackTo	Target (target object)
	Track (axis to track)
Floor	Target (target object)
StretchTo	Target (target object)
CopyLocation	Copy (which location component(s) to copy)

Note that it is possible to animate the influence of a constraint as well, in which case an Object will have an associated constraint type IPO.

Programming with constraints

Blender has many constraints that you may apply to an object. Some of them are quite like drivers, in the sense that they do not restrict a motion of an object but copy some parameters such as rotation or location. From a developer's point of view, each Blender Object has a constraints attribute that is a sequence of constraint objects. This sequence can be appended and items from this sequence can be deleted. It is also possible to alter the order of the items.

Method	Action	Example
append (*type*)	Appends a new constraint to an object and returns the constraint	`ob.constraints.append(` `Constraint.Type.TRACKTO)`
remove (*constraint*)	Removes a constraint from an object	`ob.constraints.remove(` `ob.constraints[0])`
moveUp (*constraint*) moveDown (*constraint*)	Change the position of a constraint in the list of constraints	`ob.constraints.moveDown(` `ob.constraints[0])`
[]	Accesses an attribute of a constraint	`Con = ob.constraints[0]` `Con[Constraint.Settings.` `TARGET] = other`

New `Constraint` objects are not instanced by way of a constructor, but by calling the `append()` method of the `constraints` attribute with the type of the constraint to add. `append()` will then return the new `Constraint` whose settings may then be altered.

Programming with IPOs

IPO channels can be changed from a script just as constraints can but they are rather more diverse than constraints because there are many different types of IPO channels and some of them, notably texture channels and shape keys, need a special treatment. They have a separate chapter of their own (*Chapter 6: Shape keys, IPOs, and Poses*) but a different use of Python for IPO channels is shown in the next section.

PyDrivers

There are many cases where we would like to change some property by referring to another property but where the relationship cannot be captured by driving an IPO channel by another one. Often, this is because the relation is not a simple linear dependency, for example, a piston driven by a circular motion. Another case would be if the relation is non continuous, for example, a light that is turned on when a switch is in a certain position.

In these cases the relationship may be defined by a Python expression or by the so-called *pydriver*. A pydriver takes the IPO channel of another object as input and produces output that will drive a channel on the current object. Because these Python expressions can access the complete Blender API, these relations can be made very complex indeed.

PyConstraints

Where pydrivers may be used to bypass limitations in the built-in possibilities to drive IPO channels, **PyConstraints** allow us to conquer difficulties in situations where the built-in constraints will not suffice. For example, it is not possible to restrict the position of an object to the surface of another object with holes in it. The built-in constraints offer ways to limit the position to a location not lower than another object (the `floor` constraint). But if we would like it to be possible for our object to drop below the surface at locations where there is a hole, we would have to program such a constraint ourselves. As we will see, PyConstraints allow us to do just that.

With all these introductory remarks behind us we can finally turn to programming again in the next section.

Setting the time—one to rule them all

What use is a clock if you cannot set the time in a convenient way? Instead of positioning each hand, we would like to turn a single knob to move both the big hand and the little hand where the little hand would have to move twelve times as slow as the big hand.

Therefore, we would have to define a `knob` object (that we probably would not render) and drive the rotation of the bones in the clock by the rotation of this knob.

To set up the driven channels we follow these steps:

1. In the 3D View, select the `bighand` object.

2. In the IPO window, make sure that you have the object IPO types selected. On the right-hand side, there will be a list of channels. Select the one labeled **RotZ** by left-clicking on it. It will be highlighted.

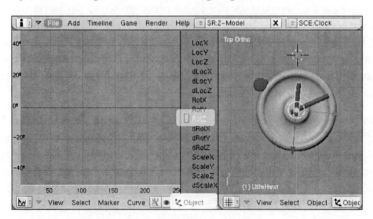

3. Select **Curve | Transform Properties**. A pop-up window will appear. Click on the **Add Driver** button.

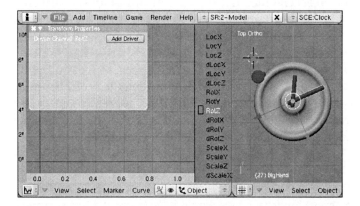

4. With the **Transform Properties** pop up still present, select **Curve | Insert 1:1 mapping** and next click on the **Default one-to-one mapping** pop up (or press *Enter*). The resulting graph will show up as a straight, pale blue line in the IPO editor window.

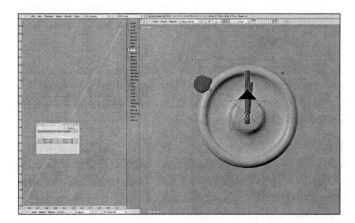

5. In the **Transform Properties** pop-up window, click on the pale green python icon. The python icon will turn dark green and it is now possible to enter a pydriver expression in the adjacent text field. Enter the following line of code:

```
ob('Knob').RotZ*(360/(2*m.pi))/10
```

Et voila! If you now rotate the `knob` object about its z-axis the big hand follows suit. The pydriver expression does need some clarification though. The highlighted part is the driver—the object channel that supplies the input for our driven channel. The `ob('Knob')` part is the shorthand allowed in pydriver expressions for `Blender. Object.Get('Knob')` and the `RotZ` attribute supplies us with the rotation about the z-axis. This rotation, however, is given in radians, whereas the result of a pydriver expression for a rotation channel should be in degrees, so we multiply by 360 degrees and divide by 2 times pi. Finally, we divide our calculated number of degrees by ten because for some obscure reason, Blender does not really expect degrees but the number of degrees divided by 10! (Note that this "divide by ten" business is valid only for rotation channels and not for any of the other channels!)

1-on-1 mappings

You may wonder why we would have to insert a 1-on-1 curve first. Well, the relation between a driven channel and its driver contains one more layer and that is a curve translating the output of the pydriver to the final output. This curve can be tweaked of course, but normally we would do all the fine-tuning in our pydriver and just put in a 1-on-1 curve. This way of working is so common that Blender provides a menu entry especially for this situation since it is quite tedious to create the necessary curves again and again for each driven channel.

Of course, we could have accomplished the same feat by driving the rotation channel directly by the rotation channel of the `knob` object or even by a copy rotation constraint. That would have saved us the strange conversion issues but the purpose of this section is to show the basics.

The little hand is an example where using a pydriver really is a valid solution. (Although by tweaking the IPO curve itself we could alter the pace of the driven channel but that would not be as clear as a simple expression and almost impossible for more complex relations) We repeat the list of actions shown earlier but now for the little hand object and enter the following pydriver expression:

```
ob('Knob').RotZ*(360/(2*m.pi))/10/12
```

Because the little hand runs twelve times as slow as the big hand, we use the same pydriver expression as for the big hand but divide that result by twelve. Now when we rotate the `knob` object about its z-axis, the big hand will follow as will the little hand at its set pace. Instead of manually rotating the knob it is also possible to animate the rotation of the knob to animate both clock hands. The complete result is available as `clock-pydriver.blend` and a rendered image of the clock, with the knob driving the motion of the hands visible on the top left, is shown in the next screenshot:

Shortcuts

Within pydriver expressions some useful shortcuts can be used to save on typing. In the step-by-step example we already made use of the `ob('<name>')` shortcut that refers to Blender objects by name and likewise, it is possible to access `Mesh` objects and materials by `me('<name>')` and `ma('<name>')` respectively. Furthermore, the `Blender` module is available as `b`, the `Blender.Noise` module as `n`, and Python's `math` module as `m`. This allows for expressions using trigonometric functions such as sinus, for example. These facilities are sufficient to cover many issues but they still might not be enough, for instance if we would like to import external modules. There is a way around these difficulties though as we will see in the next section.

Overcoming limitations: pydrivers.py

The input field for pydrivers is limited to 125 characters and even though the shortcuts provided to access Python's `math` module and some of the Blender modules allow for shorter expressions, the space provided is often not enough. Also, as pydrivers must be Python expressions, it is quite difficult to debug them (because you cannot insert `print` statements for example) or to attain something like an `if/then` functionality. The latter can be overcome, to a certain extent, by clever tricks based on the fact that `True` and `False` in Python are converted to 1 and 0 respectively inside numerical expressions, so the statement:

```
if a>b:
    c=14
else:
    c=109
```

may be expressed as:

```
c = (a>b)*14 + (a<=b)*109
```

However, this feels awkward and evaluates the condition twice. Fortunately, both the space problem and the limitation to a single expression can be solved by using a text block named `pydrivers.py`. If such a text block is present, its contents are accessible as a module called p. So, for example, if we define a function `clamp()` in `pydrivers.py` that looks like this:

```
def clamp(a,low,high):
    if a<low : a=low
    if a>high: a=high
    return a
```

We may invoke this function in our pydriver expression as `p.clamp(a,14,109)`.

We will use `pydrivers.py` quite a bit in the following examples, not only because it allows for more complex expressions, but also because the width of the pydriver field is even smaller than the length of its allowed content making it very hard to read as you have to scroll about to access all parts of an expression.

Internal combustion—correlating complex changes

Imagine that we want to demonstrate how a four-stroke internal combustion engine works. Such an engine has a lot of moving parts and many of them are related in complex ways.

To see what these exact relations are, it might be useful to have a look at the following illustration. It lists the names that we will use when we refer to the various parts. (I am neither an automotive engineer nor a mechanic so these part names may not be accurate but at least we will be talking about the same things. For more information you may want to read
`http://en.wikipedia.org/wiki/Four-stroke_cycle`.)

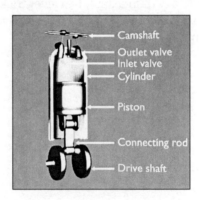

Before we start to configure the parts to have their rotation and position driven by another part, it is a good thing to think ahead: in real life, the pistons inside the cylinders are propelled by the expansion of the ignited fuel and the pistons drive the drive shaft (or crank-shaft) with the attached flywheel and a distribution belt (or in our case some gears, that are not shown here) transfers that motion back to the camshafts that drive the motion of the inlet and outlet valves. Obviously, we cannot follow this concept directly as there is no fuel object of some sort to drive other objects so it makes more sense to reverse the chain of relations. In our setup the flywheel will drive the drive shaft and the different gears and the drive shaft will drive most other objects, including the piston and its connecting rod. We will also drive the energy of the lamp positioned at the tip of the spark plug by the rotation of the drive shaft.

The drive shaft will simply follow the rotation of the flywheel as will the lower gear (this could be implemented with a `copy rotation` constraint just as well but here we choose to implement everything by pydrivers). The corresponding pydrivers for the `RotX` channel will look like this:

```
ob('Flywheel').RotX/(2*m.pi)*36
```

This may look awkward for something just copying a rotation but remember that rotations are stored as radians while pydriver expressions should return rotations as degrees divided by 10.

The top gear and both the camshafts will also follow the rotation of the flywheel but with the speed reduced to half and with the direction of the rotation reversed:

```
m.degrees(ob('Flywheel').RotX*-0.5)/10.0
```

To illustrate how to access functions in Python's `math` module we did not do the conversion to degrees ourselves but used the `degrees()` function supplied by the `math` module.

We modeled the camshafts with the cam pointing exactly downward. If we want to drive the x-axis rotation of the inlet camshaft by the rotation of the drive shaft we have to take into account that it moves at half the speed. Also, its rotation lags behind a bit to match the ignition cycle of the cylinder as it opens the inlet valve on the first downstroke and closes the valve just before the ignition spark:

```
ob('DriveShaftPart').RotX/(2*m.pi)*18+9
```

The expression for the outlet camshaft is almost identical except for the amount it lags behind (here 24, but tuning this engine is left to real mechanics):

```
ob('DriveShaftPart').RotX/(2*m.pi)*18+24
```

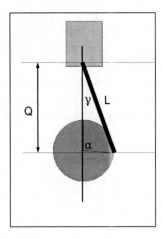

The movement of the piston is limited to just the vertical, but the exact motion is somewhat more involved to calculate. We are interested in the position of the quantity **Q**—see the preceding figure—and the distance between the center of the drive shaft and point where the connecting rod (**L** in the diagram) connects to the piston. Because the length of the connecting rod is fixed, **Q** will vary as a function of the rotation angle **α** of the drive shaft. The distance from the center of the drive shaft to point where the connecting rod is connected to the drive shaft is also fixed. We call this distance R. Now we have a triangle with sides **Q**, **L**, and **R** and a known angle **α**. As three of these quantities (L, R, and α) are known, we can calculate the fourth, **Q**, by using the cosine rule (http://en.wikipedia.org/wiki/Law_of_cosines). Therefore, we define a function q() in pydrivers.py that will return the length **Q** when **L,R**, and **α** are given:

```
def q(l,r,a): return r*cos(a)+sqrt(l**2-(r*sin(a))**2)
```

The expression for the LocZ channel of the piston will then simply call this function with the appropriate values for the arguments:

```
p.q(1.542,0.655,ob('DriveShaftPart').RotX)
```

The precise values for **L** and **R** were taken from the mesh by noting the position of appropriate vertices of the connecting rod and the drive shaft in the Transform Properties window. (*N* key in the 3D View)

The connecting rod itself may use the same expression for its LocZ channel as we carefully made the mesh origins of the piston and the connecting rod to coincide.

However, the motion of the connecting rod is not limited to the z-location as it will rotate around the x-axis centered on the point connecting it to the piston. The angle of this rotation (γ in the diagram) can be derived from the quantities **L**, **R**, and **α**:

```
def topa(l,r,a):
    Q=q(l,r,a)
    ac=acos((Q**2+l**2-r**2)/(2*Q*l))
    if a%(2*pi)>pi : ac = -ac
    return -ac
```

The pydriver expression for `RotX` will then look like this:

```
m.degrees(p.topa(1.542,0.655,ob('DriveShaftPart').RotX))/10.0
```

The inlet and outlet valves are driven by the rotation of their respective camshafts. The outline of the actual cam is quite complex so here, we use not the actual form of that outline but approximate it by something that looks good enough (that is, open the valve in a fluent yet brisk motion at the correct moment). The following graph shows the valve travel as a function of rotation angle:

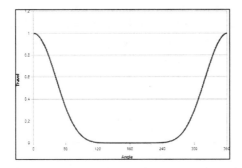

To this end, in `pydrivers.py` we define a function `spike()` that will take the rotation of the camshaft as its argument and returns a value between `0.0` and `1.0` that rises steeply around the zero angle:

```
def spike(angle):
    t = (cos(angle)+1.0)/2.0
    return t**4
```

Now the motion of the valve is linear but the line it follows is tilted by 10 degrees (forward for the inlet valve, backward for the outlet valve) so we have to drive two channels, `LocZ` and `LocY`, each multiplied by the correct amount to effect the slanted motion. We therefore define two functions in `pydrivers.py`:

```
def valveZ(angle,tilt,travel,offset):
    return cos(radians(tilt))*spike(angle)*travel+offset
def valveY(angle,tilt,travel,offset):
    return sin(radians(tilt))*spike(angle)*travel+offset
```

Both functions will return a distance given the rotation angle of the object driving it. The `tilt` is the amount that the valve is tilted (in degrees), `travel` is the maximum distance the valve will travel along the tilted line, and `offset` is a value that allows us to tweak the position of the valve. The corresponding pydriver expressions for the `LocZ` and `LocY` channels of the inlet valve will then become:

```
p.valveZ(ob('CamInlet').RotX+m.pi,-10.0,-0.1,6.55)
```

and

```
p.valveY(ob('CamInlet').RotX+m.pi,-10.0,-0.1,-0.03)
```

(The expressions for the outlet valve look the same but with a positive tilt angle.)

Until now, all channels have been object channels, that is, locations and rotations. But it is also possible to drive other channels, and that is precisely what we need to drive the energy of the lamp positioned at the tip of our spark plug. In `pydrivers.py` we first define a helper function `topi()` that, besides the rotation angle of the driving object, will take an angle h (in radians) and an intensity i as arguments. It will return that intensity if the angle of the driving object is between 0 and h and will return zero outside this range. Because the input angle may be larger than two times pi (when the driving object is rotated more than full circle), we correct this by the highlighted *modulo* operation:

```
def topi(a,h,i):
    m = a%(2*pi)
    r=0.0
    if m<h: r=i
    return r
```

The pydriver expression for the energy channel (called "Energ" in the IPO editor window) can then be expressed as follows:

```
p.topi(ob('DriveShaftPart').RotX/2+m.pi,0.3,0.5)
```

As shown, this expression will 'fire' the spark plug for the first 17 degrees or so (0.3 radians) of its cycle by setting the energy to 0.5.

More power—combining multiple cylinders to an engine

Once we have modeled a single cylinder and taken care of driving the motions of the individual parts, our next step is to duplicate the cylinders to create a set like the opening illustration of this chapter. In principle we can select all parts, duplicate them by pressing *Shift + D*, and adjust the timing of the individual driven channels.

There is a snag, however. When using *Shift + D* rather than *Alt + D* we make actual copies of the object meshes instead of merely referring to the same. We would expect the same for other items associated with an object, such as materials, textures, and IPOs. This is not the case however as Blender, by default, does not duplicate those last three categories when duplicating an object. This would be awkward, as a change in the IPO of the first piston for example would affect all duplicated pistons as well.

We could make those copies unique afterward (by clicking on the user count field of those IPOs for instance and confirm the **make single user?** popup) but this is tedious as it would have to be repeated for each copy.

A better way is to alter the **Duplicate with object** settings in the **Edit Methods** screen of the **User Preferences** window as shown in the preceding screenshot. In this way, IPOs associated with an object will be made into unique copies when duplicating an object. A screenshot of the **User Preferences** window with buttons to duplicate IPOs (highlighted) is shown above.

The result of our labors, a four cylinder engine with gears to transfer the motion of the drive shaft to the camshafts is available as engine001.blend. A still image from the animation available at http://vimeo.com/7170769 is shown in the next screenshot:

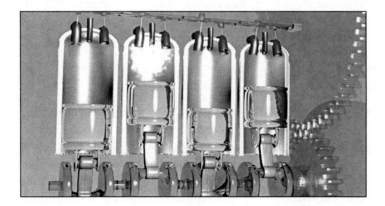

Adding simple constraints

Constraints may be applied to objects as well as to bones. In both instances a new constraint is added by calling the `append()` method of the `constraints` attribute. Our next example will show how we may restrict the movement of the clock hands from the rigged clock (from *Chapter 3, Vertex Groups and Materials*) to rotate around the z-axis. The code defining the function to accomplish this starts off with two `import` statements that will save us some typing:

```
from Blender.Constraint import Type
from Blender.Constraint import Settings
```

The function itself will take two arguments: `obbones`, a reference to a Blender object whose data is an armature (that is, not the armature object itself) and `bone`, the name of the bone whose motion we would like to restrict. It is important to understand that the constraint that we will associate with a bone is not a property of the armature but of the pose of the object containing the armature. Many objects may refer to the same armature and any poses are associated with the object so different objects referring to the same armature may strike different poses.

So the function starts off by getting the pose first and then a reference to the bone that we want to constrain. The highlighted line shows how to associate the constraint (this would be similar if we would associate a constraint with a Blender object instead of a bone):

```
def zrotonly(obbones,bone):
    poseob = obbones.getPose()
    bigarmpose = poseob.bones[bone]
    c=bigarmpose.constraints.append(Type.LIMITROT)
    c[Settings.LIMIT]=Settings.LIMIT_XROT|Settings.LIMIT_YROT
    c[Settings.XMIN]=0.0
    c[Settings.XMAX]=0.0
    c[Settings.YMIN]=0.0
    c[Settings.YMAX]=0.0
    poseob.update()
```

The newly appended constraint is retained as the variable `c` and the subsequent lines show that the different attributes of a constraint may be accessed like a dictionary. First, we configure the `LIMIT` attribute (a bitmap) to limit the rotation of the x and y axes. Next, we set the minimum and maximum of the rotations around these axes to `0.0`, as we disallow any movement. In the rigging of a realistic animal skeleton, for example, these values could be set to limit the extent of the rotation to values comparable with a real joint. Finally, to make the changes to our `Pose` object visible, we call its `update()` method.

Defining complex constraints

Where pydrivers enable us to drive the change of one IPOCurve by the change in another, PyConstraints provide us with ways to let object properties change only in a limited way.

Of course, Blender has many simple constraints predefined as we saw in previous sections and often a combination of simple constraints may be exactly what you want. But say you want your objects to move about freely within a non-rectangular area, for example to simplify the allowed placement of traffic lights and phone booths on a street grid. How would we achieve that? Enter pyconstraints.

PyConstraints are Python scripts that should be present as a text block in Blender's text editor and start with a comment line identifying it as a constraint:

    #BPYCONSTRAINT

A Python constraint should contain three functions called doConstraint(), doTarget(), and getSettings(). The first two are invoked anytime we move either the target or the constrained object and the last one is called when the user clicks the **Options** button that is present once the user has selected a pyconstraint. The following screenshot shows the **Constraints** tab once a pyconstraint is selected.

The easiest way to understand what these functions do is by looking at the built-in constraint template that we can use as a basis to write our own constraints. It is accessible in the text editor from the menu **Text | Script Templates | Script Constraint**. If clicked, it will create a new text block that can be selected from the dropdown at the bottom of the text editor.

The Blender constraint template

The Blender constraint template contains a lot of helpful comments as well, but here we list mostly the bare functions. Also, the template creates a dummy properties window. We will encounter properties in the next section so our example of `getSettings()` here will be almost empty. As shown the functions will implement a functional constraint, however, nothing is actually constrained. Location, rotation, and scale of the constrained object are all kept the same.

```
def doConstraint(obmatrix, targetmatrices, idprop):
    # Separate out the transformation components for easy access.
    obloc = obmatrix.translationPart()   # Translation
    obrot = obmatrix.toEuler()           # Rotation
    obsca = obmatrix.scalePart()         # Scale

    # code to actually change location, rotation or scale goes here

    # Convert back into a matrix for loc, scale, rotation,
    mtxloc = Mathutils.TranslationMatrix(obloc)
    mtxrot = obrot.toMatrix().resize4x4()
    mtxsca = Mathutils.Matrix([obsca[0],0,0,0], [0,obsca[1],0,0],
                              [0,0,obsca[2],0], [0,0,0,1])

    # Recombine the separate elements into a transform matrix.
    outputmatrix = mtxsca * mtxrot * mtxloc

    # Return the new matrix.
    return outputmatrix
```

The `doConstraint()` function will be passed the transformation matrix of the constrained object and a list of transformation matrices for every target object. It will also receive a dictionary of properties of the constraint that may be accessed by name.

The first thing we do is to separate out the translation, rotation, and scale components of the constrained objects' transformation matrix. The translation part will be a vector with the x, y, z position and the scale part will be a vector with scaling factors along the x, y, and z-axis. The rotation part will be represented by a Euler vector with the rotation about the three principal axes. (Eulers greatly simplify working with rotations in 3D but are rather difficult to grasp at first. Wikipedia has a great page on Euler angles http://en.wikipedia.org/wiki/Euler_angle but for now, it is easiest to think of Eulers as a rotation separated out as rotations around the local x, y, and z axes.) We could separate any of the target object's transformation matrices as well, if we wanted, and then modify the transformation components of the transformation matrix of the constrained object in any way we wish.

The function as shown here does nothing but converts the different transformation components back to matrices by using API methods (where available) and then recombines them by using matrix multiplication to a single matrix that is subsequently returned.

The `doTarget()` function is called prior to calling `doConstraint()` and gives us the opportunity to manipulate the target matrix before it is passed to `doConstraint()`. Its arguments are the target object, the subtarget (either a `Bone` or a vertex group for a target armature or mesh respectively), the target matrix, and the properties of the constraint. In a later section, we exploit this opportunity to store a reference to the target object in the properties so that `doConstraint()` may access that information that it otherwise could not access. If we do not wish to alter anything then returning the target matrix as is will suffice, as shown in the following code:

```
def doTarget(target_object, subtarget_bone, target_matrix,
             id_properties_of_constraint):
    return target_matrix
```

Likewise, if there is no need to offer the user the possibility to specify additional properties, `getSettings()` may simply return. If we *do* want to show a pop up, `getSettings()` is the place where it should happen. We see an example of that in a later section as well. The following code is a valid "do nothing" implementation:

```
def getSettings(idprop):
    return
```

Do you find me attractive too?

As the moon and earth revolve around each other they feel each other's gravitational attraction. On earth this will result in tides, but the solid body of the earth and moon will be distorted as well, although this effect is small. Now there is a lot more to tides than attraction alone (http://en.wikipedia.org/wiki/Tides), but we can show the gravitational distortion in an exaggerated way by applying constraints.

One way of doing this is to use a `TrackTo` constraint to orient an axis of our constrained object towards the attracting object and add a second constraint that scales the constrained object along the same axis. The size of the scale will depend on the inverse distance between the constrained object and the target object. The effect is illustrated in the next screenshot where the effect of a `TrackTo` constraint is combined with the script constraint `moon_constraint.py`.

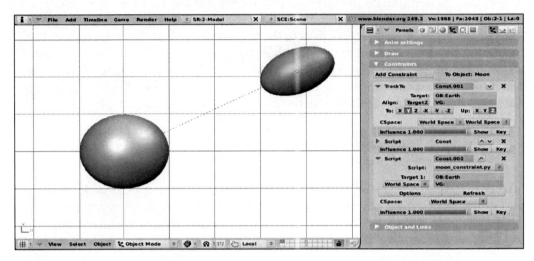

We will have to write this distance-dependent scaling ourselves. If we take the constraint template provided by Blender we can leave the `doTarget()` and `getSettings()` functions as is, but we do have to write a suitable `doConstraint()` function (full code available as `moon_constraint.py`):

```
def doConstraint(obmatrix, targetmatrices, idprop):
    obloc = obmatrix.translationPart()   # Translation
    obrot = obmatrix.toEuler()            # Rotation
    obsca = obmatrix.scalePart()          # Scale

    tloc = targetmatrices[0].translationPart()
    d = abs((obloc-tloc).length)
    d = max(0.01,d)
    f = 1.0+1.0/d
    obsca[1]*=f

    mtxloc = Mathutils.TranslationMatrix(obloc)
    mtxrot = obrot.toMatrix().resize4x4()
    mtxsca = Mathutils.Matrix([obsca[0],0,0,0], [0,obsca[1],0,0],
                              [0,0,obsca[2],0], [0,0,0,1])

    outputmatrix = mtxsca * mtxrot * mtxloc

    return outputmatrix
```

We left out any lines related to properties as we do not implement any user-configurable properties for this constraint. The highlighted lines show what we have to do to calculate the distance-dependent scaling.

The first line gets the location of our target. Next, we calculate the distance between the constrained object and the target and limit this to a minimum (slightly larger than zero) to prevent a division by zero in the next highlighted line. The formula used here is nowhere near an approximation of any gravitational influence but behaves nicely enough for our purpose; the scale factor will be 1.0 if d is very large and will smoothly increase as the distance d becomes smaller. The final highlighted line shows that we alter the scale only of the y-axis, that is, the axis we orient towards the target object with the TrackTo constraint.

Cyclic dependencies:

If both objects have a comparable mass, the gravitational distortion would be of comparable size on both objects. We might be tempted to add the TrackTo and moon_constraint.py constraints to both objects to see the effect they assert on each other, but unfortunately that will not work because it will create a cyclic dependency and Blender will protest.

Snapping to mesh vertices

This is like the "snap to vertex" mode that is available in Blender from the menu **Object | Transform | Snap** (see http://wiki.blender.org/index.php/Doc:Manual/Modelling/Meshes/Snap_to_Mesh for more about snapping) except that the effect is not permanent (the object reverts to its unconstrained position once the constraint is removed) and the strength of the constraint can be modulated (animated even) by changing the Influence slider.

In the constraints that we designed so far, only the position of the target object was needed to calculate the effects on the constrained object. This position was readily available to the doConstraint() function as the matrices of the targets were passed as arguments. Now we are facing a different challenge though: if we want to snap to a vertex we must have access to the mesh data of the target object, but the target object is not passed to the doConstraint() function.

The way around this obstacle is the `idprop` argument that is passed to `doConstraint()`. Before `doConstraint()` is called, Blender first calls `doTarget()` for each target object. This function is passed as a reference to the target object and to the properties of the constraint. This allows us to insert a reference to the target object in these properties and because these properties are passed to `doConstraint()`, this provides us with a means to pass the necessary information to `doConstraint()` to get at the `Mesh` data. There is a minor point to consider here though: Blender properties can only be numbers or strings so we cannot actually store a reference to an object but have to settle for its name. Because a name is unique and Blender's `Object.Get()` provides a way to retrieve an object by name, this is not a problem.

The code for `doConstraint()` and `doTarget()` will look like this (the full code is provided as `zoning_constraint.py`):

```python
def doConstraint(obmatrix, targetmatrices, idprop):

    obloc = obmatrix.translationPart().resize3D()
    obrot = obmatrix.toEuler()
    obsca = obmatrix.scalePart()

    # get the target mesh
    to = Blender.Object.Get(idprop['target_object'])
    me = to.getData(mesh=1)

    # get the location of the target object
    tloc = targetmatrices[0].translationPart().resize3D()

    # find the nearest vertex in the target object
    smallest = 1000000.0
    delta_ob=tloc-obloc
    for v in me.verts:
        d = (v.co+delta_ob).length
        if d < smallest:
            smallest=d
            sv=v
    obloc = sv.co + tloc

    # reconstruct the object matrix
    mtxrot = obrot.toMatrix().resize4x4()
    mtxloc = Mathutils.TranslationMatrix(obloc)
    mtxsca = Mathutils.Matrix([obsca[0],0,0,0], [0,obsca[1],0,0],
                              [0,0,obsca[2],0], [0,0,0,1])
    outputmatrix = mtxsca * mtxrot * mtxloc
    return outputmatrix

def doTarget(target_object, subtarget_bone, target_matrix,
             id_properties_of_constraint):
    id_properties_of_constraint['target_object']=target_object.name
    return target_matrix
```

The highlighted lines show how we pass the name of the target object to `doConstraint()`. In `doConstraint()` we first retrieve the target mesh. This may throw an exception, for example, if the target object is not a mesh, but this will be caught by Blender itself. The constraint will not be affected then and an error is shown on the console, but Blender will proceed happily.

Once we have the mesh data of the target object we retrieve the object location of the target object. We need this because all vertex coordinates are relative to this. Next we compare the location of the constrained object to all the vertex locations of the target mesh and remember the closest one to calculate the object location of the constrained object. Finally, we reconstruct the transformation matrix of the constrained object by combining various transformation components as before.

Aligning along a vertex normal

Now that we can constrain an object to the closest vertex on a target mesh we can see that something is missing: the object is not oriented in a meaningful way. This might not always be a problem, for example, trees will normally point upward, but in many situations it would be nice if we could orient the constrained object perpendicular to the surface. This is the same for all practical purposes, as orienting the constrained object along the vertex normal of the vertex it has been snapped to.

Therefore, after finding the closest vertex we determine the angle between the vertex normal and the z-axis (that is, we arbitrarily define the z direction as 'up') and then rotate the constrained object by the same amount around the axis perpendicular to both the vertex normal and the z-axis. This will orient the constrained object along that vertex normal. If the constrained object was rotated manually before adding the constraint these previous rotations would be lost. If that is not what we want, we can apply any rotations permanently before adding the constraint.

To implement this alignment feature, our code will change (`zoning_constraint.py` contains these changes already): `doConstraint()` will have to calculate the rotation part of the transformation matrix. We have to calculate the rotation angle, the rotation axis, and then the new rotation matrix. The highlighted part of the following code shows that the essential tools for these calculations are already provided by the `Mathutils` module:

```
vnormal = sv.no
if idprop['NormalAlign'] :
    zunit=Mathutils.Vector(0,0,1)
    a=Mathutils.AngleBetweenVecs(vnormal,zunit)
    rotaxis=zunit.cross(vnormal)
    rotmatrix=Mathutils.RotationMatrix(a,4,"r",rotaxis)
    mtxrot = rotmatrix
else:
    mtxrot = obrot.toMatrix().resize4x4()
```

In the preceding code we can see that we have made an alignment dependent on the `NormalAlign` property. Only if it is set do we calculate the necessary transformation. Therefore, we need to adapt `getSettings()` as well because the user needs a way to select whether he wants alignment or not:

```
def getSettings(idprop):
    if not idprop.has_key('NormalAlign'): idprop['NormalAlign'] = True

    align = Draw.Create(idprop['NormalAlign'])

    block = []
    block.append("Additional restrictions: ")
    block.append(("Alignment: ",align,"Align along vertex normal"))

    retval = Draw.PupBlock("Zoning Constraint", block)

    if (retval):
        idprop['NormalAlign']= align.val
```

As shown, the `NormalAlign` property will be set to `True` by default. The option is then presented as a simple pop up with a toggle button. If the user clicks outside the pop up or presses the *Esc* key, the return value from `PupBlock()` will be `None` and we won't change the `NormalAlign` property. Otherwise, it will be set to the value of the toggle button.

The effects are shown in the illustrations. The first one shows a small pine tree constrained to a vertex of a simple subdivided ground plane. It is snapped to the exact vertex location but its z-axis points straight up along the global z-axis. The following screenshot shows a fir tree constrained to a vertex in a craggy landscape.

If we turn on the `NormalAlign` property we see that the tree model is no longer pointing straight up, but that its z-axis is aligned along the direction of the vertex normal of the vertex it is snapped to. The following screenshot shows a fir tree constrained to a vertex and aligned along the vertex normal.

It is possible to restrict the vertices the model can snap to even further, for example, to just the vertices belonging to a vertex group. In the following illustration, our model cannot move beyond the extent of the vertex group that is shown in white. How this might be accomplished is shown in the next section.

Snap to vertices in a vertex group

What if we want to restrict the vertices we can snap an object to? This can be achieved by defining a vertex group and then consider only vertices from this vertex group as candidates to snap to. The code needed for this would take just a couple of lines and the relevant part of doConstraint() would look like this (the highlighted code shows the additional lines dealing with the matching against a vertex group):

```
# get the target mesh
to = Blender.Object.Get(idprop['target_object'])
me = to.getData(mesh=1)

# get the location of the target object
tloc = targetmatrices[0].translationPart().resize3D()

# find the nearest vertex in the target object
smallest = 1000000.0
delta_ob=tloc-obloc

try:
    verts = me.getVertsFromGroup(idprop['VertexGroup'])
    for vi in verts:
        d = (me.verts[vi].co+delta_ob).length
        if d < smallest :
            smallest = d
            si = vi
    obloc = me.verts[si].co+tloc
    vnormal = me.verts[si].no
except AttributeError:
    for v in me.verts:
        d = (v.co+delta_ob).length
        if d < smallest:
            smallest=d
            sv=v
    obloc = sv.co + tloc
    vnormal = sv.no
```

The try/except construction ensures that if the VertexGroup property refers to a nonexistent vertex group, we will get the chance to check all vertices. Of course, we now need a way for the user to select the vertex group, so getSettings() will have to be adapted too. We settle for a simple string input field where the name of a vertex group can be typed. There is no checking if the vertex group exists and if we do not want to restrict the snapping to a vertex group, then we can either leave this input field blank or type in the name of a nonexistent group. Not very elegant but it works (added lines highlighted):

```
def getSettings(idprop):
    if not idprop.has_key('VertexGroup'): idprop['VertexGroup'] =
    'Zone'
    if not idprop.has_key('NormalAlign'): idprop['NormalAlign'] = True

    vgroup = Draw.Create(idprop['VertexGroup'])
    align = Draw.Create(idprop['NormalAlign'])

    block = []
    block.append("Additional restrictions: ")
    block.append(("Vertex Group: ",vgroup,0,30,"Vertex Group to
                   restrict location to"))
    block.append(("Alignment: ",align,"Align along vertex normal"))

    retval = Draw.PupBlock("Zoning Constraint", block)

    if (retval):
        idprop['VertexGroup']= vgroup.val
        idprop['NormalAlign']= align.val
```

The next screenshot shows how the input box for the vertex group may look:

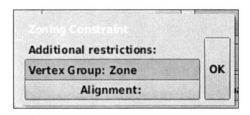

Note that the script constraint also presents the user with a VG string input field that may refer to a vertex group, but this is different from the vertex group input field that we show the user in the **Options** pop up. This VG field will alter the way the constraint looks at a target. If a valid vertex group is set here, the target matrix passed to doConstraint() will be that of the median position of the vertices in the vertex group.

Summary

In this chapter, we saw how different animated properties can be linked together and how we could constrain the spatial properties of objects to complex limitations. We have learned how to:

- Drive one **IPO** from another by a Python expression
- Work around some limitations inherent in pydrivers
- Restrict the motion of objects and bones by adding constraints
- Write a constraint in Python that will snap an object to the closest vertex on another object

Next we take a look at how to perform some action every time we advance a frame in our animation.

5
Acting on Frame Changes

Besides the many places we have encountered where Python can be used in Blender, we will now look at scripts that may be used to act on certain events. These scripts come in two flavors — **script links** and **space handlers**.

Script links are scripts that may be associated with Blender objects (Meshes, Cameras, and so on, but also Scenes and World objects) and that can be set up to run automatically on the following occasions:

- Just before rendering a frame
- Just after rendering a frame
- When a frame is changed
- When an object is updated
- When the object data is updated

Scene objects may have script links associated with them that may be invoked on two additional occasions:

- On loading a .blend file
- On saving a .blend file

Space handlers are Python scripts that are invoked each time the 3D view window is redrawn or a key or mouse action is detected. Their primary use is to extend the capabilities of Blender's user interface.

In this chapter, you will learn:

- What script links and space handlers are
- How to perform activities on each frame change in an animation
- How to associate additional information with an object

- How to make an object appear or disappear by changing its layout or changing its transparency
- How to implement a scheme to associate a different mesh with an object on each frame
- How to augment the functionality of the 3D View

Animating the visibility of objects

An often recurring issue in making an animation is the wish to make an object disappear or fade away at a certain frame, either for the sake of the effect itself or to replace the object by another one to achieve some dramatic impact (such as an explosion or a bunny rabbit changing into a ball).

There are many ways to engineer these effects, and most of them are not specifically tied to script links reacting on a frame change (many can simply be keyed as well). Nevertheless, we will look at two techniques that may easily be adapted to all sorts of situations, even ones that are not easily keyed. For example, we demand some specific behavior of a parameter that is easy to formulate in an expression but awkward to catch in an IPO.

Fading a material

Our first example will change the **diffuse color** of a material. It would be just as simple to change the transparency, but it is easier to see changes in diffuse color in illustrations.

Our goal is to fade the diffuse color from black to white and back again, spaced over a period of two seconds. We therefore define a function `setcolor()` that takes a material and changes its diffuse color (the `rgbColor` attribute). It assumes a frame rate of 25 frames per second and, therefore, the first line fetches the current frame number and performs a *modulo* operation to determine what fraction of the current whole second is elapsed.

The highlighted line in the following code snippet determines whether we are in an odd or even second. If we are in an even second, we ramp up the diffuse color to white so we just keep our computed fraction. If we are in an odd second, we tone down the diffuse color to black so we subtract the fraction from the maximum possible value (25). Finally, we scale our value to lie between 0 and 1 and assign it to all three color components to obtain a shade of gray:

```
import Blender

def setcolor(mat):
```

```
s = Blender.Get('curframe')%25
if int(Blender.Get('curframe')/25.0)%2 == 0:
    c = s
else:
    c = 25-s
c /= 25.0
mat.rgbCol = [c,c,c]

if Blender.bylink and Blender.event == 'FrameChanged':
    setcolor(Blender.link)
```

The script ends with an important check: `Blender.bylink` is `True` only if this script is called as a script handler and in that case `Blender.event` holds the event type. We only want to act on frame changes so that is what we check for here. If these conditions are satisfied, we pass `Blender.link` to our `setcolor()` function as it holds the object our `scriptlink` script is associated with—in this case that will be a `Material` object. (This script is available as `MaterialScriptLink.py` in `scriptlinks.blend`.)

The next thing on our list is to associate the script with the object whose material we want to change. We therefore select the object and in the **Buttons Window** we select the **Script panel**. In the **Scriptlinks** tab, we enable script links and select the **MaterialScriptLinks** button. (If there is no **MaterialScriptLinks** button then the selected object has no material assigned to it. Make sure it has.) There should now be a label **Select Script link** visible with a **New** button. Clicking on **New** will show a dropdown with available script links (files in the text editor). In this case, we will select `MaterialScriptLink.py` and we are done. We can now test our script link by changing the frame in the 3D view (with the arrow keys). The color of our object should change with the changing frame number. (If the color doesn't seem to change, check whether solid or shaded viewing is on in the 3D view.)

Changing layers

If we want to change the **visibility** of an object, changing the layer(s) it is assigned to is a more general and powerful technique than changing material properties. Changing its assigned layer has, for instance, the advantage that we can make the object completely invisible for lamps that are configured to illuminate only certain layers and many aspects of an animation (for example, deflection of particles by force fields) may be limited to certain layers as well. Also, changing layers is not limited to objects with associated materials. You can just as easily change the layer of a Lamp or Camera.

For our next example, we want to assign an object to layer 1 if the number of elapsed seconds is even and to layer 2 if the number of seconds is odd. The script to implement this is very similar to our material changing script. The real work is done by the function setlayer(). The first line calculates the layer the object should be on in the current frame and the next line (highlighted) assigns the list of layer indices (consisting of a single layer in this case) to the layers attribute of the object. The final two lines of the setlayer() function ensure that the layer's change is actually visible in Blender.

```python
import Blender

def setlayer(ob):
    layer = 1+int(Blender.Get('curframe')/25.0)%2
    ob.layers = [ layer ]
    ob.makeDisplayList()
    Blender.Window.RedrawAll()

if Blender.bylink and Blender.event == 'FrameChanged':
    setlayer(Blender.link)
```

As in our previous script, the final lines of our script check whether we are called as a script link and on a frame change event, and if so, pass the associated object to the setlayer() function. (The script is available as OddEvenScriptlink.py in scriptlinks.blend.)

All that is left to do is to assign the script as a scriptlink to a selected object. Again, this is accomplished in the **Buttons Window | Script panel** by clicking on **Enabling Script Links** in the **Scriptlinks** tab (if necessary, it might still be selected because of our previous example. It is a global choice, that is, it is enabled or disabled for all objects). This time, we select the object scriptlinks instead of the material scriptlinks and click on **New** to select OddEvenScriptlink.py from the dropdown.

Countdown—animating a timer with script links

One of the possibilities of using a script link that acts on frame changes is the ability to modify the actual mesh either by changing the vertices of a `Mesh` object or by associating a completely different mesh with a Blender object. This is not possible when using IPOs as these are limited to shape keys that interpolate between predefined shapes with the same mesh topology (the same number of vertices connected in the same way). The same is true for curves and text objects.

One application of that technique is to implement a `counter` object that will display the number of seconds since the start of the animation. This is accomplished by changing the text of a `Text3d` object by way of its `setText()` method. The `setcounter()` function in the following code does exactly that together with the necessary actions to update Blender's display. (The script is available as `CounterScriptLink.py` in `scriptlinks.blend`.)

```python
import Blender

objectname='Counter'
scriptname='CounterScriptLink.py'

def setcounter(counterob):
    seconds = int(Blender.Get('curframe')/25.0)+1
    counterob.getData().setText(str(seconds))
    counterob.makeDisplayList()
    Blender.Window.RedrawAll()

if Blender.bylink:
    setcounter(Blender.link)
else:
    countertxt   = Blender.Text3d.New(objectname)
    scn          = Blender.Scene.GetCurrent()
    counterob    = scn.objects.new(countertxt)
    setcounter(counterob)

    counterob.clearScriptLinks([scriptname])
    counterob.addScriptLink(scriptname,'FrameChanged')
```

This script may be associated as a script link with any `Text3d` object as shown before. However, if run with *Alt + P* from the text editor it will create a new `Text3d` object and will associate itself to this object as a script link. The highlighted lines show how we check for this just like in the previous scripts, but in this case we take some action when not called as a script link as well (the `else` clause). The final two highlighted lines show how we associate the script with the newly created object. First, we remove (clear) any script links with the same name that might have been associated earlier. This is done to prevent associating the same script link more than once, which is valid but hardly useful. Next, we add the script as a script link that will be called when a frame change occurs. The screenshot shows the 3D view with a frame from the animation together with the **Buttons window** (top-left) that lists the association of the script link with the object.

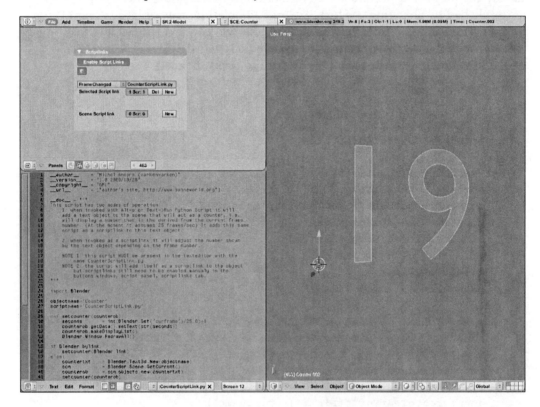

 Note that although it is possible to *associate* a script link with a Blender object from within a Python script, script links must be *enabled* manually for them to actually run! (In the **ScriptLinks** tab.) There is no functionality in the Blender Python API to do this from a script.

I'll keep an eye on you

Sometimes, when working with a complex object, it is difficult to keep track of a relevant feature as it may be obscured by other parts of the geometry. In such a situation, it would be nice to highlight certain vertices in a way that keeps them visible, no matter the orientation, and independent of the *edit* mode.

Space handlers provide us with a way to perform actions each time the 3D view window is redrawn or a key or mouse action is detected. These actions may include drawing inside the 3D view area as well, so we will be able to add **highlights** at any position we like.

How do we determine which vertices we would like to highlight? Blender already provides us with a uniform way to group collections of vertices as vertex groups so all we have to do is let the user indicate which vertex group he would like to highlight. We then store the name of this selected vertex group as an object property. Object properties are designed to be used in the game engine but there is no reason why we shouldn't reuse them as a way to persistently store our choice of vertex group.

So again, we have a script that will be called in two ways: as a space handler (that is, each time the 3D view window is redrawn to highlight our vertices) or by running it from the text editor with *Alt + P* to prompt the user to choose a vertex group to highlight.

Code outline: AuraSpaceHandler.py

The following outline shows which steps we will take in each situation:

1. Get active object and mesh.
2. If running standalone:
   ○ Get list of vertex groups
   ○ Prompt user for choice
   ○ Store choice as property of object
3. Else:
   ○ Get the property that holds the vertex group
   ○ Get a list of vertex coordinates
   ○ For each vertex:
     • draw a small disk

The resulting code is available as `AuraSpaceHandler.py` in `scriptlinks.blend`:

```
# SPACEHANDLER.VIEW3D.DRAW
```

It starts with a line of comment that is essential, as it signals to Blender that this is a space handler script that can be associated with the 3D view (no other area can have space handlers associated at present) and should be called on a `redraw` event.

```python
import Blender
from Blender import *

scn = Scene.GetCurrent()
ob  = scn.objects.active
if ob.type == 'Mesh':
    me = ob.getData(mesh = True)
    if Blender.bylink:
        p=ob.getProperty('Highlight')
        vlist = me.getVertsFromGroup(p.getData())
        matrix = ob.matrix
        drawAuras([me.verts[vi].co*matrix for vi in vlist],p.getData())
    else:
        groups = ['Select vertexgroup to highlight%t']
        groups.extend(me.getVertGroupNames())
        result = Draw.PupMenu( '|'.join(groups) )
        if result>0:
            try:
                p=ob.getProperty('Highlight')
                p.setData(groups[result])
            except:
                ob.addProperty('Highlight',groups[result])
```

The script proper then proceeds to retrieve the active object from the current scene and gets the object's mesh if it is a `Mesh`. At the highlighted line, we check if we are running as space handler and if so, we fetch the property that we named `Highlight`. The data of this property is the name of the vertex group that we want to highlight. We proceed by getting a list of all vertices in this vertex group and by getting the matrix of the object. We need this because vertex locations are stored relative to the object's matrix. We then construct a list of vertex locations and pass this along with the name of the vertex group to the `drawAuras()` function that will take care of the actual drawing.

The second highlighted line marks the beginning of the code that will be executed when we run the script from the text editor. It creates a string consisting of the names of all vertex groups associated with the active object separated by pipe characters (|) and prepended by a suitable title. This string is passed to PopMenu() which will display the menu, and will either return with the user's choice or with -1, if nothing was chosen.

If there was a vertex group chosen, we try to retrieve the Highlight property. If this succeeds we set its data to the name of the chosen vertex group. If the property did not yet exist, we add a new one with the name Highlight and again with the name of the chosen vertex group as data.

Next we have to make sure that scriptlinks are enabled (**Buttons window | Scripts panel | Scriptlinks**. Click on **enable scriptlinks** if not yet selected.). Note that to Blender it makes no difference whether we are dealing with space handlers or script links as far as enabling them is concerned.

The final step in using our space handler is associating it with the 3D view. To do this toggle the entry Draw: AuraSpaceHandler.py in the view (**Space Handler Scripts** menu of the 3D view).

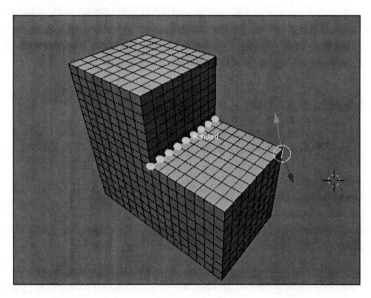

Using themes

The code we haven't seen yet deals with the actual drawing of the highlights and the name of the vertex group to identify what we are highlighting. It starts off by determining the colors we will use for the highlights and the text by retrieving these from the current theme. This way the user can customize these colors in a convenient way from the **User Preferences** window:

```
theme     = Window.Theme.Get()[0]
textcolor = [float(v)/255 for v in theme.get(
            Window.Types.VIEW3D ).text_hi[:3]]
color     = [float(v)/255 for v in
            theme.get(Window.Types.VIEW3D).active[:3]]
```

The first line will retrieve a list of **themes** that are present. The first one is the active theme. From this theme we retrieve the VIEW3D theme space and its text_hi attribute is a list of four integers representing a RGBA color. The list comprehension discards the alpha component and converts it to a list of three floats in the range [0, 1] that we will use as our text color. Likewise, we construct the color of the highlights from the active attribute.

Our next challenge is to draw a disk-shaped highlight at a specified location. As the size of the disk is quite small (it can be adjusted by altering the size variable), we can approximate it well enough by an octagonal shape. We store the list of x, y coordinates of such an octagon in the diskvertices list:

```
size=0.2
diskvertices=[( 0.0, 1.0),( 0.7, 0.7),
              ( 1.0, 0.0),( 0.7,-0.7),
              ( 0.0,-1.0),(-0.7,-0.7),
              (-1.0, 0.0),(-0.7, 0.7)]

def drawDisk(loc):
    BGL.glBegin(BGL.GL_POLYGON)
    for x,y in diskvertices:
        BGL.glVertex3f(loc[0]+x*size,loc[1]+y*size,loc[2])
    BGL.glEnd()
```

The actual drawing of the octagon depends heavily on the functions provided by Blender's BGL module (highlighted in the previous code). We start by stating that we will be drawing a polygon and then add a vertex for each tuple in the diskvertices list. The location passed to drawDisk() will be the center and the vertices will all lie on a circle with a radius equal to size. When we call the glEnd() function, the filled-in polygon will be drawn in the current color.

You might wonder how these drawing functions know how to translate locations in 3D to coordinates on the screen and there is indeed more here than meets the eye as we will see in the next section of code. The necessary function calls to inform the graphics system how to convert 3D coordinates to screen coordinates is not implemented in the `drawDisk()` function (preceding code snippet). This is because calculating this information for each disk separately would incur an unnecessary performance penalty as this information is the same for each disk we draw.

We therefore define a function, `drawAuras()`, which will take a list of locations and a `groupname` argument (a string). It will calculate the transformation parameters, call `drawDisk()` for each location in the list, and will then add the group name as an on-screen label at approximately just right of the center the highlights. Blender's `Window` module provides us with the `GetPerspMatrix()` function that will retrieve the matrix that will correctly convert a point in 3D space to a point on the screen. This 4 by 4 matrix is a Python object that will have to be converted to a single list of floats that can be used by the graphics system. The highlighted lines in the following code take care of that. The next three lines reset the projection mode and tell the graphics system to use our suitably converted perspective matrix to calculate screen coordinates. Note that changing these projection modes and other graphics settings does not affect how Blender itself draws things on screen, as these settings are saved before calling our script handler and restored afterward:

```
def drawAuras(locations,groupname):
    viewMatrix = Window.GetPerspMatrix()
    viewBuff = [viewMatrix[i][j] for i in xrange(4)
                for j in xrange(4)]
    viewBuff = BGL.Buffer(BGL.GL_FLOAT, 16, viewBuff)

    BGL.glLoadIdentity()
    BGL.glMatrixMode(BGL.GL_PROJECTION)
    BGL.glLoadMatrixf(viewBuff)

    BGL.glColor3f(*color)
    for loc in locations:
        drawDisk(loc)
    n=len(locations)
    if n>0:
        BGL.glColor3f(*textcolor)
        x=sum([l[0] for l in locations])/n
        y=sum([l[1] for l in locations])/n
        z=sum([l[2] for l in locations])/n
        BGL.glRasterPos3f(x+2*size,y,z)
        Draw.Text(groupname,'small')
```

With the preliminary calculations out of the way we can set the color we will draw our disks in with the glColor3f() function. As we stored the color as a list of three floats and the glColor3f() function takes three separate arguments, we unpack this list with the asterisk operator. Next, we call drawDisk() for each item in locations.

Blender OpenGL functions:

The documentation of Blenders BGL module lists a large number of functions from the **OpenGL** library. Many of these functions come in a large number of variants that perform the same action but receive their arguments in different ways. For example, BGL.glRasterPos3f() is a close relation to BGL.glRasterPos3fv() that will take a list of three single-precision float values instead of three separate arguments. For more information, refer to the API documentation of the Blender.BGL and Blender.Draw modules and the OpenGL reference manual on http://www.opengl.org/sdk/docs/man/.

If the number of highlights we have drawn is not zero, we set the drawing color to textcolor and then calculate the average coordinates of all the highlights. We then use the glRasterPos3f() function to set the starting position of the text that we want to draw to these average coordinates with some extra space added to the x-coordinate to offset the text a little to the right. Blender's Draw.Text() function will then draw the group name in a small font at the chosen location.

Revisiting mesh—making an impression

Although **softbody** and **cloth** simulators that are available in Blender do an excellent job in many situations, sometimes you want to have more control over the way a mesh is deformed or simulate some specific behavior that is not quite covered by Blender's built-in simulators. This exercise shows how to calculate the deformation of a mesh that is touched, but not penetrated by another mesh. This is not meant to be physically accurate. The aim is to give believable results for solid things touching an easily deformable or gooey surface such as a finger taking a lick of butter or a wheel running through a soft shoulder.

The following illustration gives some impression of what is possible. The tracks are created by animating a rolling car tire on a subdivided plane:

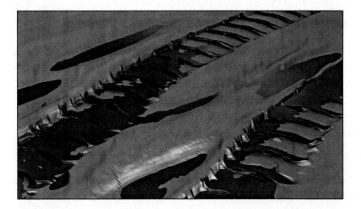

In the following part, we will refer to the object mesh being deformed as the source and the object, or objects, doing the deforming as targets. In a sense, this is much like a constraint and we might have implemented these deformations as pycontraints. However, that wouldn't be feasible because constraints get evaluated each time the source or targets move; thereby causing the user interface to come to a grinding halt as calculating the intersections and the resulting deformation of meshes is computationally intensive. Therefore, we choose an approach where we calculate and cache the results each time the frame is changed.

Our script will have to serve several functions, it must:

- Calculate and cache the deformations on each frame change
- Change vertex coordinates when cached information is present

And when run standalone, the script should:

- Save or restore the original mesh
- Prompt the user for targets
- Associate itself as a script link with the source object
- Possibly remove itself as a script link

An important consideration in designing the script is how we will store or cache the original mesh and the intermediate, deformed meshes. Because we will not change the topology of the mesh (that is, the way vertices are connected to each other), but just the vertex coordinates, it will be sufficient to store just those coordinates. That leaves us with the question: where to store this information.

If we do not want to write our own persistent storage solution, we have two options:

- Use Blender's registry
- Associate the data with the source object as a property

Blender's **registry** is easy to use but we must have some method of associating the data with an object because it is possible that the user might want to associate more than one object with an impression calculation. We could use the name of the object as a key, but if the user would change that name, we would lose the reference with the stored information while the script link functionality would still be there. This would leave the user responsible for removing the stored data if the name of the object was changed.

Associating all data as a **property** would not suffer from any renaming and the data would be cleared when the object is deleted, but the types of data that may be stored in a property are limited to an integer, a floating point value, or a string. There are ways to convert arbitrary data to strings by using Python's standard `pickle` module, but, unfortunately, this scenario is thwarted by two problems:

- Vertex coordinates in Blender are `Vector` instances and these do not support the pickle protocol
- The size of **string properties** is limited to 127 characters and that is far too small to store even a single frame of vertex coordinates for a moderately sized mesh

Despite the drawbacks of using the registry, we will use it to devise two functions — one to store vertex coordinates for a given frame number and one to retrieve that data and apply it to the vertices of the mesh. First, we define a utility function `ckey()` that will return a key to use with the registry functions based on the name of the object whose mesh data we want to cache:

```
def ckey(ob):
    return meshcache+ob.name
```

Not all registries are the same

Do not confuse Blender's registry with the Windows registry. Both serve the similar purpose of providing a persistent storage for all sorts of data, but both are distinct entities. The actual data for Blender registry items that are written to disk resides in `.blender/scripts/bpydata/config/` by default and this location may be altered by setting the `datadir` property with `Blender.Set()`.

Our `storemesh()` function will take an object and a frame number as arguments. Its first action is to extract just the vertex coordinates from the mesh data associated with the object. Next, it retrieves any data stored in Blender's registry for the object that we are dealing with and we pass the extra `True` parameter to indicate that if there is no data present in memory, `GetKey()` should check for it on disk. If there is no data stored for our object whatsoever, `GetKey()` will return `None`, in which case we initialize our cache to an empty dictionary.

Subsequently, we store our mesh coordinates in this dictionary indexed by the frame number (highlighted in the next code snippet). We convert this integer frame number to a string to be used as the actual key because Blender's `SetKey()` function assumes all of the keys to be strings when saving registry data to disk, and will raise an exception if it encounters an integer. The final line calls `SetKey()` again with an extra `True` argument to indicate that we want the data to be stored to disk as well.

```
def storemesh(ob,frame):
    coords = [(v.co.x,v.co.y,v.co.z) for v in ob.getData().verts]
    d=Blender.Registry.GetKey(ckey(ob),True)
    if d == None: d={}
    d[str(frame)]=coords
    Blender.Registry.SetKey(ckey(ob),d,True)
```

The `retrievemesh()` function will take an object and a frame number as arguments. If it finds cached data for the given object and frame, it will assign the stored vertex coordinates to vertices in the mesh. We first define two new exceptions to indicate some specific error conditions `retrievemesh()` may encounter:

```
class NoSuchProperty(RuntimeError): pass;
class NoFrameCached(RuntimeError): pass;
```

`retrievemesh()` will raise the `NoSuchProperty` exception if the object has no associated cached mesh data and a `NoFrameCached` exception if the data is present but not for the indicated frame. The highlighted line in the next code deserves some attention. We fetch the associated mesh data of the object with `mesh=True`. This will yield a wrapped mesh, not a copy, so any vertex data we access or alter will refer to the actual data. Also, we encounter Python's built-in `zip()` function that will take two lists and returns a list consisting of tuples of two elements, one from each list. It effectively lets us traverse two lists in parallel. In our case, these lists are a list of vertices and a list of coordinates and we simply convert these coordinates to vectors and assign them to the co-attribute of each vertex:

```
def retrievemesh(ob,frame):
    d=Blender.Registry.GetKey(ckey(ob),True)
    if d == None:
        raise NoSuchProperty("no property %s for object %s"
```

```
                    %(meshcache,ob.name))
        try:
            coords = d[str(frame)]
        except KeyError:
            raise NoFrameCached("frame %d not cached on object %s"
                                %(frame,ob.name))
        for v,c in zip(ob.getData(mesh=True).verts,coords):
            v.co = Blender.Mathutils.Vector(c)
```

To complete our set of cache functions we define a function `clearcache()` that will attempt to remove the registry data associated with our object. The `try` ... `except` ... clause will ensure that the absence of stored data is silently ignored:

```
def clearcache(ob):
    try:
        Blender.Registry.RemoveKey(ckey(ob))
    except:
        pass
```

The user interface

Our script will not only be used as a script link associated with an object but it will also be used standalone (by pressing *Alt* + *P* in the text editor for example) to provide the user with the means to identify a target that will make the impression to clear the cache, and to associate the script link with the active object. If used in this fashion, it will present the end user with a few pop-up menus, both shown in the screenshots. The first one shows the possible actions:

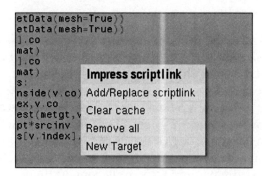

The second screenshot shows the pop up offered to select an object from a list of Mesh objects that the user can choose to make an impression:

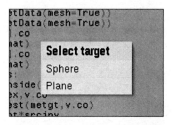

We first define a utility function that will be used by the pop-up menu that will present the user with a choice of Mesh objects to be used as a target to make an impression. getmeshobjects() will take a scene argument and will return a list of names of all Mesh objects. As depicted in the screenshot, the list of target objects includes the source object as well. Although this is legal, it is debatable whether this is very useful:

```
def getmeshobjects(scene):
    return [ob.name for ob in scene.objects if ob.type=='Mesh']
```

The menu itself is implemented by the targetmenu() function defined as follows:

```
def targetmenu(ob):
    meshobjects=getmeshobjects(Blender.Scene.GetCurrent())
    menu='Select target%t|'+ "|".join(meshobjects)
    ret = Blender.Draw.PupMenu(menu)
    if ret>0:
        try:
            p = ob.getProperty(impresstarget)
            p.setData(meshobjects[ret-1])
        except:
            ob.addProperty(impresstarget,meshobjects[ret-1])
```

It will fetch the list of all of the Mesh objects in the scene and present this list as a choice to the user by using Blender's Draw.PupMenu() function. If the user selects one of the menu entries (the return value will be positive and non-zero, see the highlighted line of the preceding code), it will store the name of this Mesh object as a property associated with our object. impresstarget is defined elsewhere as the name for the property. First, the code checks whether there already is such a property associated with the object by calling the getProperty() method and setting the properties data, if there is. If getProperty() raises an exception because the property does not yet exist, we then add the new property to the object and assign data to it with a single call to the addProperty() method.

The main user interface is defined in the top level of the script. It verifies that it is not running as a script link and then presents the user with a number of choices:

```
if not Blender.bylink:
    ret = Blender.Draw.PupMenu('Impress scriptlink%t|Add/Replace' +
                               'scriptlink|Clear cache|Remove' +
                               'all|New Target')
    active = Blender.Scene.GetCurrent().objects.active
    if ret > 0:
        clearcache(active)
    if ret== 1:
        active.clearScriptLinks([scriptname])
        active.addScriptLink(scriptname,'FrameChanged')
        targetmenu(active)
    elif ret== 2:
        pass
    elif ret== 3:
        active.removeProperty(meshcache)
        active.clearScriptLinks([scriptname])
    elif ret== 4:
        targetmenu(active)
```

Any valid choice will clear the cache (highlighted) and the subsequent checks perform the necessary actions associated with each individual choice: **Add/Replace scriptlink** will remove the script link, if it is already present, to prevent duplicates and then add it to the active object. It then presents the target menu to select a Mesh object to use to make an impression. As we already cleared the cache, the second choice, **Clear cache**, will do nothing specific, so we just pass. **Remove All** will try to remove the cache and attempt to dissociate itself as a script link and the final **New target** menu will present the target selection menu to allow the user to select a new target object without removing any cached results.

If we *are* running as a script link we first check that we are acting on a FrameChanged event and then try to retrieve any stored vertex coordinates for the current frame (highlighted in the next code). If there is no previously stored data, we have to calculate the effects of the target object for this frame. We therefore get a list of target objects for the object under consideration by calling the utility function gettargetobjects() (for now, a list of just one object will be returned) and for each object we calculate the effect on our mesh by calling impress(). Then, we store these possibly changed vertex coordinates and update the display list so that the Blender GUI knows how to display our altered mesh:

```
elif Blender.event == 'FrameChanged':
    try:
        retrievemesh(Blender.link,Blender.Get('curframe'))
```

```
except Exception as e: # we catch anything
    objects = gettargetobjects(Blender.link)
    for ob in objects:
        impress(Blender.link,ob)
    storemesh(Blender.link,Blender.Get('curframe'))
Blender.link.makeDisplayList()
```

That leaves us with the actual calculation of the impression of a target object on our mesh.

Calculating an impression

When determining the effect of a target object making an impression, we will approach this as follows:

For each vertex in the mesh receiving the impression:

1. Determine if it is located inside the target object and if so:
2. Set the location of the vertex to the location of the closest vertex on the object making the impression

There are some important issues to address here. The location of a vertex in a mesh is stored relative to the object's transformation matrix. In other words, if we want to compare vertex coordinates in two different meshes, we have to transform each vertex by the transformation matrices of their respective objects before doing any comparison.

Also, a Blender.Mesh object has a pointInside() method that will return True if a given point is inside the mesh. This will, however, only work reliably on closed meshes so the user has to verify that the objects that will make the impression are in fact closed. (They may have interior bubbles but their surfaces must not contain edges that are not shared by exactly two faces. These so-called non-manifold edges can be selected in *edge select* mode by selecting **Select | Non Manifold** in the 3D view or pressing *Ctrl + Shift + Alt + M*.)

Finally, moving vertices to the closest vertex on the target object may be quite inaccurate when the target mesh is rather coarse. Performance wise, however, it is good to have relatively few points—as our algorithm is rather inefficient because by first determining whether a point is inside a mesh and then separately calculating the closest vertex duplicates a lot of calculations. However, as the performance is acceptable even for meshes consisting of hundreds of points, we stick with our approach, as it keeps our code simple and saves us having to write and test very intricate code.

The implementation starts with a function to return the distance to and the coordinates of the vertex closest to a given point `pt`:

```
def closest(me,pt):
    min = None
    vm = None
    for v in me.verts:
        d=(v.co-pt).length
        if min == None or d<min:
            min = d
            vm = v.co
    return min,vm
```

The `impress()` function itself takes a source and a target object as arguments and will modify the mesh data of the source object if the target mesh makes an impression. The first thing that it does is retrieve the transformation matrices of the objects. As indicated before, these will be needed to transform the coordinates of the vertices so that they might be compared. We also retrieve the inverse matrix of the source object. This will be needed to transform coordinates back to the space of the source object.

The highlighted line retrieves the wrapped mesh data of the source object. We need wrapped data because we might want to change some of the vertex coordinates. The next two lines retrieve copies of the mesh data. We also need copies because the transformation we will perform may not affect the actual mesh data. Instead of copying we could have left out the `mesh=True` argument, which would have given us a reference to an `Nmesh` object instead of a `Mesh` object. However, `Nmesh` objects are not wrapped and are marked as deprecated. Also, they lack the `pointInside()` method we need, so we opt for copying the meshes ourselves.

Next, we transform these mesh copies by their respective object transform matrices. Using the `transform()` method of these meshes saves us from iterating over each vertex and multiplying the vertex coordinates by the transform matrix ourselves, and this method is probably a bit faster as well as `transform()` is completely implemented in C:

```
from copy import copy

def impress(source,target):
    srcmat=source.getMatrix()
    srcinv=source.getInverseMatrix()
    tgtmat=target.getMatrix()
```

```
orgsrc=source.getData(mesh=True)
mesrc=copy(source.getData(mesh=True))
metgt=copy(target.getData(mesh=True))

mesrc.transform(srcmat)
metgt.transform(tgtmat)

for v in mesrc.verts:
    if metgt.pointInside(v.co):
        d,pt = closest(metgt,v.co)
        orgsrc.verts[v.index].co=pt*srcinv
```

The final part of the `impress()` function loops over all of the vertices in the transformed source mesh and checks if the vertex lies enclosed within the (transformed) target mesh. If they are, it determines which vertex on the target mesh is closest and sets the affected vertex in the original mesh to these coordinates.

This original mesh is not transformed, so we have to transform this closest point back to the object space of the source object by multiplying the coordinates with the inverse transformation matrix. Because transformation calculations are expensive, modifying the transformed mesh and transforming the complete mesh back at the end may take a considerate amount of time. Keeping a reference to the untransformed mesh and just transforming back individual points may, therefore, be preferable when only relatively few vertices are affected by the impression. The full script is available as `ImpressScriptLink.py` in `scriptlinks.blend`. The following illustration shows what is possible. Here we made a small animation of a ball (an icosphere) rolling along and descending into the mud (a subdivided plane).

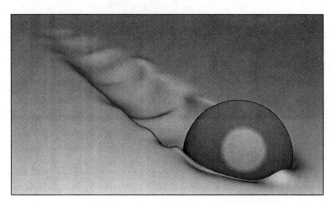

When working with the script it is important to keep in mind that when the impression is calculated, none of the vertices of the mesh that receives the impression should be located inside the target before it moves. If that happens it is possible for a vertex to be swept along with the movement of the target, distorting the source mesh along the way. For example, to make the illustration of the wheel track in the mud, we animate a rolling wheel along a path, calculating the impressions it makes at every frame. In the first frame that we animate we should make sure that the wheel is not touching the floor plane that will be distorted because if a vertex of the floor plane is inside the wheel and close to the inner rim, it will be moved to the closest vertex on that rim. If the wheel rolls slowly, this vertex will stay close to that inner rim and will thereby be effectively glued to that moving inner rim, ripping up the floor plane in the process. The same disruptive process may occur if the target object is very small compared to the source mesh or moving very fast. In these circumstances a vertex may penetrate the target object so fast that the closest vertex will not be on the leading surface making the impression but somewhere else in the target which will result in vertices being pulled outward instead of pushed inward. In the illustration of the rolling tractor tire, we carefully positioned the tire at frame one to sit just to the right of the subdivided plane before we key framed the rolling motion towards the left. The picture shown is taken at frame 171 without any smoothing or materials applied to the plane.

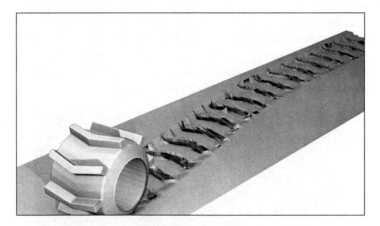

Summary

In this chapter, we learned how to link change to the progress of the animation frames and how to associate state information with an object. We also saw how to change layers, for example to render an object invisible. Specifically we saw:

- What script links and space handlers are
- How to perform activities on each frame change in an animation
- How to associate additional information with an object
- How to make an object appear or disappear by changing lay or changing its transparency
- How to implement a scheme to associate a different mesh with an object on each frame
- How to augment the functionality of the 3DView

Next up: adding shape keys and IPOs.

6
Shape Keys, IPOs, and Poses

We already encountered IPOs in *Chapter 4, Pydrivers and Constraints* when we discussed Pydrivers, but there is more to IPOs than just driving one **IPO** by another one. For example, the Blender API provides us with the means to define IPOs from scratch, enabling the definition of movements not easily re-created by setting key frames by hand. Furthermore, some types of IPOs have a somewhat different behavior than the ones that we encountered so far. **Shape keys** and **poses** are examples of (collections of) IPOs that are quite different from, for example, a location IPO. We will encounter both shape keys and poses later on in this chapter, but we will start off with looking at how we might define an IPO from scratch.

In this chapter, you will learn how to:

- Define IPOs
- Define shape keys on a mesh
- Define IPOs for those shape keys
- Pose armatures
- Group changes in poses into actions

A touchy subject—defining an IPO from scratch

Many paths of motion of objects are hard to model by hand, for example, when we want the object to follow a precise mathematical curve or if we want to coordinate the movement of multiple objects in a way that is not easily accomplished by copying IPOs or defining IPO drivers.

Imagine the following scenario: we want to interchange the position of some objects over the duration of some time in a fluid way without those objects passing through each other in the middle and without even touching each other. This would be doable by manually setting keys perhaps, but also fairly cumbersome, especially if we would want to repeat this for several sets of objects. The script that we will devise takes care of all of those details and can be applied to any two objects.

Code outline: orbit.py

The orbit.py script that we will design will take the following steps:

1. Determine the halfway point between the selected objects.
2. Determine the extent of the selected objects.
3. Define IPO for object one.
4. Define IPO for object two.

Determining the halfway point between the selected objects is easy enough: we will just take the average location of both objects. Determining the extent of the selected objects is a little bit more challenging though. An object may have an irregular shape and determining the shortest distance for any rotation of the objects along the path that the object will be taking is difficult to calculate. Fortunately, we can make a reasonable approximation, as each object has an associated **bounding box.**

This bounding box is a rectangular box that just encapsulates all of the points of an object. If we take half the body diagonal as the extent of an object, then it is easy to see that this distance may be an exaggeration of how close we can get to another object without touching, depending on the exact form of the object. But it will ensure that we never get too close. This bounding box is readily available from an object's getBoundBox() method as a list of eight vectors, each representing one of the corners of the bounding box. The concept is illustrated in the following figure where the bounding boxes of two spheres are shown:

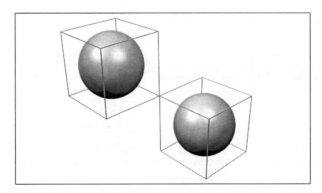

The length of the body diagonal of a bounding box can be calculated by determining both the maximum and minimum values for each x, y, and z coordinate. The components of the vector representing this body diagonal are the differences between these maximums and minimums. The length of the diagonal is subsequently obtained by taking the square root of the sum of squares of the x, y, and z components. The function `diagonal()` is a rather terse implementation as it uses many built-in functions of Python. It takes a list of vectors as an argument and then iterates over each component (highlighted. x, y, and z components of a Blender `Vector` may be accessed as 0, 1, and 2 respectively):

```
def diagonal(bb):
    maxco=[]
    minco=[]
    for i in range(3):
        maxco.append(max(b[i] for b in bb))
        minco.append(min(b[i] for b in bb))
    return sqrt(sum((a-b)**2 for a,b in zip(maxco,minco)))
```

It determines the extremes for each component by using the built-in `max()` and `min()` functions. Finally, it returns the length by pairing each minimum and maximum by using the `zip()` function.

The next step is to verify that we have exactly two objects selected and inform the user if this isn't the case by drawing a pop up (highlighted in the next code snippet). If we do have two objects selected, we retrieve their locations and bounding boxes. Then we calculate the maximum distance w each object has to veer from its path to be half the minimum distance between them, which is equal to a quarter of the sum of the lengths of the body diagonals of those objects:

```
obs=Blender.Scene.GetCurrent().objects.selected

if len(obs)!=2:
    Draw.PupMenu('Please select 2 objects%t|Ok')
else:
    loc0 = obs[0].getLocation()
    loc1 = obs[1].getLocation()

    bb0 = obs[0].getBoundBox()
    bb1 = obs[1].getBoundBox()

    w = (diagonal(bb0)+diagonal(bb1))/4.0
```

Before we can calculate the trajectories of both objects, we first create two new and empty Object IPOs:

```
ipo0 = Ipo.New('Object','ObjectIpo0')
ipo1 = Ipo.New('Object','ObjectIpo1')
```

We arbitrarily choose the start and end frames of our swapping operation to be 1 and 30 respectively, but the script could easily be adapted to prompt the user for these values. We iterate over each separate IPO curve for the Location IPO and create the first point (or key frame) and thereby the actual curve by assigning a tuple (framenumber, value) to the curve (highlighted lines of the next code). Subsequent points may be added to these curves by indexing them by frame number when assigning a value, as is done for frame 30 in the following code:

```
for i,icu in enumerate((Ipo.OB_LOCX,Ipo.OB_LOCY,Ipo.OB_LOCZ)):
    ipo0[icu] = (1,loc0[i])
    ipo0[icu][30]=loc1[i]

    ipo1[icu] = (1,loc1[i])
    ipo1[icu][30]=loc0[i]

    ipo0[icu].interpolation = IpoCurve.InterpTypes.BEZIER
    ipo1[icu].interpolation = IpoCurve.InterpTypes.BEZIER
```

Note that the location of the first object keyframed at frame 1 is its current location and the location keyframed at frame 30 is the location of the second object. For the other object this is just the other way around. We set the interpolation modes of these curves to "Bezier" to get a smooth motion. We now have two IPO curves that do interchange the location of the two objects, but as calculated they will move right through each other.

Our next step therefore is to add a key at frame 15 with an adjusted z-component. Earlier, we calculated w to hold half the distance needed to keep out of each other's way. Here we add this distance to the z-component of the halfway point of the first object and subtract it for the other:

```
mid_z = (loc0[2]+loc1[2])/2.0
ipo0[Ipo.OB_LOCZ][15] = mid_z + w
ipo1[Ipo.OB_LOCZ][15] = mid_z - w
```

Finally, we add the new IPOs to our objects:

```
obs[0].setIpo(ipo0)
obs[1].setIpo(ipo1)
```

The full code is available as `swap2.py` in the file `orbit.blend`. The resulting paths of the two objects are sketched in the next screenshot:

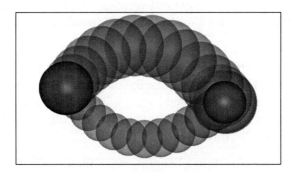

A lot to swallow—defining poses

Many cartoon characters seem to have difficulties trying to swallow their food, and even if they did enjoy a relaxing lunch, chances are they will be forced through a rain pipe too small to fit comfortably for no apparent reason.

It is difficult to animate swallowing or any other **peristaltic movement** by using shape keys as it is not the shape of the overall mesh that changes in a uniform way: we want to move along a localized deformation. One way of doing that is to associate an armature consisting of a linear chain of bones with the mesh that we want to deform (shown in the illustration) and animate the scale of each individual bone in time. This way, we can control the movement of the 'lump' inside to a great extent. It is, for example, possible to make the movement a little bit halting as it moves from bone to bone to simulate something that is hard to swallow.

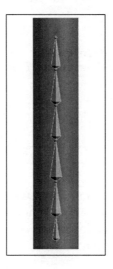

In order to synchronize the scaling of the individual bones in a way that follows the chain from parent to child, we have to sort our bones because the `bones` attribute of the `Pose` object that we get when calling `getPose()` on an armature is a dictionary. Iterating over the keys or values of this dictionary will return those values in random order.

Therefore, we define a function `sort_by_parent()` that will take a list of `Pose` bones `pbones` and will return a list of strings, each the name of a `Pose` bone. The list is sorted with the parent as the first item followed by its children. Obviously, this will not return a meaningful list for armatures that have bones with more than one child, but for our linear chain of bones it works fine.

In the following code, we maintain a list of names called `bones` that hold the names of the `Pose` bones in the correct order. We pop the list of `Pose` bones and add the name of the `Pose` bone as long as it is not already added (highlighted). We compare names instead of `Pose` bone objects because the current implementation of `Pose` bones does not reliably implement the `in` operator:

```
def sort_by_parent(pbones):
    bones=[]
    if len(pbones)<1 : return bones
    bone = pbones.pop(0)
    while(not bone.name in bones):
        bones.append(bone.name)
```

We then get the parent of the bone that we just added to our list, and as long as we can traverse the chain of parents, we insert this parent (or rather its name) in our list in front of the current item (highlighted below). If the chain cannot be followed anymore we pop a new `Pose` bone. When there are no bones left, an `IndexError` exception is raised by the pop() method and we will exit our `while-loop`:

```
        parent = bone.parent
        while(parent):
            if not parent.name in bones:
                bones.insert(bones.index(bone.name),parent.name)
            parent = parent.parent
            bone = parent
        try:
            bone = pbones.pop(0)
        except IndexError:
            break
    return bones
```

The next step is to define the script itself. First, we get the active object in the current scene and verify if it is indeed an armature. If not, we alert the user with a pop up (highlighted part of the following code), otherwise we proceed and get the associated armature data with the `getData()` method:

```
scn = Blender.Scene.GetCurrent()

arm = scn.objects.active

if arm.getType()!='Armature':
    Blender.Draw.PupMenu("Selected object is not an Armature%t|Ok")
else:
    adata = arm.getData()
```

Then, we make the armature editable and make sure that each bone has the HINGE option set (highlighted). The business with the conversion of the list of options to a set and back again to a list once we added the HINGE option is a way to ensure that the option appears only once in the list.

```
adata.makeEditable()
for ebone in adata.bones.values():
    ebone.options =
        list(set(ebone.options)|set([Blender.Armature.HINGE]))
adata.update()
```

A pose is associated with an armature object, not with its data, so we get it from arm by using the getPose() method. Bone poses are very much like ordinary IPOs but they have to be associated with an **action** that groups those poses. When working interactively with the Blender an action gets created automatically once we insert a key frame on a pose, but in a script we have to create an action explicitly if it is not present already (highlighted):

```
pose = arm.getPose()
action = arm.getAction()
if not action:
    action = Blender.Armature.NLA.NewAction()
    action.setActive(arm)
```

The next step is to sort the Pose bones as a chain of parenthood by using our previously defined function. What is left is to step along the frames in steps of ten at a time and set keys on the scale of each bone at each step, scaling up if the sequence number of the bone matches our step and resetting it if it doesn't. One of the resulting IPOs is shown in the screenshot. Note that by our setting the HINGE attribute on each bone previously, we prevent the scaling to propagate to the children of the bone:

```
bones = sort_by_parent(pose.bones.values())

for frame in range(1,161,10):
    index = int(frame/21)-1
    n = len(bones)
    for i,bone in enumerate(bones):
        if i == index :
            size = 1.3
```

```
else :
    size = 1.0
pose.bones[bone].size=Vector(size,size,size)
pose.bones[bone].insertKey(arm,frame,
                        Blender.Object.Pose.SIZE)
```

The full code is available as `peristaltic.py` in `peristaltic.blend`.

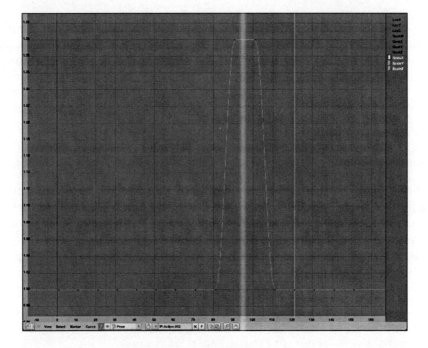

Application of peristaltic.py to an armature

To use this script you will have to run it with an armature object selected. One recipe to show its application would be the following:

1. Add an armature to a scene.

2. Go to *edit* mode and extrude any number of bones from the tip of the first bone.

3. Go to *object* mode and add a mesh centered on the position of the armature. Any mesh will do but for our illustration we use a cylinder with plenty of subdivisions.

4. Select the mesh and then shift select the armature. Both armature and `Mesh` object are now selected while the armature is the active object.

5. Press *Ctrl + P* and select **armature**. In next pop up, select **Create from bone heat**. That will create a vertex group on the mesh for each bone in the armature. These vertex groups will be used to deform the mesh when we associate the armature as a modifier with the mesh.

6. Select the mesh and add an armature modifier. Type the name of the armature in the **Ob:** field and make sure that the **Vert.Group** toggle is selected and **Envelopes** is not.

7. Select the armature and run the `peristaltic.py`.

The result will be an animated `Mesh` object resembling a lump passing through a narrow flexible pipe. A few frames are shown in the illustration:

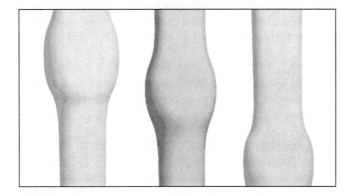

Rain pipes are of course not the only hollow objects fit for animating this way as shown in the following illustration:

Get down with the beat—syncing shape keys to sound

Many a rock video today features an animation of speaker cones reverberating with the sound of the music. And although the features for the manipulation of **sound** in the Blender API are rather sparse, we will see that this effect is rather simple to achieve.

The animation that we will construct depends mainly on the manipulation of **shape keys**. Shape keys can be understood as distortions of a base mesh. A mesh can have many of these distortions and each of them is given a distinct name. The fun part is that Blender provides us with the possibility to interpolate between the base shape and any of the distorted shapes in a continuous way, even allowing us to mix contributions from different shapes.

One way to animate our speaker cone, for instance, is to model a basic, undistorted shape of the cone; add a shape key to this base mesh; and distort it to resemble a cone that is pushed outward. We can then blend between this "pop out" shape and the base's shape depending on the loudness of the sound.

Animating by setting key frames in Blender means creating IPOs and manipulating IPO curves as we have seen earlier. Indeed, Shape or Key IPOs are very similar to other kinds of IPOs and are manipulated very much in the same way. The main difference between for example an Object IPO and a Shape IPO is that the individual IPO curves of a Shape IPO are not indexed by some predefined numerical constant (such as Ipo.OB_LOCX for an Object) but by a string because the user may define any number of named shapes.

Also, a Shape IPO is not accessed via an Object but through its underlying Mesh object (or Lattice or Curve, as these may have shape keys as well).

Manipulating sound files

So now that we know how to animate shapes, our next goal is to find out how to add some sound to our mesh, or rather to determine at each frame how much the distorted shape should be visible.

As mentioned in the previous section, Blender's API does not provide many tools for manipulating sound files, Basically the Sound module provides us with ways to load and play a sound file but that's as far as it gets. There is no way to access individual points of the waveform encoded in the file.

Fortunately, standard Python distributions come bundled with a `wave` module that provides us with the means to read files in the common `.wav` format. Although it supports only the uncompressed format, this will suffice as this format is very common and most audio tools, such as **Audacity**, can convert to this format. With this module we can open a `.wav` file, determine the sample rate and duration of the sound clip, and access individual samples. As we will see in the explanation of the following code, we still have to convert these samples to values that we can use as key values for our shape keys but the heavy lifting is already done for us.

Code outline: Sound.py

Armed with the knowledge on how to construct IPO curves and access `.wav` files, we might draw up the following code outline:

1. Determine if the active object has suitable shapes defined and provide a choice.

2. Let the user select a `.wav` file.

3. Determine the number of sound samples per second present in the file.

4. Calculate the number of animation frames needed based on the duration of the sound file and the video frame rate.

5. Then, for each animation frame:

    ° Average the sound samples occurring in this frame

    ° Set the blend value of the chosen IPO curve to this (normalized) average

The full code is available as `Sound.py` in `sound000.blend` and explained as follows:

```
import Blender
from Blender import Scene,Window,Draw
from Blender.Scene import Render

import struct
import wave
```

We start off by importing the necessary modules including Python's `wave` module to access our `.wav` file and the `struct` module that provides functions to manipulate the actual binary data that we get from the `.wav` file.

Next, we define a utility function to pop up a menu in the middle of our screen. It behaves just like the regular PupMenu() function from the Draw module but sets the cursor to a position halfway across and along the screen with the help of the GetScreenSize() and SetMouseCoords() functions from Blender's Window module:

```
def popup(msg):
    (w,h)=Window.GetScreenSize()
    Window.SetMouseCoords(w/2,h/2)
    return Draw.PupMenu(msg)
```

The bulk of the work will be done by the function sound2active(). It will take two arguments—the filename of the .wav file to use and the name of the shape key to animate based on the information in the .wav file. First, we attempt to create a WaveReader object by calling the open() function of the wave module (highlighted). If this fails, we show the error in a pop up and quit:

```
def sound2active(filename,shapekey='Pop out'):
    try:
        wr = wave.open(filename,'rb')
    except wave.Error,e:
        return popup(str(e)+'%t|Ok')
```

Then we do some sanity checks: we first check if the .wav file is a MONO file. If you want to use a stereo file, convert it to mono first, for example with the free Audacity package (http://audacity.sourceforge.net/). Then we check if we are dealing with an uncompressed .wav file because the wave module cannot handle other types. (most .wav files are uncompressed but if needed, Audacity can convert them as well) and we verify that the samples are 16-bits. If any of these checks fail, we pop up an appropriate error message:

```
c = wr.getnchannels()
if c!=1 : return popup('Only mono files are supported%t|Ok')
t = wr.getcomptype()
w = wr.getsampwidth()
if t!='NONE' or w!=2 :
    return popup('Only 16-bit, uncompresses files are supported%t|Ok')
```

Now that we can process the file, we get its **frame rate** (the number of audio samples per second) and the total number of bytes (oddly enough by using the awkwardly named function getnframes() from the wave module). Then, we read all of these bytes and store them in the variable b.

```
fr= wr.getframerate()
n = wr.getnframes()

b = wr.readframes(n)
```

Our next task is to get the rendering context from the current scene to retrieve the number of video frames per second. The number of seconds our animation will play is determined by the length of our audio sample, something we can calculate by dividing the total number of audio frames in the `.wav` file by the number of audio frames per second (highlighted in the following piece of code). We then define a constant `sampleratio`—the number of audio frames per video frame:

```
scn         = Scene.GetCurrent()
context     = scn.getRenderingContext()
seconds     = float(n)/fr
sampleratio = fr/float(context.framesPerSec())
```

As mentioned before, the `wave` module gives us access to a number of properties of a `.wav` file and the raw audio samples, but provides no functions to convert these raw samples to usable integer values. We therefore need to do this ourselves. Fortunately, this is not as hard as it may seem. Because we know that the 16-bit audio samples are present as 2 byte integers in the "little-endian" format, we can use the `unpack()` function from Python's `struct` module to efficiently convert the list of bytes to a list of integers by passing a fitting format specification. (You can read more about the way `.wav` files are laid out on `https://ccrma.stanford.edu/courses/422/projects/WaveFormat/`.)

```
samples  = struct.unpack('<%dh'%n,b)
```

Now we can start animating the shape key. We get the start frame from the rendering context and calculate the end frame by multiplying the number of seconds in the `.wav` file with the video frame rate. Note that this may be longer or shorter than the end frame that we may get from the rendering context. The latter determines the last frame that will get rendered when the user clicks on the **Anim** button, but we will animate the movement of our active object regardless of this value.

Then for each frame we calculate from start frame to end frame (exclusive) the average value of the audio samples that occur in each video frame by summing these audio samples (present in the `samples` list) and dividing them by the number of audio samples per video frame (highlighted in the next code snippet).

We will set the chosen shape key to a value in the range [0:1] so we will have to normalize the calculated averages by determining the minimum and maximum values and calculate a scale:

```
staframe = context.startFrame()
endframe = int(staframe + seconds*context.framesPerSec())

popout=[]
for i in range(staframe,endframe):
```

```
    popout.append(sum(samples[int(
    (i-1)*sampleratio):int(i*sampleratio)])/sampleratio)
minvalue = min(popout)
maxvalue = max(popout)
scale = 1.0/(maxvalue-minvalue)
```

Finally, we get the active object in the current scene and get its `Shape` IPO (highlighted). We conclude by setting the value of the shape key for each frame in the range we are considering to the scaled average of the audio samples:

```
ob=Blender.Scene.GetCurrent().objects.active

ipo = ob.getData().getKey().getIpo()

for i,frame in enumerate(range(staframe,endframe)):
    ipo[shapekey][frame]=(popout[i]-minvalue)*scale
```

The remaining script itself is now rather simple. It fetches the active object and then tries to retrieve a list of shape key names from it (highlighted in the next part). This may fail (hence the `try ... except` clause) if for example the active object is not a mesh or has no associated shape keys, in which case we alert the user with a pop up:

```
if __name__ == "__main__":
    ob=Blender.Scene.GetCurrent().objects.active

    try:
        shapekeys = ob.getData().getKey().getIpo().curveConsts
        key = popup('Select a shape key%t|'+'|'.join(shapekeys))
        if key>0:
            Window.FileSelector
            (lambda f:sound2active(f,shapekeys[key-1]),
            "Select a .wav file",
            Blender.Get('soundsdir'))
    except:
        popup('Not a mesh or no shapekeys defined%t|Ok')
```

If we were able to retrieve a list of shape keys, we present the user with a pop-up menu to choose from this list. If the user selects one of the items, `key` will be positive and we present the user with a file selector dialog (highlighted). This file selector dialog is passed a `lambda` function that will be called if the user selects a file, passing the name of this selected file as an argument. In our case we construct this `lambda` function to call the `sound2active()` function defined previously with this filename and the selected shape key.

The initial directory that will be presented to the user in the file selector to pick a file from is determined by the last argument to the `FileSelector()` function. We set it to the contents of Blender's `soundsdir` parameter. This usually is `//` (that is, a relative path pointing to the same directory as the `.blend` file the user is working on) but may be set in the user preferences window (**File Paths** section) to something else.

Animating a mesh by a .wav file: the workflow

Now that we have our `Sounds.py` script we can apply it as follows:

1. Select a `Mesh` object.
2. Add a "Basis" shape key to it (**Buttons window, Editing context, Shapes panel**). This will correspond to the least distorted shape of the mesh.
3. Add a second shape key and give it a meaningful name.
4. Edit this mesh to represent the most distorted shape.
5. In *object* mode, run `Sound.py` from the text editor by pressing *Alt + P*.
6. Select the shape key name defined earlier (not the "Basis" one) from the pop up.
7. Select the `.wav` file to apply.

The result will be an object with an `IPOcurve` for the chosen shape key that will fluctuate according to the beat of the sound as shown in the next screenshot:

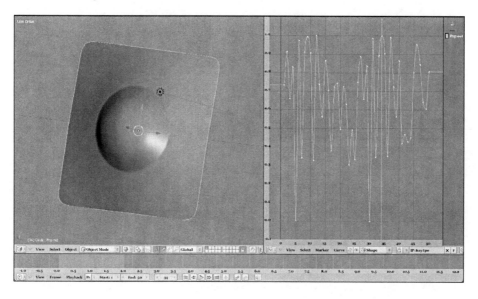

Summary

In this chapter we saw how to associate shape keys with a mesh and how to add an IPO to animate transitions between those shape keys. Specifically, we learned how to:

- Define IPOs
- Define shape keys on a mesh
- Define IPOs for those shape keys
- Pose armatures
- Group changes in poses into actions

In the next chapter, we shall learn how to create custom textures and shaders.

7
Creating Custom Shaders and Textures with Pynodes

It is sometimes said that although Blender has a powerful and versatile system to define materials, it lacks a proper shader language to define completely new **shaders**, for example, to create materials that react to light in novel ways. This is, however, not entirely true.

Blender does not have a compiled shader language but it does a have a powerful **node** system to combine textures and materials and these nodes can be Python scripts. This enables users to define completely new textures and materials.

In this chapter, we will learn:

- How to write Pynodes that create simple color patterns
- How to write Pynodes that produce patterns with normals
- How to write animated Pynodes
- How to write height-and slope-dependent materials
- How to create shaders that react to the angle of incident light

To illustrate some of its power, we start by looking at a script that creates regular color patterns made of triangles, rectangles, or hexagons.

Materials, shaders, and textures are terms that are often used as synonyms although there are differences in meaning. For our purposes we try to adhere to the following definitions: A **texture** is a basic building block, for example, a color or normal pattern or simply some function that returns a value depending on the position on a surface. A **shader** will take any number of textures or just a basic color and will return a color based on the influence of incident light and possibly the view direction. A **material** is a collection of textures, shaders, and all sorts of properties that can be applied to an object. Pynodes can be textures as well as shaders.

The basics

When we design a Pynode we basically design something that provides a function that is called for every pixel on the screen that needs to be shaded by that node (or even more than once, if **oversampling** is in effect). This function gets among other things the x, y, and z coordinates of the point on the object being shaded that corresponds to the pixel on the screen we are currently calculating. The function is then expected to return something useful such as a color, an intensity value, or something a little less intuitive such as a normal.

In Blender's Node editor window every material node, including a Pynode, is represented by a box which has its inputs on the left and its outputs on the right. These inputs and outputs are often called **sockets** and are represented by little colored circles (see the next screenshot). These sockets can be used to string nodes together; by clicking on an output socket of one node and dragging the mouse to the input socket of another node, these nodes will be connected. By combining as many different nodes as needed, very complex and powerful shaders can be created.

From nodes to Pynodes

The power of Blender's Node system not only stems from its many predefined node types and the many ways these nodes may be connected, but also from the fact that we can write new nodes in Python that may be connected in the same way as ordinary nodes.

Pynodes need a way to access the information provided by the input sockets and a way to send their calculated results to the output sockets. The concept of a node and its sockets is structured along an object-oriented model. Let's first look at some example code to prove that this doesn't need to be scary (object-oriented veterans: look the other way or peek through your fingers to just pick up the class definition from the following example):

```
from Blender import Node

class MyNode(Node.Scripted):

    def __init__(self, sockets):
        sockets.input   = [Node.Socket('Coords', val= 3*[1.0])]
        sockets.output  = [Node.Socket('Color', val = 4*[1.0])]

    def __call__(self):
        x,y,z = self.input.Coords
        self.output.Color = [abs(x),abs(y),abs(z),1.0]
```

Before we look at this code in detail try it in Blender to see how it actually works:

1. Open a new file in the text editor and give it a distinguishable name.
2. Copy the example code.
3. Create a simple scene, for example, a simple UV sphere at the origin with a couple of lamps and a camera.
4. Assign a `Node` material to the sphere like you normally would.
5. Finally, add in a *dynamic* node in the Node editor (**Add | Dynamic**) and select the name of the file that you edited by clicking on the selection button of the *dynamic* node and picking the file.

The resulting network of nodes (often called a **noodle**) may look like this:

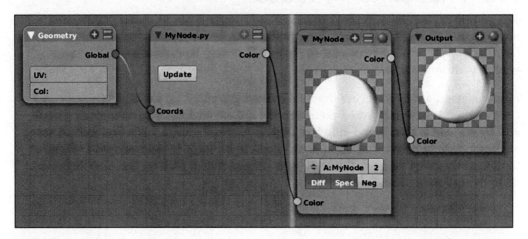

If you render the sphere the result is a colorful ball not unlike a color selection widget.

Now back to the code.

In the first line we import the Node module from Blender because we will be implementing a new type of node, but most of its behavior is already defined in the Node module.

Then we define a class MyNode, a subclass of Node.Scripted, which will behave just like a Scripted node except for the parts that we will redefine.

Next, we define the __init__() function that will be called the first time we create this type of Pynode in the node editor or any time we click on the **Update** button. When this happens Blender will pass two arguments to this function: self, a pointer to the node we are using, and sockets, a reference to an object that will point to our lists of input and output sockets. These are the nodes in the node editor we will receive input from or send data to.

In the highlighted line we define a list of input socket definitions; only one in this case and it is called Coords. It is a vector input because it is initialized with a list of three floats that define the default values, if this input socket is not connected to another node. Vector nodes are represented as blue circles in the node editor.

Other types of input socket are possible as well and the type is determined by the value of the val argument. Output sockets are defined in the same way. A list of three floats will define a vector socket, a list of four floats a color socket (with a red, green, blue, and alpha component), and a socket representing a simple value such as intensity is initialized by a single float. Note that we cannot distinguish between inputs that need to be filled in by the user or ones that should be connected to another node. We use input sockets for both and will have to document their intended use. Currently, there is no facility to add buttons or other widgets to a Pynode.

Our sample Pynode needs output as well so we define a list consisting of a single output socket called `Color`. It has four float values as a default specifying the red, green, blue, and alpha values respectively.

Next we define a function `__call__()` that is called each time a pixel is shaded. It takes no arguments but `self` — a reference to the current node that is used in the following lines to access the input and output sockets.

In the body of `__call__()` we retrieve the three components from the input socket called `Coords` and assign them to easy-to-remember variables. Finally, we create a new four-component list that represents our calculated color and assign it to the output socket called `Color`.

This is the basis to define simple textures but there is more information available to the node (as we will see in the following sections) so some pretty sophisticated effects can be designed. We end this section with a slightly more elaborate node that builds on the same principles we saw earlier but creates more useful patterns.

Regular tilings

The checkerboard texture is perhaps the simplest texture that you can imagine and is therefore often used as an example when programming textures. Because Blender already has a built-in checker texture (since version 2.49, in the texture context of the nodes window) we go one step further and create a texture node that displays not only a checkerboard texture but **tilings** of triangles and hexagons as well.

```
from Blender import Node,Noise,Scene
from math import sqrt,sin,cos,pi,exp,floor
from Blender.Mathutils import Vector as vec

# create regular tilings to be used as a color map

class Tilings(Node.Scripted):
    def __init__(self, sockets):
        sockets.input = [Node.Socket('type' , val= 2.0, min = 1.0,
                                max = 3.0),
                    Node.Socket('scale' , val= 2.0, min = 0.1,
                                max = 10.0),
                    Node.Socket('color1', val= [1.0,0.0,0.0,1.0]),
```

```
                Node.Socket('color2', val= [0.0,1.0,0.0,1.0]),
                Node.Socket('color3', val= [0.0,0.0,1.0,1.0]),
                Node.Socket('Coords', val= 3*[1.0])]

    sockets.output = [Node.Socket('Color', val = 4*[1.0])]
```

The first few lines start off by defining our input and output sockets. The output will simply be a color in all cases but we have a more varied set of input sockets. We define three different input colors because the hexagon pattern needs three colors to give each hexagon a color that is distinguishable from its neighbor.

We also define a `Coords` input. This input socket may hook up to any output of a geometry socket. In this way we have many possibilities to map our color texture to the object that we are texturing. A `Scale` socket is defined as well to control the size of our texture.

Finally, we define a `Type` socket to select the pattern that we wish to generate. As the Pynode API does not provide a drop-down box or any other simple selection widget we make do with a value socket and arbitrarily pick values to represent our choice: `1.0` for triangles, `2.0` for checkers, and `3.0` for hexagons.

We end our `__init__()` function with the definition of a number of constants and a dictionary of color mappings that we will use when generating a hexagonal texture.

```
    self.cos45 = cos(pi/4)
    self.sin45 = sin(pi/4)
    self.stretch = 1/sqrt(3.0)
    self.cmap = { (0,0):None, (0,1):2,    (0,2):0,
                  (1,0):0,    (1,1):1,    (1,2):None,
                  (2,0):2,    (2,1):None, (2,2):1 }
```

The next step is to define the `__call__()` function:

```
    def __call__(self):

        tex_coord = self.input.Coords
        # we disregard any z coordinate
        x = tex_coord[0]*self.input.scale
        y = tex_coord[1]*self.input.scale

        c1 = self.input.color1
        c2 = self.input.color2
        c3 = self.input.color3

        col= c1
```

The `__call__()` function starts off by defining some shorthands for input values and multiplying the input coordinates by the chosen scale to stretch or shrink the generated pattern. The next step is to establish the kind of pattern that is desired and call the appropriate function to calculate the output color for the given coordinates. The resulting color is assigned to our only output socket:

```
if self.input.type<= 1.0:
    col = self.triangle(x,y,c1,c2)
elif self.input.type <= 2.0:
    col = self.checker(x,y,c1,c2)
else:
    col = self.hexagon(x,y,c1,c2,c3)

self.output.Color = col
```

The various pattern-generating functions are all very similar; they take x and y coordinates and two or three colors as arguments and return a single color. As these are member functions of a class, they take an additional first argument of `self` as well.

```
def checker(self,x,y,c1,c2):
    if int(floor(x%2)) ^ int(floor(y%2)):
        return c1
    return c2
```

The `checker` function checks in which row and column we are and if the row number and the column number are both odd or even (that is what the exclusive `or` operator establishes) it returns one color, if not it returns the other color.

```
def triangle(self,x,y,c1,c2):
    y *= self.stretch
    x,y = self.cos45*x - self.sin45*y, self.sin45*x + self.cos45*y
    if int(floor(x%2)) ^ int(floor(y%2)) ^ int(y%2>x%2) : return c1
    return c2
```

The `triangle` function first rotates both x and y coordinates together by a 45 degree angle (changing squares into upright lozenges). It then determines the color based on row and column numbers just like in the `checker` function but with a twist: the third term (highlighted) checks whether we are on the left of the diagonal crossing a square and because we have rotated our grid, we really check whether or not the coordinates are above the horizontal line dividing our lozenge. This may sound a bit complicated but you can check the following screenshot to get the idea:

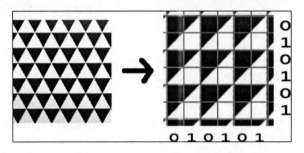

```
def hexagon(self,x,y,c1,c2,c3):
    y *= self.stretch
    x,y = self.cos45*x - self.sin45*y, self.sin45*x + self.cos45*y
    xf = int(floor(x%3))
    yf = int(floor(y%3))
    top = int((y%1)>(x%1))
    c = self.cmap[(xf,yf)]
    if c == None:
        if top :
            c = self.cmap[(xf,(yf+1)%3)]
        else :
            c = self.cmap[(xf,(yf+2)%3)]
    return (c1,c2,c3)[c]
```

The `hexagon` function is like the `triangle` function in many respects (after all a hexagon is six triangles glued together). Therefore, it performs the same rotation trick but instead of picking the color by using a straightforward formula, things are a bit more involved and hence we use a color map here (highlighted in the previous code snippet). Basically, we divide the screen into horizontal and vertical strips and pick the color based on the strips we are in.

The final piece of magic is in the last line of our script:

```
__node__ = Tilings
```

The way Pynodes are currently implemented, Blender needs this assignment to identify a class as a node. Our node will show up in the pop-up menu of a script node as **Tilings**. The full code is available as `tilings.py` in `tilings.blend` together with a sample node setup. Some of the possible patterns are shown in the next screenshot:

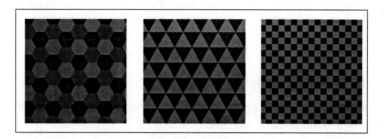

The corresponding node setup is shown in the next screenshot. Note that we have not connected any node to the color inputs but even more elaborate patterns can be created if we do.

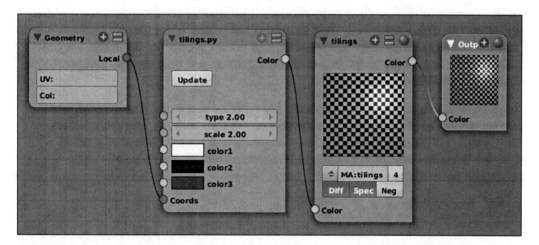

Anti-aliasing

If you would look closely at the diagonal boundaries of the hexagonal or triangular tilings you would notice some staircase-like artifacts even if oversampling was set to a high value.

Blender itself is smart enough to apply the chosen **anti-aliasing** level to things such as object boundaries, but in most cases textures on a surface will have to take care of anti-aliasing themselves. Blender's built-in textures are designed that way of course, but our own textures produced with Pynodes should address this explicitly.

There are numerous mathematical techniques available to reduce aliasing in generated textures but most are not easy to implement or require specific knowledge about the way a pattern is generated. Fortunately, Blender provides us with the **Full OSA** option (**Buttons windows | Shading context | Material buttons | Links and pipeline tab**). If we enable this option, Blender is forced to oversample each pixel in our texture by the amount selected in the render buttons. This is an expensive option but will get rid of aliasing effects without the need to implement specific filtering options in our Pynode texture.

Indexing a texture by vector

In our tiling patterns we have limited the colors to the minimum number needed to distinguish each neighboring tile. But would it be possible to assign random colors based on some noise texture? This way we might color fish scales in a way that follows an overall random pattern yet colors each individual scale uniformly.

We cannot simply connect a colored texture to the color inputs as this leads to interesting patterns, perhaps, but each tile would not have a uniform color. The solution is to modify our Pynode to produce a unique vector that is uniform within any given tile. This vector may then be connected to any noise texture that takes a vector as input as all Blender textures do. This vector is used by the noise texture node to point to a single point in the random texture and this way we can produce randomly colored but uniform tiles.

To provide this functionality we modify our code by removing the color inputs and replacing the color output by a vector output (not shown). The code inside the __call__() function will now have to produce a vector instead of a color. Here we show the modified triangle function (full code available as tilingsv.py in tilingsv.blend):

```
def triangle(self,x,y):
    y *= self.stretch
    x,y = self.cos45*x - self.sin45*y, self.sin45*x + self.cos45*y

    if int(floor(x%2)) ^ int(floor(y%2)) ^ int(y%2>x%2) :
        return [floor(x),floor(y),0.0]
    return [floor(x)+0.5,floor(y),0.0]
```

The logic is largely the same but, as shown in the highlighted line, we return a vector that is dependent on the position. However, due to the floor() operation it is constant within a triangle. Note that for the alternate triangle we add a slight offset; it doesn't matter which offset we choose as long as it is constant and produces a vector distinct from the other triangle.

The results show a random pattern of triangles that follows the large correlations in the noise yet leaves each individual triangle with a uniform color. The sample on the right has a larger noise size for the cloud texture used:

A possible node setup is shown in the following screenshot:

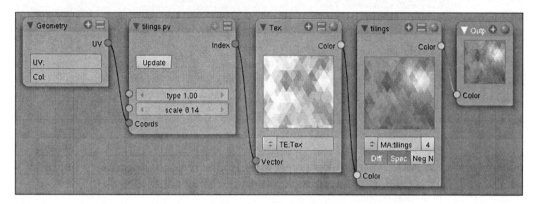

A fresh breeze—textures with normals

A texture can have more than just a geometric input. If you need a texture to change its behavior based on another texture in a way that cannot be achieved by a simple node setup you may provide it with extra input sockets. We will develop a Pynode that generates a normal map that simulates the little patches of **wavelets** on a pond on an almost windless day.

Where those patches appear is controlled by an extra input socket that may be linked to almost any noise texture. We will give this input socket the name amplitude because we use it to multiply it with our calculated **normal**. This way our wavelets will disappear wherever our noisy texture is zero.

The wavelength of the ripples is controlled by yet another input called wavelength and our Ripples node will have an input socket for the coordinates as well.

The fourth and final input is called direction—a vector that controls the orientation of our wavelets. It may be set by hand by the user but if desired, may be linked up to a normal node that provides an easy way to manipulate the direction with the mouse.

The resulting node setup that combines all of this is shown in the screenshot of the node editor:

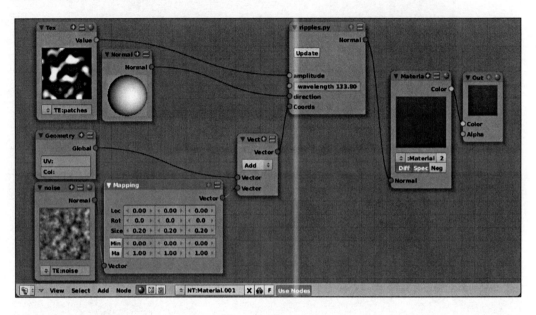

The script for the node is straightforward; after importing some necessary definitions we then define the numerous input sockets and our single output socket:

```
from Blender import Node
from math import cos
from Blender.Mathutils import Vector as vec

class Ripples(Node.Scripted):
    def __init__(self, sockets):
        sockets.input = [Node.Socket('amplitude' , val= 1.0,
                                     min = 0.001, max = 1.0),
                         Node.Socket('wavelength', val= 1.0,
                                     min = 0.01, max = 1000.0),
                         Node.Socket('direction' , val= [1.0,0.0,0.0]),
                         Node.Socket('Coords'     , val= 3*[1.0])]

        sockets.output = [Node.Socket('Normal', val = [0.0,0.0,1.0])]

    def __call__(self):

        norm = vec(0.0,0.0,1.0)
```

```
p = vec(self.input.Coords)
d = vec(self.input.direction)
x = p.dot(d)*self.input.wavelength
norm.x=-self.input.amplitude*cos(x)

n = norm.normalize()

self.output.Normal = n*.01

__node__ = Ripples
```

Again, all real work is done in the __call__() function (highlighted in the preceding code snippet). We first define the shorthands p and d for the coordinates and the direction vectors respectively. Our wavelets are sinus functions and the location on this sinus curve is determined by the projection of the position on the direction vector. This projection is calculated by taking the "in product" or "dot product"—an operation provided by the dot() method of a Vector object.

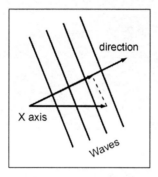

The projection is then multiplied by the wavelength. If we would calculate the sinus we would have the height of our wave. We are, however, not interested in the height but in the normal. The normal always points upward and moves along with our sine wave (see the next diagram). It can be shown that this normal is a vector with a z-component of 1.0 and an x-component equal to the negative derivative of the sine function, that is, minus cosine. The script (ripples.py) and an example node setup are available as ripples.blend.

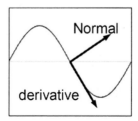

In the node setup that we showed earlier you might have noticed that instead of linking up the geometry node directly to our ripples node, we added a second texture node and combined this node with the geometry input by adding and scaling the normal output of the texture node. We could have mixed in some noise in the ripples node itself but this way we give the user far more control over the type and amount of noise he wants to add (if any). This is a general pattern: nodes should be designed as simple as possible to facilitate reuse in different settings.

These ripples were not designed to be animated but in the following section we will design a node that can.

Raindrops—animated Pynodes

Many patterns are not static but change in time. One example is the ripples formed by **raindrops** falling in a pond. Blender exposes render-time parameters such as start frame, frame rate, and current frame so we have plenty of hooks to make our Pynodes time dependent. We will see how to use those hooks in a script that generates a raindrop pattern. A pattern that changes realistically resembling the outward expanding ripples caused by drops falling in a pond. On the way we also pick up some useful tricks to speed up calculations by storing the results of expensive calculations in the Pynode itself for later reuse.

Render-time parameters

The most relevant render parameters when dealing with time-dependent things are the current frame number and the frame rate (the number of frames per second). These parameters are provided grouped together as a rendering context by the `Scene` module, most via function calls, some as variables:

```
scn                 = Scene.GetCurrent()
context             = scn.getRenderingContext()
current_frame       = context.currentFrame()
start_frame         = context.startFrame()
end_frame           = context.endFrame()
frames_per_second   = context.fps
```

With this information we can now calculate the time, either absolute or relative to the start frame:

```
absolute_time = current_frame/float(frames_per_second)
relative_time = (current_frame-start_frame)/float(frames_per_second)
```

Note the conversion to float in the denominator (highlighted). That way we ensure that the division is treated as a floating point operation. This is not strictly necessary since `fps` is returned as a float but many people assume the frame rate to be some integer value such as 25 or 30. This is, however, not always the case (for example, NTSC encoding uses a fractional frame rate) so we better make this explicit. Also note that we cannot do away with this division, otherwise when people would change their mind about their chosen frame rate the speed of the animation would change.

What looks good, *is* good

Accurately simulating the look of ripples caused by falling droplets may seem difficult but is straightforward, albeit a bit involved. Readers interested in the underlying mathematics might want to check some reference (for example `http://en.wikipedia.org/wiki/Wave`). Our goal, however, is not to simulate the real world as accurately as possible but to provide the artist with a texture that looks good and is controllable so that the texture may even be applied in situations which are not realistic.

So instead of making the speed at which the ripple travels dependent on things, such as the viscosity of the water, we provide speed as a tunable input to our Pynode. Likewise for the height and width of the ripple and the rate at which the height of the ripple diminishes as it expands. Basically, we approximate our little packet of ripples as it radiates outward from the point of impact of a droplet by a cosine function multiplied by an exponential function and a damping factor. This may sound dangerously like mathematics again, but it can be easily visualized:

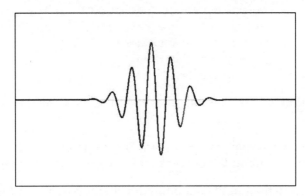

To calculate the height at any position x, y in our texture the above can be implemented as follows:

```
position_of_maximum=speed*time
damping = 1.0/(1.0+dampf*position_of_maximum)
distance = sqrt((x-dropx)**2+(y-dropy)**2)
height = damping*a*exp(-(distance-position_of_maximum)**2/c)* \
         cos(freq*(distance-position_of_maximum))
```

Here, `dropx` and `dropy` are the positions of impact of a drop and `a` is our tunable height parameter.

The effects of more drops dropped at different times and at different locations may simply be calculated by summing the resulting heights.

Storing expensive results for reuse

A single drop is not rain of course, so we would like to see the effects of many random drops added together. Therefore, we have to choose random impact locations and times for as many droplets as we'd like to simulate.

We would have to do this every time a call to the `__call__()` method is made (this is, for every visible pixel in our texture). However, this would be a tremendous waste of processing power because calculating many random numbers and allocating and releasing memory for possibly a large number of drops is expensive.

Fortunately, we can store these results as instance variables of our Pynode. Of course, we should be careful to check that no input parameters have changed between invocations of __call__() and take appropriate action if they have changed. The general pattern would look like this:

```
class MyNode(Node.Scripted):

    def __init__(self, sockets):
        sockets.input    = [Node.Socket('InputParam', val = 1.0)]
        sockets.output   = [Node.Socket('OutputVal' , val = 1.0)]
        self.InputParam = None
        self.Result     = None

    def __call__(self):
        if self.InputParam == None or \
            self.InputParam != self.input.InputParam :
            self.InputParam = self.input.InputParam
            self.Result     = expensive_calculation ...
        self.output.OutputVal = other_calculations_using_Result ...
```

This pattern works only if the input parameter changes infrequently, for example, only if the user changes it. If the input changes every pixel because the input socket is connected to the output of another node—the suggested scheme only costs time instead of saving some.

Calculating normals

Our goal is to generate a ripple pattern that can be used as a normal. so we need some way to derive the normal from the calculated heights. Blender does not provide us with such a conversion node for materials so we have to devise a scheme ourselves.

 Contrary to materials nodes, Blender's texture nodes do provide a conversion function called 'Value to Normal' that is available in the texture node editor from the menu **Add|Convertor|Value** to Normal.

Now, as in the case of ripples, we could, in principle, calculate an exact normal for our rain drops as well, but instead of going the mathematical way again we adapt a method used by many built-in noise textures to calculate the normal that works irrespective of the underlying function.

As long as we can evaluate a function at three points: f(x,y),f(x+nabla,y), and f(x,y+nabla) we can estimate the direction of the normal at x,y by looking at the slopes of our function in the x and y direction. The surface normal will be the unit vector perpendicular to the plane defined by these two slopes. We can take any small value for nabla to start and if it doesn't look good, we can make it smaller.

Putting it all together

Taking all of these ideas from the preceding paragraphs, we can cook up the
following code for our raindrops Pynode (with `import` statements omitted):

```
class Raindrops(Node.Scripted):
    def __init__(self, sockets):
        sockets.input = [Node.Socket('Drops_per_second'  , val = 5.0,
                                      min = 0.01, max = 100.0),
                         Node.Socket('a',val=5.0,min=0.01,max=100.0),
                         Node.Socket('c',val=0.04,min=0.001,max=10.0),
                         Node.Socket('speed',val=1.0,min=0.001,
                                      max=10.0),
                         Node.Socket('freq',val=25.0,min=0.1,
                                      max=100.0),
                         Node.Socket('dampf',val=1.0,min=0.01,
                                      max=100.0),
                         Node.Socket('Coords', val = 3*[1.0])]

        sockets.output = [Node.Socket('Height', val = 1.0),
                          Node.Socket('Normal', val = 3 *[0.0])]

        self.drops_per_second = None
        self.ndrops = None
```

The initialization code defines a number of input sockets besides the coordinates.
`Drops_per_second` should be self explanatory. a and c are the overall height and
width of the ripples traveling outward from the point of impact. `speed` and `freq`
determine how fast our ripples travel and how close ripples are together. How fast
the height of the ripples diminishes as they travel outward is determined by `dampf`.

We also define two output sockets: `Height` will contain the calculated height and
`Normal` will contain the corresponding normal at that same point. The `Normal` is
what you would normally use to obtain the rippling surface effect, but the calculated
height might be useful for example to attenuate the reflectance value of the surface.

The initialization ends with the definition of some instance variables that will be
used to determine if we need to calculate the position of the drop impacts again
as we will see in the definition of the __call__() function.

The definition of the __call__() function starts off with the initialization of a
number of local variables. One notable point is that we set the random seed used
by the functions of the `Noise` module (highlighted in the following code). In this
way, we make sure that each time we recalculate the points of impact we get
repeatable results, that is if we set the number of drops per second first to ten, later
to twenty, and then back to ten, the generated pattern will be the same. If you would
like to change this you could add an extra input socket to be used as input for the
`setRandomSeed()` function:

```
def __call__(self):

    twopi = 2*pi

    col = [0,0,0,1]
    nor = [0,0,1]
    tex_coord = self.input.Coords
    x = tex_coord[0]
    y = tex_coord[1]

    a = self.input.a
    c = self.input.c

    Noise.setRandomSeed(42)

    scn                 = Scene.GetCurrent()
    context             = scn.getRenderingContext()
    current_frame       = context.currentFrame()
    start_frame         = context.startFrame()
    end_frame           = context.endFrame()
    frames_per_second   = context.fps
    time                = current_frame/float(frames_per_second)
```

The next step is to determine whether we have to calculate the positions of the points of impact of the drops anew. This is necessary only when the value of the input socket `Drops_per_second` is changed by the user (you could hook up this input to some other node that changes this value at every pixel, but that wouldn't be a good idea) or when the start or stop frame of the animation changes, as this influences the number of drops we have to calculate. This test is performed in the highlighted line of the following code by comparing the newly obtained values to the ones stored in the instance variables:

```
drops_per_second = self.input.Drops_per_second
# calculate the number of drops to generate
# in the animated timeframe
ndrops = 1 + int(drops_per_second * (float(end_frame) -
        start_frame+1)/frames_per_second )

if self.drops_per_second != drops_per_second
or self.ndrops != ndrops:
    self.drop = [ (Noise.random(), Noise.random(),
                Noise.random() + 0.5) for i in range(ndrops)]
    self.drops_per_second = drops_per_second
    self.ndrops = ndrops
```

If we do have to calculate the position of the drops anew we assign a list of tuples to the self.drop instance variable, each consisting of the x and y position of the drop and a random drop size that will attenuate the height of the ripples.

The rest of the lines are all executed each time __call__() is called but the highlighted line does show a significant optimization. Because drops that have not yet fallen in the current frame do not contribute to the height, we exclude those from the calculation:

```
speed=self.input.speed
freq=self.input.freq
dampf=self.input.dampf

height = 0.0
height_dx = 0.0
height_dy = 0.0
nabla = 0.01
for i in range(1+int(drops_per_second*time)):
    dropx,dropy,dropsize = self.drop[i]
    position_of_maximum=speed*time-i/float(drops_per_second)
    damping = 1.0/(1.0+dampf*position_of_maximum)
    distance = sqrt((x-dropx)**2+(y-dropy)**2)
    height += damping*a*dropsize*
            exp(-(distance-position_of_maximum)**2/c)*
            cos(freq*(distance-position_of_maximum))
    distance_dx = sqrt((x+nabla-dropx)**2+(y-dropy)**2)
    height_dx += damping*a*dropsize*
            exp(-(distance_dx-position_of_maximum)**2/c)*
            cos(freq*(distance_dx-position_of_maximum))
    distance_dy = sqrt((x-dropx)**2+(y+nabla-dropy)**2)
    height_dy += damping*a*dropsize*
            exp(-(distance_dy-position_of_maximum)**2/c)*
            cos(freq*(distance_dy-position_of_maximum))
```

In the preceding code we actually calculate the height at three different positions to be able to approximate the normal (as explained previously). These values are used in the following lines to determine the x and y components of the normal (the z component is set to one). The calculated height itself is divided by the number of drops (so the average height will not change when the number of drops is changed) and by the overall scaling factor a, which may be set by the user before it is assigned to the output socket (highlighted):

```
nor[0]=height-height_dx
nor[1]=height-height_dy

height /= ndrops * a
```

```
self.output.Height = height

N = (vec(self.shi.surfaceNormal)+0.2*vec(nor)).normalize()
self.output.Normal= N

__node__ = Raindrops
```

The calculated normal is then added to the surface normal at the pixel where we are calculating so the ripples will still look good on a curved surface and normalized before assigning it to the output socket. The final line as usual defines a meaningful name for this Pynode. The full code and a sample node setup are available as `raindrops.py` in `raindrops.blend`. A sample frame from an animation is shown in the next screenshot:

A sample node setup is shown in the following screenshot:

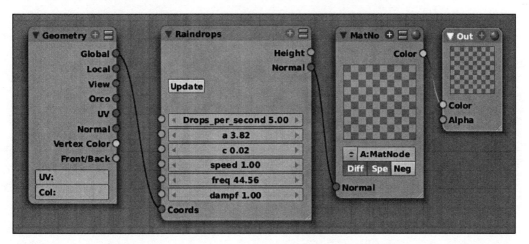

Wuthering heights—a slope-dependent material

In Blender it is quite simple to generate a fractal terrain (just add a plane, go to *edit* mode, select all, and then subdivide fractal a few times $W \rightarrow 3$). If you want something more elaborate a few excellent scripts exist to help you (see for example `http://sites.google.com/site/androcto/Home/python-scripts/ ANTLandscape_104b_249.py`). But how would you apply textures to such a terrain? In this example, we will examine a method to choose between different material inputs based on the slope of the surface that we're shading. This will allow us to create the effect that very steep slopes are generally devoid of greenery even though they might be well below the tree line. Combined with a height-dependent material we should be able to shade a mountainous terrain in a pretty convincing way.

Reducing computation time:

Pynodes are computationally intensive as they are called for every visible pixel. Clever coding can sometimes reduce the amount of computation needed but if a further speedup is required a just-in-time compiler might help. **psyco** is such a compiler and we will encounter it in the last chapter where we will apply it on Pynodes and see whether it has any appreciable effect.

Determining the slope

The **slope** can be defined as the angle between the floor plane and a line tangent to the surface at the point of interest.

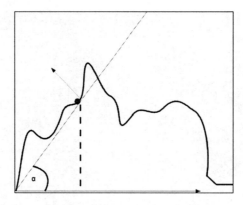

Because we assume our (imaginary) floor plane to stretch horizontally along the x and y axis this angle is completely determined by the z-component of the surface normal at the same point. Now we can calculate this angle exactly (it is $\arctan(z/\sqrt{x^2+y^2})$), but as artists we may want to have some extra control anyway so we simply take the normalized z-component of the surface normal and modify this output intensity with any color ramp node that we like. Within a Pynode a surface normal is a readily available vector entity: `self.input.shi.surfaceNormal`. There is a snag however...

World space versus camera space

The surface normal that we have available happens to be defined in camera space. This means that, for example, when the surface normal is pointing straight at the camera it is defined as (0, 0,-1). Now we want our surface normals to be defined in world space. A normal that is pointing straight up for instance should have a value of (0,0,1) irrespective of the position or tilt of the camera (after all, mountainside vegetation does not normally change with the camera angle). Fortunately, we can convert from **camera space** to **world space** by taking the camera's world space matrix and multiplying the surface normal with the rotation part of this matrix. The resulting code looks like this:

```
class Slope(Node.Scripted):
    def __init__(self, sockets):
        sockets.output = [Node.Socket('SlopeX', val = 1.0),
                          Node.Socket('SlopeY', val = 1.0),
                          Node.Socket('SlopeZ', val = 1.0),]
        self.offset =  vec([1,1,1])
        self.scale =   0.5
```

Note that the initialization code does not define an input socket. We will get the surface normal at the position of the pixel that we are shading from the shader input (highlighted in the next piece of code). We do define three separate output sockets for the x, y, and z components of the slope for ease of use in a node setup. As we mostly will be using just the z-component of the slope, having it available in a separate socket saves use from extracting it from a vector with an additional vector manipulation node.

```
    def __call__(self):

        scn=Scene.GetCurrent()
        cam=scn.objects.camera
        rot=cam.getMatrix('worldspace').rotationPart().resize4x4();
```

```
N = vec(self.shi.surfaceNormal).normalize().resize4D() * rot
N = (N + self.offset ) * self.scale
self.output.SlopeX=N[0]
self.output.SlopeY=N[1]
self.output.SlopeZ=N[2]


  __node__ = Slope
```

The transformation from camera space to world space is done in the line that references the surface normal (highlighted). The orientation is dependent only on the rotation, therefore we extract only the rotation part of the camera's transformation matrix before we multiply the surface normal with it. As the normalized result may point downward we force the z-component to lie in the range [0, 1] by adding 1 and multiplying by 0.5. The full code is available as `slope.py` in `slope.blend`.

There is one important thing to be aware of: the surface normal that we use here is not interpolated and hence equal everywhere along the surface of a single face, even if the `smooth` attribute of a face is set. This shouldn't be a problem in a finely subdivided landscape where the slope input is not used directly, However, this is different from what you might expect. In the present implementation of Pynodes, this limitation is difficult if not impossible to overcome.

The following illustration shows an example of what is possible.

The effects shown above were realized by combining different materials in the node setup shown in the next screenshot. This setup is available in `slope.blend` as well. The lower two materials were mixed using our slope-dependent node and the resulting material was mixed with the upper material based on a Pynode that calculates the height.

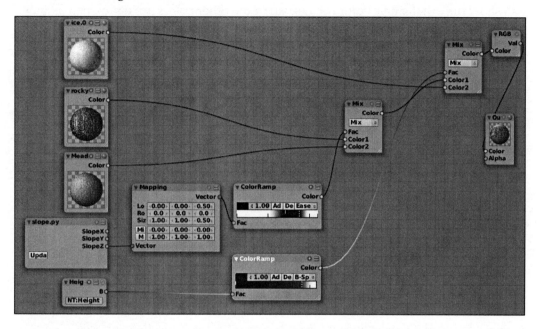

Soap bubbles—a view-dependent shader

Some materials change the way they look depending on the angle at which we look at them. Bird feathers, some fancy car paints, oil spills on water, and **soap bubbles** are some examples. This phenomenon of changing colors is known as **iridescence**. If we want to implement something like that we need access to the view vector and the surface normal. In our soap bubble shader we see one way of doing this.

First some mathematics: Why is it that soap bubbles show all those different colors? Soap bubbles are basically curved sheets of water (with a little soap), and at the interface between air and water, light is reflected. An incident ray will therefore be partially reflected when it hits the outer surface of the bubble and be reflected again when it reaches the inner surface. The reflected light that reaches the eye is therefore a mixture of light that has traveled different distances; part of it has traveled the extra distance of twice the thickness of the soap bubble.

Now, light behaves like a wave and waves that interfere can either dampen or amplify each other depending on their phase, and two light rays that have traveled distances whose difference is not an exact multiple of their wavelength will cancel each other. The result is that white light (a continuum of colors) reflecting off a soap bubble with a thickness equal to half the wavelength of some specific color will show only that single color because all of the other colors are dampened as they do not "fit" properly between the inner and outer surface. (There is much more to soap bubbles. For more and more accurate information refer to: `http://www.exploratorium.edu/ronh/bubbles/bubble_colors.html`.)

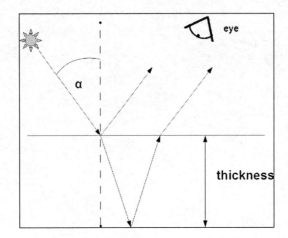

Now we know that the distance traveled between the two reflecting surfaces determines the color we perceive, we can also understand why there will be color variations in a soap bubble. The first factor is the curvature of the bubble. The distance traveled will be dependent on the angle between the incident light and the surface: the shallower this angle, the longer the distance the light has to travel between the surfaces will be. As the angle of incidence changes as the surface curves so will the distance and, hence the color. The second source of color variation is the unevenness of the surface; slight variations due to gravity or swirls caused by air currents or temperature differences also cause different colors.

All this information translates to a surprisingly short piece of code (the full code is available as `irridescence.py` in `irridescence.blend` together with a sample node setup).

Beside the coordinates, we have two input sockets—one for the thickness of the water film and one for the variation. The variation will get added to the thickness and can be hooked up to a texture node to generate swirls and the like. We have a single output socket for the calculated distance:

```
class Iridescence(Node.Scripted):
    def __init__(self, sockets):
        sockets.input = [ Node.Socket('Coords', val= 3*[1.0]),
                          Node.Socket('Thickness', val=275.0,
                                      min=100.0, max=1000.0),
                          Node.Socket('Variation', val=0.5, min=0.0,
                                      max=1.0)]

        sockets.output = [Node.Socket('Distance', val=0.5, min=0.0,
                                      max=1.0)]
```

The calculations of the reflected color start off with getting a list of all lamps in the scene as we will want to calculate the angle of the incident light rays. For now, we take into account only the contribution of the first lamp that we find. However, a more complete implementation would consider all lamps and maybe even their color. For our calculations we have to make certain that the surface normal N and the incidence vector of the light L are in the same space. As the surface normal provided will be in camera space we will have to transform this vector by the transformation matrix of the camera as we did for our slope-dependent shader (highlighted in the following code snippet):

```
def __call__(self):

    P = vec(self.input.Coords)
    scn=Scene.GetCurrent()
    lamps = [ob for ob in scn.objects if ob.type == 'Lamp']

    lamp = lamps[0]

    cam=scn.objects.camera
    rot=cam.getMatrix('worldspace').rotationPart().resize4x4();
    N = vec(self.shi.surfaceNormal).normalize().resize4D() * rot

    N = N.negate().resize3D()
    L = vec(lamp.getLocation('worldspace'))
    I = (P - L).normalize()
```

Next, we calculate the angle between the surface normal and the incidence vector (`VecT` is an alias for `Mathutils.angleBetweenVecs()`) and use this incidence angle to calculate the angle between the surface normal *inside* the water film as this will determine the distance the light travels. We use **Snell's law** to calculate this and use `1.31` as the index of refraction of the water film. Calculating the distance is then a matter of simple trigonometry (highlighted below):

```
angle = VecT(I,N)

angle_in = pi*angle/180
sin_in = sin(angle_in)
sin_out = sin_in/1.31
angle_out = asin(sin_out)

thickness = self.input.Thickness + self.input.Variation
distance = 2.0 * (thickness / cos (angle_out))
```

The calculated distance is equal to the wavelength of the color that we will perceive. However, Blender does not work with wavelengths but with RGB colors so we still need to convert this wavelength to a (R, G, B) tuple that represents the same color. This might be done by applying some spectral formula (see for example `http://www.philiplaven.com/p19.html`) but it might even be more versatile to scale this calculated distance and use it as an input for a color band. In this way we might produce non-physically accurate iridescence (if desired):

```
self.output.Distance = distance
```

To use this Pynode there are some things to keep in mind. First, make sure that the calculated color only affects the specular color of the soap bubble material otherwise everything will show up washed out.

Furthermore, it is important to add some variation to the thickness of the layer as no real soap bubble has an exactly uniform thickness. The choice of noise texture can make quite a difference to the appearance. In the next node setup example, we have added the contribution of a slightly noisy wood texture to obtain the swirly bands often seen on soap films.

Finally, make the material of the soap film very transparent but with a high specular reflectance. Experiment with the values to get the exact effect desired and do take into account the lighting setup. The example shown in the illustration has been tweaked to get some of the issues across in a black and white rendition and is therefore not realistic, but the setup in the example file `iridescence.blend` is tweaked to produce a pleasingly colorful result when rendered.

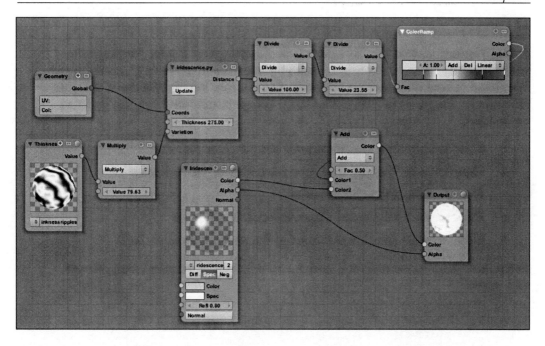

The use of a color ramp and a noise texture is shown in the previous screenshot where we added some division nodes to scale our distance to a range within [0,1] that can be used as input for the color ramp:

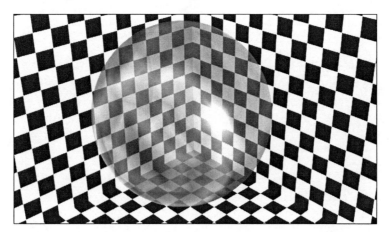

Summary

In this chapter, we saw that Blender's lack of a compiled shader language does not prevent its use from designing custom patterns and shaders. Pynodes are an integrated part of Blender's node system and we saw how to use them to create effects from simple color patterns to fairly-complex animated ripples. Specifically, we learned:

- How to write Pynodes that create simple color patterns
- How to write Pynodes that produce patterns with normals
- How to write animated Pynodes
- How to write height and slope dependent materials
- How to create shaders that react to the angle of incident light

In the next chapter, we will look into the automation of the rendering process as a whole.

8

Rendering and Image Manipulation

In the previous chapters, we looked mainly at the scripting aspects of the individual components that make up a Blender scene such as meshes, lamps, materials, and so on. In this chapter, we will turn to the rendering process as a whole. We will automate this rendering process, combine the resulting images in various ways, and even turn Blender into a specialized web server.

In this chapter, you will learn how to:

- Automate the rendering process
- Create multiple views for product presentations
- Create billboards from complex objects
- Manipulate images, including render results, by using the Python Imaging Library (PIL)
- Create a server that creates on-demand images that may be used as CAPTCHA challenges
- Create a contact sheet

A different view—combining multiple camera angles

By now, you might expect that rendering can be automated as well, and you're quite right. The Blender Python API provides access to almost all parameters of the rendering process and lets you render individual frames as well as animations. This allows for automating many tasks that would be tedious to do by hand.

Say you have created an object and want to create a single image that shows it from different angles. You could render these out separately and combine them in an external application, but we will write a script that not only renders these views but also combines them in a single image by using Blender's image manipulation capabilities and an external module called PIL. The effect we try to achieve is shown in the illustration of Suzanne, showing her from all of her best sides.

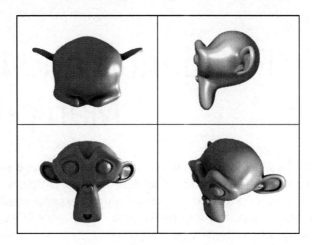

Blender is an excellent tool that provides you not only with modeling, animating, and rendering options but has compositing functionality as well. One area that it does not excel in is "image manipulation". It does have an UV-editor/Image window of course, but that is very specifically engineered to manipulate UV maps and to view images rather than to manipulate them. The Node editor is also capable of sophisticated image manipulation but it has no documented API so it can't be configured from a script.

Of course, Blender cannot do everything and surely it doesn't try to compete with packages such as **GIMP** (www.gimp.org), but some built-in image manipulation functions would have been welcomed. (Each image can be manipulated on the pixel level but this would be fairly slow on large images and we still would have to implement high-level functionality, such as alpha blending or rotating images.)

Fortunately, we can access any image generated by Blender from Python, and in Python it is fairly simple to add additional packages that do provide the extra functionality and use them from our scripts. The only drawback is that any script that uses these additional libraries is not automatically portable so users would have to check that the relevant libraries are available to them.

The **Python Imaging Library** (**PIL**) that we will be using is freely available and easy to install. Therefore, it should pose no problem for the average user. However, as it is possible to implement the simple pasting functionality (we will see below) using just Blender's Image module, we do provide in the full code a minimalist module pim that implements just the bare minimum to be able to use our example without the need to install PIL. This independence comes at a price: our paste() function is almost 40 times slower than the one provided by PIL and the resulting image can be saved only in TARGA (.tga) format. But you probably won't notice that as Blender can display TARGA files just fine. The full code is equipped with some trickery to use PIL (if it's available) and our replacement module if it isn't. (This is not shown in the book.)

The Python Imaging Library (PIL)

PIL is an open source package available for free from `http://www.pythonware.com/products/pil/index.htm`. It consists of a number of Python modules and a core library that comes precompiled for Windows (and is easy enough to compile on Linux or might even be available in the distribution already). Just follow the instructions on the site to install it (just remember to use the correct python version to install PIL; if you have more than one version of Python installed, use the one Blender uses as well to install).

Code outline—combine.py

What steps do we have to take to create our combined image? We will have to:

1. Create cameras if needed.

2. Frame the cameras on the subject.

3. Render views from all cameras.

4. Combine the rendered images to a single image.

The code starts off by importing all of the necessary modules. From the PIL package we need the Image module, but we import it under a different name (pim) to prevent name clashes with Blender's Image module, which we will be using as well:

```
from PIL import Image as pim
import Blender
from Blender import Camera, Scene, Image, Object, Mathutils, Window
import bpy
import os
```

The first utility function that we encounter is `paste()`. This function will combine four images into one. The images are passed as filenames and the result is saved as `result.png` unless another output filename is specified. We assume all four images to have the same dimensions, which we determine by opening the first file as a PIL image and examining its `size` attribute (highlighted in the next code). The images will be separated and bordered by a small line with a solid color. The width and color are hardcoded as the `edge` and `edgecolor` variables, although you might consider passing them as arguments:

```
def paste(top,right,front,free,output="result.png"):
    im = pim.open(top)
    w,h= im.size
    edge=4
    edgecolor=(0.0,0.0,0.0)
```

Next, we create an empty image big enough to hold the four images with the appropriate borders. We will not be drawing any borders specifically, but just defining the new image with a solid color onto which the four images will be pasted at a fitting offset:

```
comp = pim.new(im.mode, (w*2+3*edge,h*2+3*edge),edgecolor)
```

We already opened the top image so all we have to do is paste it in the upper-left quadrant of our combined image offset in both the horizontal and vertical directions by the border width:

```
comp.paste(im, (edge,edge))
```

Pasting the three other images follows the same line: open the image and paste it at the correct position. Finally, the combined image is saved (highlighted). The file type of the saved image is determined by its extension (for example, png) but might have been overridden had we passed a format argument to the `save()` method. Note that there was no reason to specify a format for the input files as the image type is determined from its contents by the `open()` function.

```
im = pim.open(right)
comp.paste(im, (w+2*edge,edge))
im = pim.open(front)
comp.paste(im, (edge,h+2*edge))
im = pim.open(free)
comp.paste(im, (w+2*edge,h+2*edge))
comp.save(output)
```

Our next function renders the view from a specific camera and saves the result to a file. The camera to render is passed as the name of the Blender Object (that is, not the name of the underlying `Camera` object). The first line retrieves the `Camera` object and the current scene and makes the camera current in the scene—the one that will be rendered (highlighted below). `setCurrentCamera()` takes a Blender Object, not a `Camera` object, and that's the reason we passed the name of the object.

```
def render(camera):
    cam = Object.Get(camera)
    scn = Scene.GetCurrent()
    scn.setCurrentCamera(cam)
    context = scn.getRenderingContext()
```

As we might use this function in a **background process** we will be using the `renderAnim()` method of the rendering context rather than the `render()` method. This is because the `render()` method cannot be used in a background process. Therefore, we set the current frame and both the start and end frames to the same value to ensure that `renderAnim()` will render just a single frame. We also set `displayMode` to `0` to prevent an extra render window popping up (highlighted in the next code snippet):

```
frame = context.currentFrame()
context.endFrame(frame)
context.startFrame(frame)
context.displayMode=0
context.renderAnim()
```

The `renderAnim()` method renders frames to files so our next task is to retrieve the filename of the frame that we just rendered. The exact format of the filename may be specified by the user in the **User Preferences** window, but by calling `getFrameFilename()` explicitly we ensure that we get the right one:

```
filename= context.getFrameFilename()
```

As the frame number will be the same for each camera view that we render, we will have to rename this file otherwise it would be overwritten. Therefore, we create a suitable new name consisting of the path of the frame we just rendered and the name of the camera. We use portable path manipulation functions from Python's `os.path` module so everything will work just as well under Windows as on Linux, for example.

As our script may have been used already, we try to remove any existing file with the same name because renaming a file to an existing filename will fail under Windows. Of course, there might not be a file yet—a situation we guard against in the `try` block. Finally, our function returns the name of the newly created file:

```
camera = os.path.join(os.path.dirname(filename),camera)
try:
    os.remove(camera)
```

```
except:
    pass
os.rename(filename,camera)
return camera
```

The next important task is to frame the cameras, that is, to choose a suitable **camera angle** for all of the cameras in such a way that the subject fits the available area in the picture in an optimal way. We want the camera angle to be the same for all cameras to provide the viewer with a consistent perspective from all viewing angles. Of course, this could be done manually, but this is tedious so we define a function to do the work for us.

The way we do this is to take the **bounding box** of our subject and determine the viewing angle of the camera by assuming that this bounding box must just fill our view. Because we can calculate the distance of the camera to the center of the bounding box, the viewing angle must be the same as the acute angle of the triangle formed by the bounding box and the camera distance.

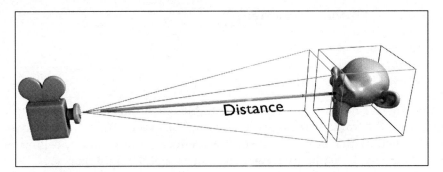

We calculate this angle for all of the cameras and then set the camera angle for each camera to the widest angle calculated to prevent unwanted clipping of our subject. Note that this algorithm may fail if the cameras are too close to the subject (or equivalently, if the subject is too large), in which case some clipping may occur.

The code is pretty heavy on the math, so we start off by importing the necessary functions:

```
from math import asin,tan,pi,radians
```

The function itself will take a list of names of Blender objects (the cameras) and a bounding box (a list of vectors, one for each corner of the bounding box). It starts off by determining the minimum and maximum extents of the bounding box for all three axes and the widths. We assume that our subject is centered on the origin. maxw will hold the largest width along any axis.

```
def frame(cameras,bb):
    maxx = max(v.x for v in bb)
    maxy = max(v.y for v in bb)
    maxz = max(v.z for v in bb)
    minx = min(v.x for v in bb)
    miny = min(v.y for v in bb)
    minz = min(v.z for v in bb)
    wx=maxx-minx
    wy=maxy-miny
    wz=maxz-minz
    m=Mathutils.Vector((wx/2.0,wy/2.0,wz/2.0))
    maxw=max((wx,wy,wz))/2.0
```

Next, we get the world space coordinates for each `Camera` object to calculate the distance `d` to the midpoint of the bounding box (highlighted in the next code). We store the quotient of maximum width and distance:

```
sins=[]
for cam in cameras:
    p=Mathutils.Vector(Object.Get(cam).getLocation('worldspace'))
    d=(p-m).length
    sins.append(maxw/d)
```

We take the largest quotient calculated (as this will amount to the widest angle) and determine the angle by calculating the arc sinus and finish by setting the `lens` attribute of the `Camera` object. The relation between camera's viewing angle and the value of the `lens` attribute in Blender is complex and scarcely documented (`lens` holds an approximation of the focal length of an ideal lens). The formula shown is the one taken from Blender's source code (highlighted).

```
maxsin=max(sins)
angle=asin(maxsin)
for cam in cameras:
    Object.Get(cam).getData().lens = 16.0/tan(angle)
```

Another convenience function is the one that defines four cameras and puts them into the scene suitably arranged around the origin. The function is straightforward in principle but is a little bit complicated because it tries to reuse existing cameras with the same name to prevent unwanted proliferation of cameras if the script is run more than once. The `cameras` dictionary is indexed by name and holds a list of positions, rotations, and lens values:

```
def createcams():
    cameras = {
            'Top'  : (( 0.0,  0.0,10.0),( 0.0,0.0, 0.0),35.0),
            'Right': ((10.0,  0.0, 0.0),(90.0,0.0,90.0),35.0),
            'Front': (( 0.0,-10.0, 0.0),(90.0,0.0, 0.0),35.0),
            'Free' : (( 5.8, -5.8, 5.8),(54.7,0.0,45.0),35.0)
            }
```

For each camera in the `cameras` dictionary we check if it already exists as a Blender object. If it does, we check whether the Blender object has a `Camera` object associated with it. If the latter is not true we create a perspective camera with the same name as the top-level object (highlighted) and associate it with the top-level object by way of the `link()` method:

```
for cam in cameras:
    try:
        ob = Object.Get(cam)
        camob = ob.getData()
        if camob == None:
            camob = Camera.New('persp',cam)
            ob.link(camob)
```

If there wasn't a top-level object present already we create one and associate a new perspective `Camera` object with it:

```
    except ValueError:
        ob = Object.New('Camera',cam)
        Scene.GetCurrent().link(ob)
        camob = Camera.New('persp',cam)
        ob.link(camob)
```

We end by setting the `location`, `rotation`, and `lens` attributes. Note that the rotation angles are in radians so we convert them from the more intuitive degrees that we used in our table (highlighted). We end by calling `Redraw()` to make the changes show up in the user interface:

```
        ob.setLocation(cameras[cam][0])
        ob.setEuler([radians(a) for a in cameras[cam][1]])
        camob.lens=cameras[cam][2]
        Blender.Redraw()
```

Finally, we define a `run()` method that strings all components together. It determines the active object and then cycles through a list of camera names to render each view and add the resulting filename to a list (highlighted):

```
def run():
    ob = Scene.GetCurrent().objects.active
    cameras = ('Top','Right','Front','Free')
    frame(cameras,ob.getBoundBox())
    files = []
    for cam in cameras:
        files.append(render(cam))
```

We will put the combined pictures in the same directory as the individual views and call it `result.png`:

```
outfile = os.path.join(os.path.dirname(files[0]),'result.png')
```

We then call our `paste()` function, passing the list of component filenames expanded as individual arguments by the asterisk (*) operator and end with a finishing touch of loading the result file as a Blender image and showing it in the image editor window (highlighted below). The `reload` is necessary to ensure that a previous image of the same name is refreshed:

```
paste(*files,output=outfile)
im=Image.Load(outfile)
bpy.data.images.active = im
im.reload()
Window.RedrawAll()
```

The `run()` function deliberately did not create any cameras because the user might want to do that himself. The final script itself does take care of creating the cameras, but this might be changed quite easily and is as usual quite simple. After the check to see if it runs standalone it just creates the cameras and calls the `run` method:

```
if __name__ == "__main__":
    createcams()
    run()
```

The full code is available as `combine.py` in `combine.blend`.

Workflow—how to showcase your model

The script can be used in the following way:

1. Put your subject at the origin (position (0, 0, 0)).
2. Create suitable lighting conditions.
3. Run `combine.py`.

The script may be loaded into the text editor to run with *Alt* + *P* but you may also put the script in Blender's `scripts` directory to make it available from the **Scripts | Render** menu.

Now, strip—creating a film strip from an animation

Fitting multiple camera views to a single image is just one example where multiple images might be effectively combined to a single image. Another example is when we would like to show frames from an animation where we don't have access to facilities to replay the animation. In such situations we would like to show something resembling a film strip where we combine a small rendition of, for example, every tenth frame to a single sheet of images. An example is shown in the following illustration.

Although there are more images to combine than in the multiple camera view, the code to create such a film strip is fairly similar.

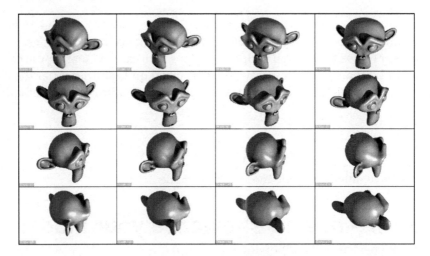

The first function that we develop is `strip()` that takes a list of filenames of images to combine and an optional `name` that will be given to the combined image. A third optional argument is `cols`, which is the number of columns in the combined image. The default is four, but for long sequences it might be more natural to print on landscape paper and use a higher value here. The function will return a Blender `Image` object containing the combined image.

We again use the `pim` module, which is either an alias for the PIL module if it's available or will refer to our bare bones implementation if PIL is not available. The important difference with our previous image combination code is highlighted. The first highlighted part shows how to calculate the dimensions of the combined image based on the number of rows and columns plus the amount of pixels needed for the colored edges around images. The second highlighted line shows where we paste an image in the destination image:

```
def strip(files,name='Strip',cols=4):
    rows = int(len(files)/cols)
    if len(files)%int(cols) : rows += 1

    im = pim.open(files.pop(0))
    w,h= im.size
    edge=2
    edgecolor=(0.0,0.0,0.0)

    comp =  pim.new(im.mode,
                    (w*cols+(cols+1)*edge,h*rows+(rows+1)*edge),
                    edgecolor)

    for y in range(rows):
        for x in range(cols):
            comp.paste(im,(edge+x*(w+edge),edge+y*(h+edge)))
            if len(files)>0:
                im = pim.open(files.pop(0))
            else:
                comp.save(name,format='png')
                return Image.Load(name)
```

The `render()` function that we define here will take the number of frames to skip as an argument and will render any number of frames between the start and end frames. These start and end frames may be set by the user in the render buttons. The render buttons also contain a step value, but this value is not provided to the Python API. This means that our function is a little bit more verbose than we like as we have to create a loop that renders each frame ourselves (highlighted in the next code) instead of just calling `renderAnim()`. We therefore have to manipulate the `startFrame` and `endFrame` attributes of the render context (as before) but we take care to restore those attributes before returning a list of filenames of the rendered images. If we did not need any programmatic control of setting the `skip` value, we could have simply replaced a call to `render()` by a call to `renderAnim()`:

```
def render(skip=10):
    context = Scene.GetCurrent().getRenderingContext()
    filenames = []
    e = context.endFrame()
    s = context.startFrame()
    context.displayMode=0
    for frame in range(s,e+1,skip):
        context.currentFrame(frame)
        context.startFrame(frame)
        context.endFrame(frame)
        context.renderAnim()
        filenames.append(context.getFrameFilename())
    context.startFrame(s)
    context.endFrame(e)
    return filenames
```

With these functions defined the script itself now simply calls `render()` to create the images and `strip()` to combine them. The resulting Blender image is reloaded to force an update if an image with the same name was already present and all windows are prompted to redraw themselves (highlighted):

```
def run():
    files = render()
    im=strip(files)
    bpy.data.images.active = im
    im.reload()
    Window.RedrawAll()

if __name__ == "__main__":
    run()
```

The full code is available as `strip.py` in `combine.blend`.

Workflow—using strip.py

Creating a strip of animated frames can now be done as follows:

1. Create your animation.

2. Run `strip.py` from the text editor.

3. The combined image will show up in the UV-editor/image window.

4. Save the image with a name of your choice.

Rendering billboards

Realism in scenes is often accomplished by providing lots of detail, especially in natural objects. However, this kind of realism comes with a price as detailed models often contain many faces and these faces consume memory and take time to render. A realistic tree model may contain as much as half a million faces so a forest of these would be almost impossible to render, even more so, if this forest is part of the scenery in a fast-paced game.

Blender comes with a number of tools to reduce the amount of memory needed when rendering many copies of an object; different `Mesh` objects may refer to the same mesh data as may **DupliVerts**. (Child objects that are replicated at the position of each vertex of a parent object. See `http://wiki.blender.org/index.php/Doc:Manual/Modeling/Objects/Duplication/DupliVerts` for more information.) Duplication of objects in particle systems also allows us to create many instances of the same object without actually duplicating all the data. These techniques may save huge amounts of memory but detailed objects still may take a lot of CPU power to render because the details are still there to be rendered.

Billboards are a technique used to apply a picture of a complex object to a simple object, such as a single square face, and replicate this simple object as many times as needed. The picture must have suitable transparency otherwise each object may occlude the others in unrealistic ways. Apart from that, this technique is quite simple and may save a lot of rendering time and it will give fairly realistic results for objects placed in the middle distance or farther away. Blender's particle systems may use billboards either as simple squares with images applied or by applying an image to a simple object ourselves and using that as a duplicating object. The latter also holds for dupliverted objects.

The trick is to generate an image with suitable lighting to be used as an image that can be applied to a square. Actually, we want to create two images: one shot from the front, one from the right, and construct an object consisting of two square faces perpendicular to each other with the two images applied. Such an object will give us a limited amount of freedom later in the placement of the camera in our scene as they do not have to be seen from just one direction. This works well only for objects with a roughly cylindrical symmetry, such as trees or high-rises, but then it is quite effective.

The workflow for constructing such objects is complex enough to warrant automation:

1. Position two cameras front and right of the detailed object.
2. Frame both cameras to capture all of the object with the same angle.
3. Render the transparent images with alpha premultiplied and without sky.
4. Construct a simple object of two perpendicular squares.
5. Apply each rendered image to a square.
6. Hide the detailed object from rendering.
7. Optionally, replicate the simple object in a particle system (the user may opt not to automate this part but place the simple objects manually).

The "premultiplication" mentioned in the third step may need some clarification. Obviously, the rendered images of our complex object need not show any background sky as their replicated clones may be positioned anywhere and may show different parts of the sky through their transparent parts. As we will see, this is simple enough to accomplish but when we simply render a transparent image and overlay it later on some background the image may have unsightly glaring edges.

The way to avoid this is to adjust the rendered colors by multiplying them with the alpha value and the render context has the necessary attributes to indicate this. We should not forget to mark the images produced as "premultiplied" when using them as textures, otherwise they will look too dark. The difference is illustrated in the following screenshot where we composited and enlarged a correctly premultiplied half on the left and a sky rendered half on the right. The trunk of the tree shows a light edge on the right. (Refer to Roger Wickes' excellent book "Foundation Blender Compositing" for more details.)

The beech tree (used in these and the following illustrations) is a highly-detailed model (over 30,000 faces) created by Yorik van Havre with the free plant-modeling package **ngPlant**. (See his website for more fine examples: `http://yorik.uncreated.net/greenhouse.html`) The following first set of images shows the beech tree from the front and the resulting front facing render of the two billboards on the left. (slightly darker because of the premultiplication).

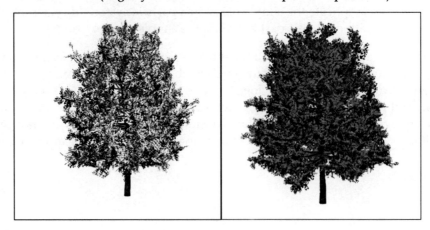

The next set of screenshots shows the same beech tree rendered from the right together with a right-facing render of the billboard on the left. As can be seen, the rendition is certainly not perfect from this angle and this closeup, but a reasonable three-dimensional aspect is retained.

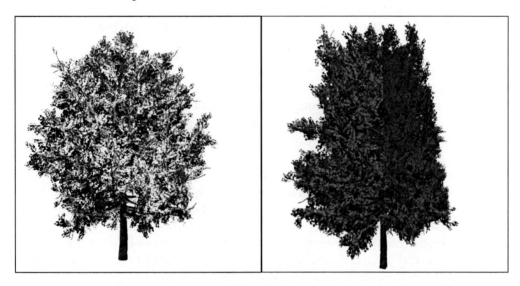

To give an impression of the construction of the billboards the next screenshot shows the two faces with the rendered images applied. The transparency is deliberately lessened to show the individual faces.

Our first challenge is to reuse some of the functions that we wrote for the generation of our contact sheet. These functions are in a text buffer called `combine.py` and we did not save this to an external file. We will create our `cardboard.py` script as a new text buffer in the same `.blend` file as `combine.py` and would like to refer to the latter just like some external module. Blender will make this possible for us as it searches for a module in the current text buffers if it cannot find an external file.

Because internal text buffers have no information on when they were last modified, we have to make sure that the latest version is loaded. That is what the `reload()` function will take care of. If we didn't do this Blender would not detect if `combine.py` had changed, which could lead to us using an older compiled version of it:

```
import combine
reload(combine)
```

We will not reuse the `render()` function from `combine.py` because we have different requirements for the rendered images that we will apply to the billboards. As explained, we have to make sure that we won't get any bright edges at points where we have partial transparency so we have to premultiply the alpha channel in advance (highlighted). We reset the rendering context to 'rendering the sky' again just before we return from this function because it's easy to forget to turn this on again manually and you may waste time wondering where your sky has gone:

```
def render(camera):
    cam = Object.Get(camera)
    scn = Scene.GetCurrent()
    scn.setCurrentCamera(cam)
    context = scn.getRenderingContext()
    frame = context.currentFrame()
    context.endFrame(frame)
    context.startFrame(frame)
    context.displayMode=0
    context.enablePremultiply()
    context.renderAnim()
    filename= context.getFrameFilename()
    camera = os.path.join(os.path.dirname(filename),camera)
    try:
        os.remove(camera) # remove otherwise rename fails on windows
    except:
        pass
    os.rename(filename,camera)

    context.enableSky()
    return camera
```

Each rendered image will have to be converted to a suitable material to apply to a UV-mapped square. The function `imagemat()` will do just that; it will take a Blender `Image` object as an argument and will return a `Material` object. This material will be made completely transparent (highlighted) but this transparency and the color will be modified by the texture we assign to the first texture channel (second highlighted line). The textures type is set to `Image` and because we rendered these images with a premultiplied alpha channel, we use the `setImageFlags()` method to indicate that we want to use this alpha channel and set the `premul` attribute of the image to `True`:

```
def imagemat(image):
    mat = Material.New()
    mat.setAlpha(0.0)
    mat.setMode(mat.getMode()|Material.Modes.ZTRANSP)
    tex = Texture.New()
    tex.setType('Image')
    tex.image = image
    tex.setImageFlags('UseAlpha')
    image.premul=True
    mat.setTexture(0,tex,Texture.TexCo.UV,
                    Texture.MapTo.COL|Texture.MapTo.ALPHA)
    return mat
```

Each face that we will apply a material to will have to be UV-mapped. In this case, this will be the simplest mapping possible as the square face will be mapped to match a rectangular image exactly once. This is often called **reset mapping** and therefore the function we define is called `reset()`. It will take a Blender `MFace` object that we assume to be a quad and set its `uv` attribute to a list of 2D vectors, one for each vertex. These vectors map each vertex to a corner of the image:

```
def reset(face):
    face.uv=[vec(0.0,0.0),vec(1.0,0.0),vec(1.0,1.0),vec(0.0,1.0)]
```

The `cardboard()` function takes care of constructing an actual `Mesh` object from the two `Image` objects passed as arguments. It starts off by constructing two square faces that cross each other along the z-axis. The next step is to add an UV-layer (highlighted) and make it the active one:

```
def cardboard(left,right):
    mesh = Mesh.New('Cardboard')
    verts=[(0.0,0.0,0.0),(1.0,0.0,0.0),(1.0,0.0,1.0),(0.0,0.0,1.0),
            (0.5,-0.5,0.0),(0.5,0.5,0.0),(0.5,0.5,1.0),(0.5,-0.5,1.0)]
    faces=[(0,1,2,3),(4,5,6,7)]
    mesh.verts.extend(verts)
    mesh.faces.extend(faces)

    mesh.addUVLayer('Reset')
    mesh.activeUVLayer='Reset'
```

Next, we construct suitable materials from both images and assign these materials to the materials attribute of the mesh. Then, we reset the UV coordinates of both faces and assign the materials to them (highlighted). We update the mesh to make the changes visible before we return it:

```
mesh.materials=[imagemat(left),imagemat(right)]

reset(mesh.faces[0])
reset(mesh.faces[1])
mesh.faces[0].mat=0
mesh.faces[1].mat=1

mesh.update()
return mesh
```

To replace the mesh of the duplication object of a particle system we implement a utility function setmesh(). It takes the name of the object with an associated particle system and a Mesh object as arguments. It locates the Object by name and retrieves the first particle system (highlighted in the next code snippet). The duplication object is stored in the duplicateObject attribute. Note that this is a *read-only* attribute so currently there is no possibility of replacing the object from Python. But we can replace the *data* of the object and that is what we do by passing the Mesh object to the link() method. Both the emitter object and the particle system's duplication object are changed so we ensure that the changes are visible by calling the makeDisplayList() method on both of them before initiating a redraw of all Blender's windows:

```
def setmesh(obname,mesh):
    ob = Object.Get(obname)
    ps = ob.getParticleSystems()[0]
    dup = ps.duplicateObject
    dup.link(mesh)
    ob.makeDisplayList()
    dup.makeDisplayList()
    Window.RedrawAll()
```

The run() function encapsulates all the work that needs to be done to convert the active object to a set of billboards and assign them to a particle system. First, we retrieve a reference to the active object and make sure that it will be visible when rendered:

```
def run():
    act_ob = Scene.GetCurrent().objects.active
    act_ob.restrictRender = False
```

The next step is to make the rest of the objects in the scene invisible before we render the billboards. Some object may have been made invisible by the user, therefore, we have to remember the states so that we can restore them later. Also,we do not alter the state of lamps or cameras as making these invisible would leave us with all black images (highlighted):

```
renderstate = {}
for ob in Scene.GetCurrent().objects:
    renderstate[ob.getName()] = ob.restrictRender
    if not ob.getType() in ('Camera','Lamp' ):
        ob.restrictRender = True
act_ob.restrictRender = False
```

Once everything is set up to render just the active object, we render front and right images with suitably framed cameras, just like we did in the `combine.py` script. In fact, here we reuse the `frame()` function (highlighted):

```
cameras = ('Front','Right')
combine.frame(cameras,act_ob.getBoundBox())
images={}
for cam in cameras:
    im=Image.Load(render(cam))
    im.reload()
    images[cam]=im
bpy.data.images.active = im
Window.RedrawAll()
```

Then we restore the previous visibility of all the objects in the scene before we construct a new mesh from the two images. We finish by making the active object invisible for rendering and replacing the mesh of the duplication object in a designated particle system by our new mesh:

```
for ob in Scene.GetCurrent().objects:
    ob.restrictRender = renderstate[ob.getName()]

mesh = cardboard(images['Front'],images['Right'])
act_ob.restrictRender = True
setmesh('CardboardP',mesh)
```

The final lines of code create the cameras necessary to render the billboards (if those cameras are not already present) by calling the `createcams()` function from the `combine` module before calling `run()`:

```
if __name__ == "__main__":
    combine.createcams()
    run()
```

The full code is available as `cardboard.py` in `combine.blend`.

Workflow—using cardboard.py

Assuming that you have a high poly object that you would like to convert to a set of billboards, a possible work flow would look like this:

1. Create an object called `CardboardP`.

2. Assign a particle system to this object.

3. Create a dummy cube.

4. Assign the dummy cube as the duplicate object on the first particle system of the `CarboardP` object.

5. Select (make active) the object to be rendered as a set of billboards.

6. Run `cardboard.py`.

7. Select the original camera and render the scene.

Of course, the script might be changed to omit the automated replacement of the duplication objects mesh if that is more suitable. For example, if we would like to use dupliverted objects instead of particles we would simply generate the cardboard object and assign its mesh to the dupliverted object. If we do use a particle system we probably do not want all replicated objects to be oriented in exactly the same way. We might, therefore, randomize their rotation, an example setup to accomplish that is shown in the following screenshot:

The next screenshot illustrates the application of billboards created from a tree model and used in a particle system:

Generating CAPTCHA challenges

In many situations such as blogs, forums, and online polls (to name a few) website operators want to guard against automated postings by spambots without wanting to burden human visitors with registration and authentication. In such situations it has become common to provide the visitor with a so-called CAPTCHA challenge (http://en.wikipedia.org/wiki/Captcha). A **CAPTCHA challenge** (or just **Captcha**) in its simplest form is a picture that should be hard to recognize for a computer, yet simple to decipher by a human as it is, typically a distorted or blurred word or number.

Of course, no method is foolproof and certainly Captchas are neither without their flaws nor immune to the ever-growing computing power available, but they still remain quite effective. Although the current consensus is that simple blurring and coloring schemes are not up to the task, computers still have a hard time separating individual characters in words when they slightly overlap where humans have hardly any problem doing that.

Given these arguments, this might be an excellent application of 3D rendering of text as presumably three-dimensional renditions of words in suitable lighting conditions (that is, harsh shadows) are even harder to interpret than two-dimensional text. Our challenge then is to design a server that will respond to requests to render three-dimensional images of some text.

We will design our server as a web server that will respond to requests addressed to it as URLs of the form http:<hostname>:<port>/captcha?text=<sometext> and that will return a PNG image—a 3D rendition of that text. In this way it will be easy to integrate this server into an architecture where some software, such as a blog, can easily incorporate this functionality by simply accessing our server through HTTP. An example of a generated challenge is shown in the illustration:

Design of a CAPTCHA server

By making use of the modules available in a full Python distribution the task of implementing an HTTP server is not as daunting as is may seem. Our Captcha server will be based on the classes provided in Python's BaseHTTPServer module so we start by importing this module along with some additional utility modules:

```
import BaseHTTPServer
import re
import os
import shutil
```

The BaseHTTPServer module defines two classes that together comprise a complete HTTP server implementation. The BaseHTTPServer class implements the basic server that will listen to incoming HTTP requests on some network port and we will use this class as is.

Upon receiving a valid HTTP request BaseHTTPServer will dispatch this request to a request handler. Our implementation of such a request handler based on the BaseHTTPRequestHandler is pretty lean as all it is expected to do is to field GET and HEAD requests for URIs of the form captcha?text=abcd. Therefore, all we have to do is override the do_GET() and do_HEAD() methods of the base class.

A HEAD request is expected to return only the headers of a requested object, not its content, to save time when the content isn't changed since the last request (something that can be determined by checking the Last-Modified header). We ignore such niceties; we will return just the headers when we receive a HEAD request but we will generate a completely new image nonetheless. This is something of a waste but does keep the code simple. If performance is important, another implementation may be devised.

Our implementation starts off by defining a do_GET() method that just calls the do_HEAD() method that will generate a Captcha challenge and return the headers to the client. do_GET() subsequently copies the contents of the file object returned by do_HEAD() to the output file, such as object of the request handler (highlighted), which will in turn return this content to the client (the browser for example):

```
class CaptchaRequestHandler(BaseHTTPServer.BaseHTTPRequestHandler):

    def do_GET(self):
        f=self.do_HEAD()
        shutil.copyfileobj(f,self.wfile)
        f.close()
```

The do_HEAD() method first determines whether we received a valid request (that is, a URI of the form captcha?text=abcd) by calling the gettext() method (highlighted, defined later in the code). If the URI is not valid, gettext() will return None and do_HEAD() will return a **File not found** error to the client by calling the send_error() method of the base class:

```
def do_HEAD(self):
    text=self.gettext()
    if text==None:
        self.send_error(404, "File not found")
        return None
```

If a valid URI was requested, the actual image is generated by the captcha() method that will return the filename of the generated image. If this method fails for any reason an **Internal server** error is returned to the client:

```
try:
        filename = self.captcha(text)
except:
        self.send_error(500, "Internal server error")
        return None
```

If everything went well we open the image file, send a **200** response to the client (indicating a successful operation), and return a Content-type header stating that we will return a png image. Next, we use the fstat() function with the number of the open file handle as argument to retrieve the length of the generate image and return this as a Content-Length header (highlighted) followed by the modification time and an empty line signifying the end of the headers before returning the open file object f:

```
f = open(filename, 'rb')
self.send_response(200)
self.send_header("Content-type", 'image/png')
fs = os.fstat(f.fileno())
self.send_header("Content-Length", str(fs[6]))
self.send_header("Last-Modified",
                self.date_time_string(fs.st_mtime))
self.end_headers()
return f
```

The gettext() method verifies that the request passed to our request handler in the path variable is a valid URI by matching it against a regular expression. The match() function from Python's re module will return a MatchObject if the regular expression matches and None if it does not. If there actually is a match we return the contents of the first match group (the characters that match the expression between the parentheses in the regular expression, in our case the value of the text argument), otherwise we return None:

```
def gettext(self):
    match = re.match(r'^.*/captcha\?text=(.*)$',self.path)
    if match != None:
        return match.group(1)

    return None
```

Now we come to the Blender-specific task of actually generating the rendered 3D text that will be returned as a `png` image. The `captcha()` method will take the text to render as an argument and will return the filename of the generated image. We will assume that the lights and camera in the `.blend` file we run `captcha.py` from are correctly set up to display our text in a readable way. Therefore, the `captcha()` method will just consider itself with configuring a suitable `Text3d` object and rendering it.

Its first task is to determine the current scene and check whether there is an Object called `Text` that can be reused (highlighted). Note that it is perfectly valid to have other objects in the scene to obfuscate the display even more:

```
def captcha(self,text):
    import Blender
    scn = Blender.Scene.GetCurrent()

    text_ob = None
    for ob in scn.objects:
        if ob.name == 'Text' :
            text_ob = ob.getData()
            break
```

If there was no reusable `Text3d` object, a new one is created:

```
if text_ob == None:
    text_ob = Blender.Text3d.New('Text')
    ob=scn.objects.new(text_ob)
    ob.setName('Text')
```

The next step is to set the text of the `Text3d` object to the argument passed to the `captcha()` method and make it 3D by setting its extrude depth. We also alter the width of the characters and shorten the spacing between them to deteriorate the separation. Adding a small bevel will soften the contours of the characters what may add to the difficulty for a robot to discern the characters if the lighting is subtle (highlighted). We could have chosen to use a different font for our text that is even harder to read for a bot and this would be the place to set this font (see the following information box).

Something is missing

Blender's API documentation has a small omission: there seems to be no way to configure a different font for a Text3d object. There is an undocumented setFont() method, however, that will take a Font object as argument. The code to accomplish the font change would look like this:

```
fancyfont=Text3d.Load( '/usr/share/fonts/ttf/myfont.ttf')
text_ob.setFont(fancyfont)
```

We have chosen not to include this code, however, partly because it is undocumented but mostly because the available fonts differ greatly from system to system. If you do have a suitable font available, by all means use it. Script type fonts which resemble handwriting for example may raise the bar even further for a computer.

The final step is to update Blender's display list for this object so that our changes will be rendered:

```
text_ob.setText(text)
text_ob.setExtrudeDepth(0.3)
text_ob.setWidth(1.003)
text_ob.setSpacing(0.8)
text_ob.setExtrudeBevelDepth(0.01)
ob.makeDisplayList()
```

Once our Text3d object is in place our next task is to actually render an image to a file. First, we retrieve the rendering context from the current scene and set the displayMode to 0 to prevent an additional render window popping up:

```
context = scn.getRenderingContext()
context.displayMode=0
```

Next, we set the image size and indicate that we want a png image. By enabling RGBA and setting the alpha mode to 2 we ensure that there won't be any sky visible and that our image will have a nice transparent background:

```
context.imageSizeX(160)
context.imageSizeY(120)
context.setImageType(Blender.Scene.Render.PNG)
context.enableRGBAColor()
context.alphaMode=2
```

Even though we will render just a still image, we will use the `renderAnim()` method of the rendering context because otherwise the results will not be rendered to a file but to a buffer. Therefore, we set the start and end frames of the animation to 1 (just like the current frame) to ensure that we generate just a single frame. We then use the `getFrameFilename()` method to return the filename (with the complete path) of the rendered frame (highlighted). We then both store this filename and return it as a result:

```
context.currentFrame(1)
context.sFrame=1
context.eFrame=1
context.renderAnim()
self.result=context.getFrameFilename()
return self.result
```

The final part of the script defines a `run()` function to start the Captcha server and calls this function if the script is running standalone (that is, not included as a module). By defining a `run()` function this way we can encapsulate the often used server defaults, such as port number to listen on (highlighted), yet allow reuse of the module if a different setup is required:

```
def run(HandlerClass = CaptchaRequestHandler,
        ServerClass = BaseHTTPServer.HTTPServer,
        protocol="HTTP/1.1"):

    port = 8080
    server_address = ('', port)

    HandlerClass.protocol_version = protocol

    httpd = ServerClass(server_address, HandlerClass)

    httpd.serve_forever()

if __name__ == '__main__':
    run()
```

The full code is available as `captcha.py` in the file `captcha.blend` and the server may be started in a number of ways: from the text editor (with *Alt + P*) from the menu **Scripts | render | captcha** or by invoking Blender in *background* mode from the command line. To stop the server again it is necessary to terminate Blender. Typically, this can be done by pressing **Ctrl + C** in the console or DOSbox

Warning

Note that as this server responds to requests from anybody it is far from secure. As a minimum it should be run behind a firewall that restricts access to it to just the server that needs the Captcha challenges. Before running it in any location that might be accessible from the Internet you should think thoroughly about your network security!

Summary

In this chapter, we automated the render process and learned how to perform a number of operations on images without the need for an external image editing program. We have learned:

- How to automate the rendering process
- How to create multiple views for product presentations
- How to create billboards from complex objects
- How to manipulate images, including render results by using the Python Imaging Library (PIL)
- How to create a server that creates on demand images that may be used as CAPTCHA challenges

In the final chapter, we will look at some housekeeping tasks.

9
Expanding your Toolset

This chapter is less about rendering and more about making life easier for the day-to-day use of Blender by extending its functionality. It uses some external libraries that need to be installed, and at some point the Python scripting used is perhaps a little bit harder to read for a novice. Also, from an artist's point of view, it might be a little less visually pleasing as these scripts don't lend themselves to pretty illustrations. Nevertheless, these scripts do add genuine useful functionality, especially for a script developer, so please read on.

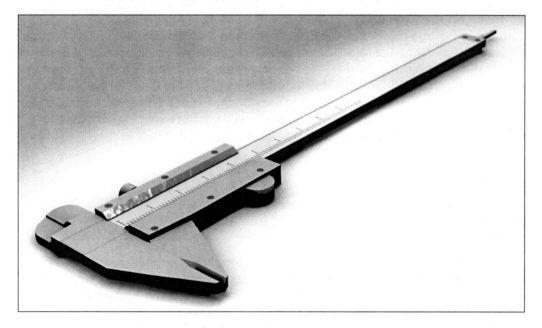

In this chapter, we will learn how to:

- List and archive assets such as image maps
- Publish a rendered image automatically with FTP
- Extend the functionality of the built-in editor with regular expression searches
- Speed up computations by using Psyco—a just-in-time compiler
- Add version control to your scripts with Subversion

To the Web and beyond—publish a finished render with FTP

We can save a rendered image to any location as long as it is visible in the filesystem, but not all platforms offer the possibility to make a remote FTP server accessible via a local directory (folder). This script offers us a simple option to store a rendered image on a remote FTP server and remembers the server name, the username, and (optionally) the password for later reuse.

The **File Transfer Protocol (FTP)** that we will be using is somewhat more complicated than, for instance, the HTTP protocol as it uses more than one connection. Fortunately for us, all the intricacies of an FTP client are nicely encapsulated in the standard Python module ftplib. We not only import this module's FTP class but a number of other standard Python modules as well, notably those for pathname manipulation (os.path) and for reading the standard .netrc file (which enables us to store passwords outside our script if we need passwords to log in to the FTP server). We will discuss each module where necessary.

```
from ftplib import FTP
import os.path
import re
import netrc
import tempfile
from Blender import Image,Registry,Draw
```

Python is almost as platform independent as it gets, but of course, sometimes there are intricacies that are not fully covered. For example, we want to use usernames and passwords stored in a .netrc file that is commonly used by FTP programs (and others) and the FTP client expects this file to reside in the user's home directory, which it hopes to find in an environment variable HOME. On Windows, however, the concept of a home directory isn't that well defined and different schemes exist to store data that is restricted to a single user; not every implementation of Python resolves this in the same way.

We, therefore, define a small utility function that checks if there is a HOME variable present in the environment (always the case on Unix-like operating systems and on some versions of Windows). If not, it checks whether the USERPROFILE variable is present (present on most versions of Windows including XP where it typically points to a directory C:\Documents and Settings\<yourusername>). If it is present it sets the HOME variable to the contents of this USERPROFILE variable:

```
def sethome():
    from os import environ
    if not 'HOME' in environ:
        if 'USERPROFILE'in environ:
            environ['HOME'] = environ['USERPROFILE']
```

Our next task is to find out which FTP server the user wants to upload the rendered result to. We store this in a Blender registry key so that we don't have to bother the user with a prompt each time he wants to upload a render. The getftphost() function takes an argument reuse that may be used to clear this key if set to False (to allow for the possibility of choosing a different FTP server), but rewriting the user interface to offer the user such an option is left as an exercise to the reader.

The actual code starts with retrieving the key from the registry (from disk if necessary, hence the True argument, highlighted). If there isn't a key present or it doesn't contain a host entry, we prompt the user for the name of the FTP server with a pop up. If the user does not specify, one we bail out by raising an exception. Otherwise, we store the hostname in the host entry — first create the dictionary if it is not present and store this dictionary in Blender's registry. Finally, we return the stored hostname.

```
def getftphost(reuse=True):
    dictname = 'ftp'
    if reuse == False:
        Registry.RemoveKey(dictname)

    d = Registry.GetKey(dictname,True)
    if d == None or not 'host' in d:
        host = Draw.PupStrInput("Ftp hostname:", "", 45)
        if host == None or len(host) == 0 :
            raise Exception("no hostname specified")
        if d == None :
            d ={}
        d['host'] = host
        Registry.SetKey(dictname,d,True)
    return d['host']
```

We need another utility function to make sure that a Blender image is stored on disk as the last rendered image is present as an image with the name Render Result, but this image isn't written to disk automatically. The function imagefilename() takes a Blender image as an argument and first checks if it has a valid filename associated with it (highlighted). If not, it creates a filename from the name of the image by appending a .tga extension (images can be saved as TARGA files only). The full path is then constructed from this filename and the path of the temp directory. Now when there is a valid filename present it is saved to call the save() method and return the filename:

```
def imagefilename(im):
    filename = im.getFilename()
    if filename == None or len(filename) == 0:
        filename = im.getName()+'.tga'
        filename = os.path.join(tempfile.gettempdir(),filename)
        im.setFilename(filename)
    im.save()
    return filename
```

When we upload a file to an FTP server we want to make sure that we do not overwrite any existing file. If we do find that a file with a given name is already present we'd like to have a function that creates a new filename in a predictable fashion—much like the way Blender behaves when creating names for Blender objects. We'd like to preserve the extension of the filename so we cannot simply stick to a numerical suffix. The nextfile() function, therefore, starts by splitting the pathname and extension parts of the filename. It uses the split() and splitext() functions from the os.path module to leave us with the bare name.

If the name already ends in a suffix consisting of a dot and some number (for example, .42) we'd like to increment this number. This is exactly what the rather daunting highlighted lines accomplish. The sub() function of Python's re module takes a regular expression as a first argument (we use a raw string here so we don't have to escape any backslashes) and checks whether this regular expression matches its third argument (name in this case). The regular expression used here (\. (\d+)$) matches a dot followed by one or more decimal digits if and only if these digits are the last characters. If this pattern does match it is replaced by the second argument of the sub() function. In this case the replacement is not a simple string but a lambda (that is, unnamed) function that will be passed a match object and is expected to return a string.

As we surrounded the digits part of our regular expression with parentheses, we can retrieve just these digits—without the leading dot—with a call to the `match` object's `group()` method. We pass it a `1` as argument, as the first opening parenthesis marks the first group (group 0 would be the whole pattern). We convert this string of digits to an integer by using the built-in `int()` function, add 1 to it, and convert it back again to a string with the `str()` function. Before this result is automatically returned from the `lambda` function we prepend a dot again to conform to our desired pattern.

We finish by checking if the resulting name is different from the original one. If they are the same the original name did not match our pattern and we just append `.1` to the name. Finally, we reconstruct the full filename by adding the extension and calling the `join()` function from `os.path` to add the path in a platform-independent way:

```
def nextfile(filename):
    (path,base) = os.path.split(filename)
    (name,ext) = os.path.splitext(base)
    new = re.sub(r'\.(\d+)$',lambda m:'.'+str(1+int(m.group(1))),name)
    if new == name :
        new = name + '.1'
    return os.path.join(path,new+ext)
```

Now, we are all set to do the real work of uploading a file to an FTP server. First, we make sure that our environment has a suitable HOME variable by calling the `sethome()` function. Then, we retrieve the hostname of the FTP server we want to upload to (it is perfectly valid, by the way, to enter an IP address instead of a hostname):

```
if __name__ == "__main__":
    sethome()
    host = getftphost()
```

Next, we retrieve the user's credentials for the selected host from the `.netrc` file if there is one present (highlighted). This may fail for various reasons (there might not be a `.netrc` file or the given host has no entry in this file); in which case an exception will be raised. If this happens we inform the user and ask for a username and password instead with suitable pop ups:

```
    try:
        (user,acct,password) = netrc.netrc().authenticators(host)
    except:
        acct=None
        user = Draw.PupStrInput('No .netrc file found, enter username:',
                    "",75)
        password = Draw.PupStrInput('Enter password:',"",75)
```

The rendered image will have been stored as a Blender `Image` object with the name `Render Result`. The next thing we do is retrieve a reference to this image and make sure it is stored on disk. The `imagefilename()` function that we defined earlier will return the filename of the stored image.

The next step is to connect to the FTP server by using the hostname and credentials we retrieved earlier (highlighted). Once the connection is established we retrieve a list of filenames with the `nlst()` method:

```
im = Image.Get('Render Result')
filename = imagefilename(im)

ftp = FTP(host,user,password,acct)
files = ftp.nlst()
```

Because we want to make sure that we do not overwrite any files on the FTP server, we strip the path from the filename of our stored image with the `basename()` function and compare the result to the list of filenames retrieved from the server (highlighted). If the filename is already present we generate a new filename with the `nextfile()` function and check again and keep on doing that until we finally have a filename that isn't used yet on the FTP server.

```
dstfilename = os.path.basename(filename)
while dstfilename in files:
    dstfilename = nextfile(dstfilename)
```

Then, we upload our image file by calling the `storbinary()` method. This method will take the destination filename prefixed with `STOR` as the first argument and an open file descriptor as the second argument. We provide the latter by calling Python's built-in `open()` function with the name of our image file as the single argument. (For more details on the rather outlandish behavior of the `ftplib` module, refer to its documentation on `http://docs.python.org/library/ftplib.html`.) We gracefully end the connection to the FTP server by calling the `quit()` method and inform the user about the completion of the task by showing a message that mentions the destination filename as this might be different than expected if a similarly named file exists:

```
ftp.storbinary('STOR '+dstfilename,open(filename))

ftp.quit()

Draw.PupMenu('Render result stored as "%s"%s|Ok'
             % (dstfilename,'%t'))
```

The full code is available as `ftp.py` in `ftp.blend`. It may be run from the text editor but in this case it is certainly far more convenient to put `ftp.py` in Blender's `scripts` directory. The script is configured to make itself available in the **File | Export** menu.

Spring cleaning—archive unused images

After a while, any long-running project gathers a lot of cruft. For example, texture images that were tried once but were discarded in favor of better ones. This script will help us retain a bit of order by finding all files in a selected directory that are not referenced by our `.blend` file and packing them into a **ZIP archive**.

We will take care not to move any `.blend` files to the ZIP archive (after all, those we normally want to be able to render) nor the ZIP archive itself (to prevent endless recursion). Any file that we archive we subsequently try to remove, and if removing a file leaves an empty directory, we remove that directory as well unless it is the directory our `.blend` file resides in.

The file manipulation functions are provided by Python's `os` and `os.path` modules and ZIP files that can be used both on Windows and open platforms can be manipulated with the use of the `zipfile` module. The `zipfile` that we move the unused files to we will name `Attic.zip`:

```
import Blender
from os import walk, remove, rmdir, removedirs
import os.path
from zipfile import ZipFile

zipname = 'Attic.zip'
```

The first challenge is to generate a list of all files in the directory where our `.blend` file sits. The function `listfiles()` uses the `walk()` function from Python's `os` module to recursively descend into the tree of directories and produces a list of files along the way.

By default, the `walk()` function traverses the directory tree's depth first that allows us to alter the list of directories on the fly. This feature is used here to remove any directories that start with a dot (highlighted). This isn't necessary for the current and parent directories (represented by `..` and `.` respectively) because `walk()` already filters them out, but this allows us, for example, to also filter out any `.svn` directories that we may encounter.

The line containing the `yield` statement returns the results one file at a time so our function may be used as an iterator. (For more on iterators, refer to the online documentation at `http://docs.python.org/reference/simple_stmts.html#yield`) We join the filename proper and the path to form a complete filename and normalize it (that is, remove double path separators and the like); although normalizing here isn't strictly necessary because `walk()` is expected to return any paths in normalized form:

```
def listfiles(dir):
    for root,dirs,files in walk(dir):
        for file in files:
            if not file.startswith('.'):
                yield os.path.normpath(os.path.join(root,file))
        for d in dirs:
            if d.startswith('.'):
                dirs.remove(d)
```

Before we can compare the list of files our `.blend` file uses to the list of files present in the directory, we make sure any packed file is unpacked to its original file location. This isn't strictly necessary but ensures that we don't move any files to the archive that are not directly used but do have a copy inside the `.blend` file:

```
def run():
    Blender.UnpackAll(Blender.UnpackModes.USE_ORIGINAL)
```

The `GetPaths()` function from the Blender module produces a list of all files used by the `.blend` file (except for the `.blend` file itself). We pass it an absolute argument set to `True` to retrieve filenames with a full path instead of paths relative to the current directory in order to compare these properly with the list produced by the `listfiles()` function.

Again, we normalize these filenames as well. The highlighted line shows how we retrieve the absolute path of the current directory by passing the shorthand for the current Bender directory (`//`) to the `expandpath()` function:

```
files = [os.path.normpath(f) for f in
        Blender.GetPaths(absolute=True)]
currentdir = Blender.sys.expandpath('//')
```

Next we create a `ZipFile` object in *write* mode. This will truncate any existing archive with the same name and enables us to add files to the archive. The full name of the archive is constructed by joining the current Blender directory and the name we want to use for the archive. The use of the `join()` function from the `os.path` module ensures that we construct the full name in a platform-independent way. We set the `debug` argument of the `ZipFile` object to 3 to report anything unusual to the console when creating the archive:

```
zip = ZipFile(os.path.join(currentdir,zipname),'w')
zip.debug = 3
```

The `removefiles` variable will record the names of the files we want to remove after we have constructed the archive. We can only safely remove files and directories after we have created the archive or we might refer to directories that no longer exist.

The archive is constructed by looping over the list of all the files in the current Blender directory and comparing them to the list of files used by our `.blend` file. Any file with an extension such as `.blend` or `.blend1` is skipped (highlighted) as is the archive itself. The files are added to the ZIP file using the `write()` method, which accepts as a parameter, the filename with a path relative to the archive (and hence the current directory). That way it is easier to unpack the archive in a new location. Any references to files outside the current directory tree are unaffected by the `relpath()` function. Any file we add to the archive is marked for removal by adding it to the `removefiles` list. Finally, we close the archive — an important step because omitting it may leave us with a corrupted archive:

```
removefiles = []
for f in listfiles(currentdir):
    if not (f in files
                or os.path.splitext(f)[1].startswith('.blend')
                or os.path.basename(f) == zipname):
        rf = os.path.relpath(f,currentdir)
        zip.write(rf)
        removefiles.append(f)

zip.close()
```

The last task left is to remove the files we moved to the archive. The `remove()` function from Python's `os` module will accomplish that but we also want to remove any directory that ends up empty after removing the files. Therefore, for each file we remove we determine the name of its directory. We also check if this directory doesn't point to the current directory because we want to make absolutely sure we do not remove it as this is where our `.blend` files reside. Although an unlikely scenario, it is possible to open a `.blend` file in Blender and remove the `.blend` file itself that might leave an empty directory. If we remove this directory any subsequent (auto) save would fail. The `relpath()` function will return a dot if the directory passed as its first argument points to the same directory as the directory passed as its second argument. (The `samefile()` function is more robust and direct but not available on Windows.)

If we made certain we are not referring to the current directory we use the `removedirs()` function to remove the directory. If the directory is not empty this will fail with an `OSError` exception (that is, the file we removed was not the last file in the directory), which we ignore. The `removedirs()` function will also remove all parent directories leading to the directory iff they are empty, which is exactly what we want:

```
for f in removefiles:
    remove(f)
    d = os.path.dirname(f)
    if os.path.relpath(d,currentdir) != '.':
        try:
            removedirs(d)
        except OSError:
            pass

if __name__ == '__main__':
    run()
```

The full code is available as `zip.py` in `attic.blend`.

Extending the editor—searching with regular expressions

The **editor** already provides basic search and replace functionality but if you are used to other editors you might miss the possibility to search using **regular expressions**. This plug-in provides this functionality.

Regular expressions are very powerful and many programmers love their versatility (and many others loathe their poor readability). Whether you love or hate them, they are very expressive: matching any decimal number can simply be expressed as \d+ for example (one or more digits). If you are looking for a word that is spelled differently in British or American English, such as colour/color, you can match any of them with the expression colou?r (color with an optional *u*).

The following code will show that Blender's built-in editor can be equipped with this useful search tool with just a few lines of code. The script provided should be installed in Blender's scripts directory and can then be invoked from the text editor menu as **Text | Text Plugins | Regular Expression Search** or by a hot key *Alt + Ctrl + R*. It will pop up a small input widget where the user may enter a regular expression (this pop up will remember the last regular expression entered) and if the user clicks on the **OK** button or hits *Enter* the cursor will be positioned at the first occurrence that matches the regular expression, highlighting the extent of the match.

```
32          default = ''
33          pattern = Draw.PupStrInput('Regex:
34          if pattern == None or len(pattern) =
35
```

```
Regex: colou?r                        OK  rn)
```

```
           except:
39              popup('Illegal expression')
40              return
```

To register the script as a text plug-in with the designated hot key the first lines of the script consist of the customary headers augmented with a Shortcut: entry (highlighted below):

```
#!BPY
"""
Name: 'Regular Expression Search'
Blender: 249
Group: 'TextPlugin'
Shortcut: 'Ctrl+Alt+R'
Tooltip: 'Find text matching a regular expression'
"""
```

The next step is to import the necessary modules. Python supplies us with a standard `re` module, which is well documented (the online docs are sufficient even for novice users unfamiliar with regular expressions), and we import Blender's `bpy` module. In this book we do not often use this module as it is marked as experimental, but in this case we need it to find out which text buffer is the active one:

```
from Blender import Draw,Text,Registry
import bpy
import re
```

To signal any error conditions, such as an illegal regular expression or when nothing matches, we define a simple `popup()` function:

```
def popup(msg):
    Draw.PupMenu(msg+'%t|Ok')
    return
```

Because we want to remember the last regular expression the user entered we will be using Blender's registry and, therefore, we define a key to use:

```
keyname = 'regex'
```

The `run()` function ties all functionality together; it retrieves the active text buffer and bails out if there isn't one:

```
def run():

    txt = bpy.data.texts.active
    if not txt: return
```

Subsequently, it retrieves the cursor position within this buffer:

```
    row,col = txt.getCursorPos()
```

Before presenting the user with a pop up to enter a regular expression we check if we stored one earlier in the registry. We simply retrieve it and if it fails we set the default expression to the empty string (highlighted). Note that we do not pass any extra parameters to the `GetKey()` function because we do want to store any information on disk in this case. If the user enters an empty string we simply return without searching:

```
    d=Registry.GetKey(keyname)
    try:
        default = d['regex']
    except:
        default = ''
    pattern = Draw.PupStrInput('Regex: ',default,40)
    if pattern == None or len(pattern) == 0 : return
```

We compile the regular expression to see if it's valid and if this fails we show a message and return:

```
try:
    po = re.compile(pattern)
except:
    popup('Illegal expression')
    return
```

Now that we know the regular expression is correct, we iterate over all lines of the text buffer starting at the line the cursor is on (highlighted). For each line we match our compiled regular expression to the string (or the part after the cursor if it is the first line).

```
first = True
for string in txt.asLines(row):
    if first :
        string = string[col:]
    mo = re.search(po,string)
```

If there is a match we note the start of the match within the line and the length of the match (suitably set off if it's the first line) and set the cursor position to the current line and the start of the match (highlighted). We also set the "select position" to the position of the match plus the length of the match so our match will be highlighted and then returned. If there is no match within the line we increment the row index and continue the iteration.

If there is nothing left to iterate over, we signal the user that we did not find any match. In all cases, we store the regular expression in the registry for reuse:

```
        if mo != None :
            i = mo.start()
            l = mo.end()-i
            if first :
                i += col
            txt.setCursorPos(row,i)
            txt.setSelectPos(row,i+1)
            break
        row += 1
        first = False

    else :
        popup('No match')
    Registry.SetKey(keyname,{'regex':pattern})

if __name__ == '__main__':
    run()
```

The full code is available as `regex.py` in `regex.blend` but should be installed in Blender's `scripts` directory with a suitable name, such as `textplugin_regex.py`.

Extending the editor—interacting with Subversion

When actively developing scripts it can be difficult to keep track of changes or to revert to previous versions. This is not unique to writing Python scripts in Blender and over the years a number of **version control** systems have evolved. One of the better known, and widely used ones is **Subversion** (`http://subversion.tigris.org`). In this section, we show how the editor can be augmented to commit or update a text file from a repository.

Interaction with a Subversion repository is not provided by a bundled Python module so we have to get that from somewhere else. The **Downloads** section of `http://pysvn.tigris.org` contains both source and binary distributions for many platforms. Be sure to get the right one since both the supported version of Subversion and the version of Python may differ. The scripts we develop here are tested against Subversion 1.6.x and Python 2.6.x but should work with earlier versions of Subversion as well.

We will be implementing the functionality to commit a text file to a repository and to update a file (that is, get the latest revision from the repository). If we try to commit a file that is not part of the repository yet we will add it, but we will not implement tools to create a repository or check out a working copy. A tool such as **TortoiseSVN** on Windows (`http://tortoisesvn.tigris.org/`) or any number of tools for open platforms are far better equipped for that. We just assume a checked-out working directory where we store our Blender text files. (This working directory might be completely different from your Blender project directory.)

Committing a file to the repository

Committing a text buffer to the repository is a two-step process. First, we have to save the contents of the text buffer to a file and then we commit this file to the repository. We have to check whether the text block has an associated filename and prompt the user to save the file first if it hasn't got one yet. The user must save the file to a checked out directory in order to commit the file to a repository.

Just like the extension that allowed us to search with regular expressions, this one starts with a suitable header to identify it as a text editor plug-in and to assign a keyboard shortcut. We define the mnemonic *Ctrl + Alt + C* for committing (highlighted) as we will define *Ctrl + Alt + U* for updating in its companion script. We also import the necessary modules, notably the `pysvn` module:

```
#!BPY
"""
Name: 'SVNCommit'
Blender: 249
Group: 'TextPlugin'
Shortcut: 'Ctrl+Alt+C'
Tooltip: 'Commit current textbuffer to svn'
"""


from Blender import Draw,Text,Registry
import bpy
import pysvn

def popup(msg):
    Draw.PupMenu(msg+'%t|Ok')
    return
```

The `run()` function first tries to get the active text buffer and will return without a croak if there isn't one. Then it checks if there is a filename defined for this text buffer (highlighted). If not, it reminds the user to save the file first (thus defining a filename and placing the file in a checked out directory) and returns.

```
def run():

    txt = bpy.data.texts.active
    if not txt: return

    fn = txt.getFilename()
    if fn == None or len(fn) == 0:
        popup('No filename defined: save it first')
        return
```

The next step is to create a `pysvn` client object that will enable us to interact with a repository. Its `info()` method allows us to retrieve information about the repository status of a file (highlighted). If there is no information the file will not have been added to the repository yet—a situation that we correct by calling the `add()` method:

```
svn = pysvn.Client()
info = svn.info(fn)
if info == None:
    popup('not yet added to repository, will do that now')
    svn.add(fn)
```

Next, we write out the current contents of the text buffer by joining all the lines in it to a single chunk of data and writing that to the file object we opened on the filename associated with the buffer:

```
file=open(fn,'wb')
file.write('\n'.join(txt.asLines()))
file.close()
```

This file will be committed to the repository with the `checkin()` method to which we pass a rather uninformative commit message. It might be a good idea to prompt the user for a more sensible message. Finally, we inform the user of the resulting revision.

> Note that Subversion revision numbers are not associated with a file but with a repository, so this number may differ by more than one from the previous file commit if meanwhile other files were committed.

```
version = svn.checkin(fn,'Blender commit')
popup('updated to rev. '+str(version))

if __name__ == '__main__':
    run()
```

The full code is available as `textplugin_commit` in `svn.blend` but should be installed in Blender's `scripts` directory.

Updating a file from the repository

The whole purpose of a repository is being able to collaborate, which means that others may change the files we are working on as well and we must be able to retrieve those committed changes. This is called updating a file and means that we copy the latest version that resides in the repository to our working directory.

Besides checking whether the text buffer is saved and the file is already added to the repository, we must also check whether our current version is newer or altered from the version in the repository. If so, we offer the user the choice of discarding these changes and reverting to the version in the repository or to commit the version residing in the text buffer. (A third option, merging the differences is not provided here; although Subversion is certainly able to do that, at least for text files, but this is better left to more versatile tools such as TortoiseSVN.)

The first part of the script is very similar to the commit script. The main difference is a different shortcut key:

```
#!BPY
"""
Name: 'SVNUpdate'
Blender: 249
Group: 'TextPlugin'
Shortcut: 'Ctrl+Alt+U'
Tooltip: 'Update current textbuffer from svn'
"""

from Blender import Draw,Text,Registry
import bpy
import re
import pysvn

def popup(msg):
    Draw.PupMenu(msg+'%t|Ok')
    return
```

The run() function also starts off quite similar as it retrieves the active text buffer (if any) and checks whether the text buffer has an associated filename (highlighted). It also checks if the filename was already added to the repository and if not, corrects this by calling the add() method and informs the user with a pop up:

```
def run():

    txt = bpy.data.texts.active
    if not txt: return

    fn = txt.getFilename()
    if fn == None or len(fn) == 0:
        popup('No filename defined: save it first')
        return
    svn = pysvn.Client()
    info = svn.info(fn)
    if info == None:
        popup('not yet added to repository, will do that now')
        svn.add(fn)
```

After writing the contents of the text buffer to its associated file it calls the status() method to see if the file we have written (and therefore the contents of the text buffer) is modified compared to the version in the repository (highlighted). The status() method may be passed a *list* of filenames as well and always returns a list of results, even when we pass it just a single filename—hence the [0] index. If our text buffer is modified we inform the user and offer a choice: either discard the changes and retrieve the version stored in the repository or commit the current version. It is also possible to cancel the action altogether by clicking outside the menu, in which case PupMenu() will return -1:

```
file=open(fn,'wb')
file.write('\n'.join(txt.asLines()))
file.close()

if svn.status(fn)[0].text_status == pysvn.wc_status_kind.modified:
    c=Draw.PupMenu('file probably newer than version in'+
                   'repository%t|Commit|Discard changes')
    if c==1:
        svn.checkin(fn,'Blender')
        return
    elif c==2:
        svn.revert(fn)
```

After retrieving the version from the repository we refresh the contents of our text buffer:

```
txt.clear()
file=open(fn)
txt.write(file.read())
file.close()
```

Finally, we inform the user with a pop up what the revision number is of the content in the text buffer by calling the `status()` method again and fetching the `commit_revision` field:

```
popup('updated to rev. '
        +str(svn.status(fn)[0].entry.commit_revision))

if __name__ == '__main__':
    run()
```

The full code is available as `textplugin_svnupdate` in `svn.blend`, and like its commit counterpart it should be installed in Blender's `scripts` directory.

Working with a repository

Although a full tutorial on working with Subversion is out of scope of this book, it might be useful to sketch a workflow for a Blender project where scripted components are versioned.

It is important to understand that a Blender project itself does not have to be under version control. We may organize our Blender project in any way that makes sense and have a `scripts` directory within it that is under version control.

Say we have created a repository for scripts on a network storage device and created a Blender project directory on our local machine. In order to bring our scripts under version control we have to perform the following steps:

1. Check out the script's repository within our Blender project directory (this is called the **working copy** of the repository).
2. Create a script within our `.blend` file with the built-in editor.
3. Save this script to the working copy.
4. Every time we change something, we press *Ctrl + Alt + C* to commit our changes.
5. Every time we start working on our script again we press *Ctrl + Alt + U* first to see if someone else has changed anything.

Note that there is nothing against bringing all assets, such as textures or `.blend` files that act as libraries under version control but we have to use a separate client to commit changes. It would be an interesting exercise to create some scripts that commit or update all files in the current Blender directory.

The need for speed—using Psyco

Python is an interpreted language: all instructions in a script are interpreted and executed again and again when they are encountered. This may sound inefficient but for a developer of a program the advantage of being able to quickly develop and test a program may outweigh the disadvantage of a slower running program. And interpreting might be inefficient but that is not identical to slow. Python is a very high-level language so a single language element might be equivalent to a lot of low-level instructions. Besides, given modern hardware even a slow script might be finished faster than a user expects a result.

Nevertheless, there are situations where any speed increase is welcome. From all the examples we have seen in this book Pynodes are probably the most computationally intensive as the instructions are run for every visible pixel in a texture or shader and often even many more times per pixel if oversampling is taken into account. Saving a few milliseconds from a script that takes less than a second to execute doesn't amount to much, but saving 20% of the rendering time amounts to a significant amount of time saved when rendering a 500 frame shot.

Enter Psyco: Psyco is a Python extension that tries to speed up the execution of a script by compiling frequently used parts of a script to machine instructions and storing them for reuse. This process is often called **just-in-time compilation** and is akin to just-in-time compilation in other languages such as Java. (The implementation is similar in concept but quite different in implementation due to Python's dynamic typing. This is of no concern to developers of Python scripts.) What matters is that Psyco may be used in any script without any changes in the code except for adding a few lines.

Psyco is available as a binary package for Windows and can be compiled from source on other platforms. Full instructions are available on the Psyco website: `http://psyco.sourceforge.net/.`

Do verify that you install the version that fits your Python installation because although the site states that the version compiled for Python 2.5 should work for 2.6 as well, it still might fail, so rather use the version specifically compiled for 2.6. Now, what speed increase might we expect? That is difficult to estimate but easy enough to measure! Just render a frame and note the time it took, then import psyco in your code, render again, and note the difference. If it is significant leave the code in, otherwise you might remove it again.

In the following table some results are listed for the test scene provided in `pysco.blend` but your mileage may vary. Also note that the test scene is a rather optimistic scenario as most of the render is covered by a texture generated by a Pynode. If this were less, the gain in speed would be less, but this does give an estimate of what is possible with Psyco. A factor two for the relevant code is readily achievable. The following table lists some illustrating sample timings:

Time in seconds	Without Psyco	With Psyco
Netbook	52.7	26.3
Desktop	14.01	6.98

Enabling Psyco

The following code shows the additional lines needed to enable psyco on our previously encountered `raindrops` Pynode. Changes are indicated in bold.

```
<... all other code unchanged ...>

__node__ = Raindrops

try:
    import psyco
    psyco.bind(Raindrops.__call__)
    print 'Psyco configured'
except ImportError:
    print 'Psycho not configured, continuing'
    pass
```

So basically, only a few lines are added after the definition of the Pynode. Make sure to click on the **Update** button on the Pynode otherwise the code will not be recompiled and changes will not be visible.

The previous code just tries to import the `psyco` module. If this fails (for any reason) an informative message is printed on the console but the code will run correctly, nevertheless. If it is imported we instruct Psyco to optimize the `__call__()` method by calling the `bind()` function with a reference to this `__call__` method as an argument and inform the user on the console that we successfully configured Psyco.

Summary

In this chapter we looked beyond 3D and rendering and saw how to make life happier for a Python developer and artist alike by providing some scripts to help in some common housekeeping tasks by extending the functionality of the built-in editor with regular expression searches and version control and showed how to save valuable rendering time in some situations by using Psyco. Specifically, we learned:

- How to list and archive assets such as image maps
- How to publish a rendered image automatically with FTP
- How to extend the functionality of the built-in editor with regular expression searches
- How to speed up computations using Psyco—a just-in-time compiler
- How to add version control to your scripts with Subversion

Links and Resources

There are many excellent resources available on the Web to provide you with additional information on almost any Blender subject you can think of. The following is not an exhaustive list, but hopes to give you some good starting points. A general word of advice might be appropriate here, especially for novices: use the Internet to your advantage and do some research before you ask questions on forums. Blender users (and developers) are quite a friendly and helpful bunch but on many forums, simple questions remain unanswered because people feel that the answers can simply be found on the Web or by searching in the forum archives itself and do not warrant the time to answer them. This may be disappointing sometimes, but many of these disappointments may be prevented by some research in advance.

General Blender-related forums and blogs

Blender's home page is an important source of information and the following pages should be considered a must read:

- `www.blender.org`: The home page with news on Blender developments.
- `wiki.blender.org`: The wiki that contains the manual, tutorials, and links to resources.

Some general Blender-related forums are worth noticing as they attract the attention of a large part of the Blender community:

- `www.blenderartists.org`: It hosts a number of forums. Of special relevance to readers of this book, is the forum on Python and Plug-ins where both novices and experienced Blender hackers will find a helpful crowd to assist with scripting-related issues. The author of this book can be found here as well, under his "varkenvarken" nickname.

- `www.blendernation.com`: This site tries to be the central hub of all Blender-related news and succeeds quite well at it. Its RSS feed is a useful addition to your browser navigation bar to stay up-to-date.

Python programming

This section lists some general Python-related resources. Blender scripting resources are listed in the next section.

- `www.python.org`: It's the main site and very well organized, nevertheless some main sections deserve to be mentioned separately here.

- `www.python.org/download/`: Download your full Python distribution here if you do not already have it installed or if the installed version doesn't match Blender's built-in version exactly.

For newcomers and seasoned programmers alike, the following pages offer some useful tutorials on Python in general and some 'how-tos' on specific subjects. All the articles on these pages have a fairly low learning curve:

- `docs.python.org/tutorial`: It is especially worth reading for people experienced in other programming languages who want to learn Python. It covers most Python-related issues and should be sufficient for most people to get started with Python.

- `docs.python.org/howto`: Detailed information on subjects such as regular expressions, Internet programming, and Python style.

More extensive information on the Python programming language and its bundled modules is available as well. These pages are a credit to their authors and maintainers because although exhaustive in their coverage and depth, they are still very readable.

- `docs.python.org/reference/`: It is the main reference on all language structures such as statements, data types, and exceptions.
- `docs.python.org/library/`: The ultimate reference for all bundled modules, built-in functions, and objects. Before you even think of programming something yourself, you should check this page to see if a module is already provided that covers your needs.
- `pypi.python.org/pypi`: If the bundled modules do not provide what you need, chances are some third-party encountered the same problem and wrote a package to deal with the issue. If so, you'll probably find it on Python's Package Index.
- `code.activestate.com/recipes/langs/python/`: Sometimes, you just need a code snippet, code example, or an algorithm to get you started. You might find it here.

Blender scripting

Specific information on Blender scripting is readily available too.

- `http://wiki.blender.org/index.php/Doc:Manual/Extensions/Python`: Gives important information on how to install and use Python with Blender on different platforms and includes information on the built-in editor.
- `http://www.blender.org/documentation/249PythonDoc/`: The official documentation of Blender's Python API. This is the page we refer to in this book when we mention "the API documentation". Before you start scripting, read this at least twice from start to finish. It will give you an excellent overview of what is possible and by reading it completely, you will find it easier to find something when you need the information.
- `wiki.blender.org/index.php/Extensions:Py/Scripts`: A catalog of the many, many scripts available for Blender, both the bundled ones and the additional ones people have written. Before trying to invent something on your own, check to see if someone already invented it for you.
- `www.opengl.org/sdk/docs/man/`: The Blender Python API also gives access to many OpenGL functions to draw things directly on screen. The API documentation refers to these pages for detailed information. OpenGL is not a subject taken up lightly so you might want to check some tutorials first if you want to get fancy. `http://www.opengl.org/code/` lists some entries that might give a start.

External packages used in this book

Most examples in this book do not need any external Python packages to get the job done, as most functionality that we need is already covered by Python's standard modules or the Blender API. However, for some specific areas we made use of freely available third-party packages.

- www.pythonware.com/products/pil/index.htm: The Python Imaging Library (PIL) contains every 2D functionality imaginable and is therefore an excellent supplement to Blender's API, as Blender's API is rather lacking in this field.
- psyco.sourceforge.net: Psyco is a just-in-time compiler for Python that may give a significant speed increase on computationally heavy Python code such as Pynodes with minimal changes to your code.
- subversion.tigris.org: Subversion (SVN) is a widely used versioning package (also used by the Blender Foundation for the development of Blender itself). The Python specific bindings can be found on a separate page http://pysvn.tigris.org/ and if you need an SVN client that is integrated with your Windows file explorer, TortoiseSVN might be worth checking out (pun intended): http://tortoisesvn.tigris.org/. The main Subversion page lists many links to SVN clients for open platforms as well.

Other sources of information

When researching ways to model or animate something, it is essential to look at real life examples. You may find images on the Web easily enough but simple images normally will not give sufficient insight on underlying principles or inner workings. For these, the Wikipedia is a very useful resource and consulted for many things in this book. Below we list some samples.

A word of warning may be in order though. Wikipedia has proven itself over the years as a readily accessible and dependable source of information and its quality seems to be comparable to that of printed encyclopedias. However, anyone can alter that information and there may be different views on the subject, so it is always wise to check other resources as well, especially if these are difficult subjects. Good Wikipedia entries generally give a list of external references as well and it is a good idea to check a few of them.

- en.wikipedia.org/wiki/Captcha
- en.wikipedia.org/wiki/Sunflower
- en.wikipedia.org/wiki/Wave
- en.wikipedia.org/wiki/Tides
- en.wikipedia.org/wiki/Four-stroke_cycle

These are some of the pages consulted when creating the examples in this book. A few of the more math oriented ones are listed here (they are referred to in the main text as well):

- `en.wikipedia.org/wiki/Mean_curvature`
- `en.wikipedia.org/wiki/Euler_angle`
- `en.wikipedia.org/wiki/Law_of_cosines`

Of course, there is more to life than just the Wikipedia and the following two sites proved exceptionally useful when implementing the iridescence shader:

- `www.exploratorium.edu/ronh/bubbles/bubble_colors.html`: Everything worth knowing on soap bubbles, especially on the way colors are formed on the surface.
- `www.philiplaven.com/p19.html` A useful resource on color issues in general but notable for an algorithm to convert a wavelength to an RGB-tuple.

Finally, these sites are worth a special mention:

- `www.blender-materials.org/`: Currently hosted at `http://matrep.parastudios.de/`, this site provides a huge database of Blender materials that can be used as is or can serve as a starting point for your own materials. Blender materials probably warrant a book of their own, but for this site offers a wealth of choices from community-generated materials that give you a head start in your projects.
- `blenderunderground.com/`: Noted here as an excellent source of tutorials.

B

Common Pitfalls

Read the API documents

It may sound pedantic but it is not an exaggeration to say that many Python-related questions asked on Blender forums can simply be answered by reading the API docs thoroughly.

Of course, these are not the easiest documents to read as they cover many topics and often it might not be clear where to start, so it might be a good idea to read them at least once in their entirety from start to finish. Not only will it give you some idea about the vast scope of the Blender API but it will also help you find specific subjects later on.

The trouble with import

One of the questions that regularly pops up is why the `import` statement isn't working as expected. The problem here is that you have to know what to expect. Blender has augmented the standard import behavior of Python to make it possible to import from the text files residing within a `.blend` file. This is a great boon because it allows you to modularize your code without the need to distribute separate files. However, the behavior of the part that imports these internal files should be absolutely clear to spare you nasty surprises but it is, at the moment, not very well-documented.

This is what happens when an `import` statement such as `import foo` is executed:

1. Check whether `foo.pyc` or `foo.py` exists in any of the directories in `sys.path`

2. If one of them exists:
    - if `foo.py` is newer
        - compile `foo.py` to `foo.pyc`
    - use `foo.pyc`

3. Else, if `foo.py` exists as an internal text file:
    - if it is not compiled already:
        - compile internal text file
    - use compiled version

4. Else
    - raise an exception

The first part is Python's regular behavior (it is a bit simplified from what really happens as we don't mention packages or `.pyo` files here) and the second part is what Blender adds to it if the required module does not exist as an external file. There are two important things to note here: if an external file exists with the same name as an internal file, the external file (or its compiled version) takes precedence. This can be annoying because many people save an external copy of an internal file with the same name. If these two are out of sync unexpected things may happen. Fortunately, Blender's internal editor reminds you of this situation by showing an **Out of Sync** button next to the name of the internal file. Still, if you haven't opened the text editor on that specific file, you may not notice it.

Furthermore, if you take a close look at the previous outline you will notice that if Blender is looking for an internal file it checks if this internal file is already compiled but does not check if the source might be newer. This means that any changes in the source code of an internal file that are to be imported will not be seen by the main program. To remedy this situation, you may force Python to compile the module by using the built-in `reload()` function. This is less efficient when running a program, but it saves a lot of headaches when developing. Once your script is production-ready you might drop the `reload()`.

So suppose you have two internal files, `main.py` and `mymodule.py`, and you want to make sure changes in `module.py`, will always be visible once `main.py` is executed, then each file might look like this:

```
# main.py

import mymodule
reload(mymodule)

mymodule.myfunction()

# mymodule.py

def myfunction():
    print "myfunction called"
```

The highlighted line shows the all important `reload()`.

Installing a full Python distribution

Two specific issues come up frequently: either a standard Python module seems to be missing (an `import` statement raises an exception telling you it can't find the requested module) or Blender warns that it cannot find the Python distribution with a version equal to the compiled version.

Both issues were addressed in *Chapter 1, Extending Blender with Python* and for additional information refer to: `http://wiki.blender.org/index.php/Doc:Manual/Introduction/Installing_Blender/Python`.

C
Future Developments

Blender

Blender is a stable and production quality package yet it has been in heavy development ever since it became open source. Almost every version of Blender brought new features—some small and some very sophisticated indeed. The changes in Blender's development are neatly documented on the Blender site at: `http://www.blender.org/development/release-logs/`.

Blender's current, stable version is 2.49 and this version will probably stay around for sometime because Blender is no longer 'just' an open source package used by 3D enthusiasts but a viable production tool used in different parts of the production pipeline by professional studios.

Nevertheless, as of writing this book, the development of a new version of Blender is in full swing. The version number, 2.50, may lead you to believe that this is just a minor change but in fact, it is almost a complete rewrite. The most visible part is a completely different graphical user interface. This interface is almost completely written in Python, which opens up endless opportunities for writing sophisticated user interfaces to replace the limited possibilities in 2.49.

Not only the user interface is changed but also the internal structure is overhauled completely and although most of the functionality exposed in the Python API stays similar in nature, there are numerous changes in most of Blender's modules.

One major drawback is that the new version is developed alongside the Durian project (which will produce the open source movie "Sintel", see `durian.blender.org`), so the main development goals for version 2.50 are providing all of the functionality for this project. This does cover most issues, but some parts, notably Pynodes and screen handlers, will not be provided in the first production release.

On the positive side it will no longer be necessary to install a full Python distribution alongside Blender as the new version will be bundled with a full Python distribution.

The road map for Blender's 2.50 development may be found at `http://www. blender.org/development/release-logs/blender-250/` but the timetable mentioned there is of course very preliminary. A full production version is expected somewhere late 2010 and will have a version number of 2.6.

Python

The new version of Blender will be bundled with a full Python 3.x distribution obviating the need for a separate installation of Python. This version of Python is already very stable and it is unlikely that major changes will be implemented in the near future.

Version 3.x is different from version 2.6 but most significant changes are below the surface and mostly won't concern a Blender scripter.

There is a notable side effect of the new Python version though: many third-party packages (that is, Python packages not bundled with the distribution) are not (yet) ported to version 3.x. In some situations this might be a considerable nuisance. From the packages used in this book the most notable one that is not yet ported to version 3.x is PIL (Python Imaging Library). That one is surely missed as it provides sophisticated 2D functionality not present in Blender.

Another package not yet ported to 3.x is Psyco—the just-in-time compiler—but Python 3 already is quite a bit faster in many situations so the speed increase attainable by a package such as Psyco might not be worth the trouble.

To increase the speed of acceptance of Python 3.x Python's developers have declared a moratorium on the addition of new features so that packages developers won't have to aim at a moving target. More on this subject can be found at `http://www.python.org/dev/peps/pep-3003/`.

Index

error pop up, creating 40, 41
new mesh object, creating 41
user's choice, remembering 39, 40
user interface, building 36, 37
user interface, creating 37, 38
object groups 66
objects
adding, from script 24
grouping 66
groups 66
parenting 66
sunflower, creating 68-71
sunflower, growing from seed 67, 68
vertex groups 66
objects visibility
animating 138
layer, changing 140
material, fading 138, 139
Object type IPO 108
open() function 172, 210, 240
orbit.py script
designing 162-164

P

parenting 66
paste() function 209, 215
peristaltic movement 165
peristaltic.py application 168, 169
PIL 209
pointInside() method 155
poles
about 55
selecting 56
selecting again 56, 57
popup() function 246
pose armature 168
poses
defining 165-167
premul attribute 223
Psyco
about 254
enabling 255
PupBlock() 132
PupMenu() function 172
PyConstraints 125
pydrivers 107

Pynode
designing 178
regular tilings, creating 181-184
writing 179-181
pysvn module 249
Python 268
Python distribution
installing 265
Python Imaging Library. *See* **PIL**
Python programming 258
Python-related resources, Blender scripting 258

Q

quads 55

R

raindrops example, Pynode
about 190
effects, calculating 191, 192
ideas, merging 194-197
normals, calculating 193
results, storing 192, 193
ray 86
redraw() 214
redraw event 144
regular expressions 245
reload() function 222, 264
relpath() function 243, 244
removedirs() function 244
removefiles variable 243
remove() function 244
remove() method 113
removeVertGroup() method 75
removeVertsFromGroup() method 75
renameVertGroup() method 75
renderAnim() method 211
RenderData class 28
rendered image
publishing, FTP used 236-240
render() function 217
rendering process
automating 207, 208
combined image, creating 209-215
combine.py, used 209
render() method 211

TrackTo constraint 128
tris 55

U

ultra sharp faces
  selecting 54, 55
unpack() function 173
utility function 88
uv attribute 223

V

version control systems
  about 248
  adding to script, Subversion used 248
vertex groups
  about 66, 74
  adding, to existing mesh object 76
  leftright.py script 76, 77
  mesh objects methods 74, 75
  using 74
  vertices, adding 75

vertex normal 85
VGROUPS property 97
view-dependent shader
  creating 201-205
volume() function 65

W

walk() function 241
warped quads
  3D-view 50, 51
  code outline 53
  flat quad, comparing with 51, 52
  identifying 51
Wikipedia 260
write() method 243

Z

ZIP archive 241
zipfile module 241
zip() function 88, 163

Thank you for buying
Blender 2.49 Scripting

About Packt Publishing

Packt, pronounced 'packed', published its first book "*Mastering phpMyAdmin for Effective MySQL Management*" in April 2004 and subsequently continued to specialize in publishing highly focused books on specific technologies and solutions.

Our books and publications share the experiences of your fellow IT professionals in adapting and customizing today's systems, applications, and frameworks. Our solution based books give you the knowledge and power to customize the software and technologies you're using to get the job done. Packt books are more specific and less general than the IT books you have seen in the past. Our unique business model allows us to bring you more focused information, giving you more of what you need to know, and less of what you don't.

Packt is a modern, yet unique publishing company, which focuses on producing quality, cutting-edge books for communities of developers, administrators, and newbies alike. For more information, please visit our website: www.packtpub.com.

About Packt Open Source

In 2010, Packt launched two new brands, Packt Open Source and Packt Enterprise, in order to continue its focus on specialization. This book is part of the Packt Open Source brand, home to books published on software built around Open Source licences, and offering information to anybody from advanced developers to budding web designers. The Open Source brand also runs Packt's Open Source Royalty Scheme, by which Packt gives a royalty to each Open Source project about whose software a book is sold.

Writing for Packt

We welcome all inquiries from people who are interested in authoring. Book proposals should be sent to author@packtpub.com. If your book idea is still at an early stage and you would like to discuss it first before writing a formal book proposal, contact us; one of our commissioning editors will get in touch with you.

We're not just looking for published authors; if you have strong technical skills but no writing experience, our experienced editors can help you develop a writing career, or simply get some additional reward for your expertise.

Blender 3D 2.49 Incredible Machines

ISBN: 978-1-847197-46-7   Paperback: 316 pages

Modeling, rendering, and animating realistic machines with Blender 3D

1. Walk through the complete process of building amazing machines

2. Model and create mechanical models and vehicles with detailed designs

3. Add advanced global illumination options to the renders created in Blender 3D using YafaRay and LuxRender

4. Create machines such as a handgun, a steam punk spacecraft, and a transforming robot

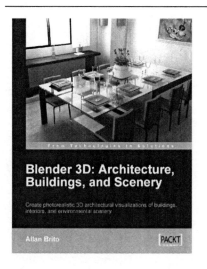

Blender 3D Architecture, Buildings, and Scenery

ISBN: 978-1-847193-67-4   Paperback: 332 pages

Create photorealistic 3D architectural visualizations of buildings, interiors, and environmental scenery

1. Turn your architectural plans into a model

2. Study modeling, materials, textures, and light basics in Blender

3. Create photo-realistic images in detail

4. Create realistic virtual tours of buildings and scenes

Please check **www.PacktPub.com** for information on our titles

Lightning Source UK Ltd.
Milton Keynes UK
31 July 2010

157606UK00002B/10/P